FORMING A CHRISTIAN MENTALITY

FORMING A CHRISTIAN MENTALITY

*Chapters for the Religious Guidance of Youth
for Priests, Parents and Teachers*

By
KILIAN J. HENNRICH
O.F.M.CAP., M.A., K.C.H.S.

Catholic Authors Press
www.CatholicAuthors.com

Nihil Obstat:
> FR. CUTHBERT GUMBINGER, O.F.M.CAP., S.T.D.
> FR. THOMAS AQUINAS HEIDENREICH, O.F.M.CAP., PH.D.
> *Censores Ordinis*

Imprimi Potest:
> FR. CLEMENT NEUBAUER, O.F.M.CAP.,
> *Minister Provincial*

DETROIT, EASTER, 1945

Imprimi Permittimus:
> FR. BENNO AICHINGER, O.F.M.CAP.
> *Delegate General*

NEW YORK, ASCENSION, 1945

DEDICATED TO

POPE PIUS X OF SAINTLY MEMORY
IN THIS FORTIETH ANNIVERSARY OF
HIS ENCYCLICAL "ACERBO NIMIS," ON
THE TEACHING OF CHRISTIAN DOCTRINE
MCMXLV

FOREWORD

IN THIS BOOK, FORMING A CHRISTIAN MENTALITY, the author presumes to set forth the place of man in the universal economy of God and his subsequent duties. These duties consist in knowing God and serving Him lovingly. The human body is not permanent and is to serve man temporarily as an abode for the soul during his time of probation which decides eternal life.

The great faculties of the soul given to man by God for co-operating with God to insure personal salvation, are the intellect and the will, or the mind and the heart. Of these two great faculties, the will is free in many ways. Good, better, and best are legitimate choices. The intellect, however, has but one objective, namely, the truth and nothing else. Owing to the fall of man, his intellect was darkened and many external influences may lead the mind into error, especially in purely material and temporal things. A deeper knowledge of God's plan will prevent many erroneous opinions, but the only entire guide to the supernatural is faith.

This faith in its purity is found only in Revelation and Tradition, contained in the Scriptures, the Liturgy, and the infallible teaching of the Church. Faith is, therefore, the principal object of the mind enlightened by grace, in all that is supernatural. The relationship between mentality, spirituality, and personality is clear. The latter two are fruits of the first.

To the knowledge of God's work, the will must add worship and service. The latter, consisting in the observance of the manifested will of God, is extensively treated in moral theology and also fundamentally in our catechisms. To this, the present volume does not add much except to provide cogent motives for observing the Commandments. The main stress is laid upon the divine worship of the whole man.

The material presented in this work divides itself logically into two parts. But this division is theoretical rather than practical, because in actual Christian life one cannot be separated from the other. The first part, entitled *Faith*, leads man through life from the cradle to the grave, guided by Revelation, principally on the basis of Holy Scripture. The second part, entitled *Worship*, conducts man through the life of grace. It is based predominantly on the Liturgy of the Mass and some Sacraments. All the latter are not included, nor are those given treated extensively, because the author has done this in his book "The Better Life," issued a few years ago by the same publisher.

In preparing the present volume, the author had in mind the improvement of the Christian mentality by showing that the principles of secularism and materialism are in contradiction to the principles of Christianity and that public and private life cannot be separated from each other and conducted on different principles.

All who are acquainted with the modern errors of the mind and heart that rock the very foundation of faith and intend to destroy the whole divinely willed structure of Christianity, will readily see that the restoration of a truly Christian mentality is of utmost importance. Among the most pernicious errors that threaten to influence even Catholics are: secularism, materialistic liberalism, atheistic totalitarianism, rationalism, moral skepticism, and moral autonomy. All persons afflicted with one or the other of these great fundamental evils will not believe the words of a preacher and will not conform their morals to the teaching of the Church.

It is the firm conviction of all Popes, beginning with Pius IX, and of many bishops, as revealed in Encyclicals and Pastorals, that Catholics should be made immune to such errors and that where the Christian mentality has been lost, it should be hopefully restored by all the means at our command.

Among the suitable means which are most promising of good results are preaching, study courses, scriptural and spiritual reading, and, above all, the catechetical instruction of youth. All these means and others have been recommended by the Supreme Pastors, and to carry out their wishes is one more important reason for writing this book. It depends greatly on man's mentality, whether Christ will continue to live in the Christian and whether man will be a living member of the Mystical Body of Christ or not.

This book, intended as a companion volume to "Youth Guidance," may also be of value to members of catechetical, scriptural, liturgical, and other religious study clubs.

A word of thanks must be added to the Reverend Cuthbert Gumbinger, O.F.M.Cap., S.T.D., who was very helpful in seeing this book through the press, to the censors, to the writers, and to the publishers who graciously granted permission to use some excerpts from their publications as indicated in the proper places.

K.J.H.

NEW YORK CITY,
EASTER, 1945.

CONTENTS

CHAPTER	PAGE
FOREWORD	vii

PART ONE: FAITH

I. CHRISTIAN MENTALITY	3
II. FOUNTAINS OF FAITH	9
III. CREATION AND PROCREATION	17
IV. REGENERATION AND SANCTIFICATION	27
V. REARING CHILDREN IN FAITH AND PIETY	38
VI. SPIRITUAL GUIDANCE TOWARDS MANHOOD	49
VII. HOLY PREPARATION FOR CHASTE WEDLOCK	61
VIII. THE GREAT SACRAMENT	75
IX. THE CHRISTIAN FAMILY IN FAITH	88

PART TWO: WORSHIP

X. THE REDEMPTION IN THE LITURGY	103
XI. ADVENT AND CHRISTMAS	110
XII. THE EPIPHANY OF THE LORD	119
XIII. MORE DIVINE MANIFESTATIONS	133
XIV. LITURGICAL PREPARATION FOR PENANCE	148
XV. THE DAYS OF SALVATION	162
XVI. LIFE THROUGH DEATH	177
XVII. A NEW LIFE IN CHRIST	191
XVIII. THE GLORIFICATION OF CHRIST	206

		PAGE
XIX.	THE FINAL PREPARATION OF MANKIND	220
XX.	THE CHURCH TRIUMPHANT IN THE LITURGY	234
XXI.	THE LITURGY AND CHRISTIAN LIFE	252
XXII.	THE DOMESTIC LITURGY	262
	BIBLIOGRAPHY	271
	INDEX	277

PART ONE: FAITH

"It is only the doctrine of Jesus Christ that makes us understand the true and wondrous dignity of man, and it is this doctrine that inspires in proud man the lowliness of mind which is the origin of all true glory."

Pope Pius X, in Encyclical on Christian Doctrine, "Acerbo nimis," April 15, 1905.

CHAPTER I

Christian Mentality

MENTALITY PERTAINS to the intellect or the mind of man. The object of the intellect is truth, and error is a deficiency caused by insufficient knowledge of principles or wrong application. The result of the application of the mind is a judgment according to individual understanding and the due consideration of all circumstances. However, the principle or laws upon which a judgment is formed can make a great difference, especially in things that pertain to religious or moral life.

The mentality is called Christian, if it is informed by the teachings and principles of Christ, and enlightened by grace. It is the only mentality that considers man as he is and does not lose sight of his eternal destiny. According to Christ Himself, the Christian mentality and its judgment are in opposition to the spirit or judgments of the world.

The intellectual process of the world, understood as being opposed to that demanded by Christ, might be called a pagan mentality. This may seem to be a harsh designation, but it is true, because the simple neglect of God, the creation of substitutes for Him, and the maintenance of a false freedom and an indifference to a future life is paganism, although it may not manifest the uglier and more apparent aspects.

It is true that all men have been endowed with a reliable conscience to guide them in morality. But it is also true that this initially reliable guide may become erroneous, blunted, and even false. The last is frequently the case in those afflicted with a worldly mentality. On the other hand, an unreliable conscience will rarely be found in those who possess an other-worldly or Christian mentality.

The lack or loss of the Christian mentality may be the cause of great evils. It practically amounts to the loss of faith and the true concept of morality. It creates from the very start a serious doubt as to whether there are such things as absolute truth and a permanent norm of morality. One who has some acquaintance with radio talks, articles, sermons, biographies, and novels of a certain type cannot fail to see how far the modern world has drifted away from the strong anchor of God's truth and law.

A pertinent statement of Archbishop William Duke, of Vancouver, in a Lenten Pastoral (1944) is here in order:

> "Our generation has lost the sense of modesty, and this mentality that nothing is a sin has led to much juvenile delinquency. Increased and open temptation does not appear in its 'naked hideousness,' but rather in a more 'attractive' form, in motion pictures, the lending library, places of amusement and night clubs, unprotected youthful company keeping, wartime crowded living rooms, the automobile, wine parties and on darkened streets. This mentality is a sign that many people have completely lost faith. But we have only to listen to the voice of Holy Church warning us that we cannot keep our souls pure and spotless except by a constant struggle."

The utterly false and pernicious theory of expediency and the total separation of religion as taught in all secular colleges and universities is a natural but nevertheless dangerous consequence. This theory of expediency maintains that for the sake of profit, greater utility, turning of events, etc., truth and morality may be dispensed with. This works great havoc in personal life, but still greater in public or international relations.

Our Holy Father, Pius XII, lamented the lack of faith and morality in nations and individuals in his first Encyclical, "Summi pontificatus," of October 20, 1939. In his Encyclical to American Catholics, "Sertum lætitæ," he clearly pointed out that there was much room for improvement in mentality as well as in morality. Nor did he fail to direct courageous statements to rulers and all who have influence in the shaping of the welfare of mankind.

Pertinently, Lon Francis wrote in the *Acolyte* for April, 1944:

> "There are only two schools of thought in Europe and the Americas. . . . Since they are mutually exclusive, both cannot be

CHRISTIAN MENTALITY 5

right. The pagan school of thought has long been dominant in the press, in the secular Universities, and now in the common schools. It is dominant in social conduct, and even the homes. It has invaded most of the churches . . . , and is responsible for the frightful wars of this century, for the totalitarian States, for the rejection of God Himself, and the persecution of religion, for the brazen attacks on morals, for the flood of printed filth, for the shocking delinquencies among tender youth, for the repudiation of the very idea of any moral law based either on nature or revelation. . . ."

These words were written during World War II and there is no indication that war will bring a change for the better. Wars never brought about a permanent religious revival among old and young. History substantiates this fully. Even wars fought for religious reasons have done more harm than good. A turn for the worse must be expected after a great war and presupposing a religious improvement to follow is mere wishful thinking without solid reasons to support it.

In this respect wars differ from religious persecutions. The latter always bring some good results. Persecutions seem to be the means Divine Providence has chosen to reestablish a Christian mentality. Without a persecution that rallies Christians around the Cross it will be difficult to form a Christian mentality, but for this reason an attempt should not be neglected.

It is not a prophecy to state that unless attempts are made to counteract an anti-Christian mentality, its signs will reappear with increased vigor when the war is ended.

There will be a greater quest after pleasure, convenience, comfort, and prosperity. How does this harmonize with the Christian principles, "Do penance" and "Seek ye first the kingdom of God"?

There will be a more unreasonable amount of care for the body, its culture and happiness. The manifestations of lust will increase. The number of divorces, broken homes, adulteries, and worse will be multiplied as they were after World War I. Wrong ideologies which the great mental errors will propagate in some pernicious form will spread over the world, because they cannot be destroyed by guns. To hold the contrary would be childish after the Popes have pointed this out time and again. How do these intellectual as well as moral evils agree with that quality of the mind possessed by those whom the Saviour calls "clean of heart" and for which He promised the vision of God?

And all these things will come about under the slogans of right and justice. Present trends like the application of force, neglect of principles, etc. show the spirit. Moreover, having happened after the first World War, why should it not happen after the second or third? Christ has told us: "Blessed are the meek," for only they "shall possess the land."

It must be kept in mind that all the evils mentioned are predominantly mental and about their existence there can be no reasonable doubt. Anyone denying these conditions might manifest a low standard of Christian mentality. However, the picture drawn may be considered one-sided. This is true. Undoubtedly, there has been an increase in works of piety, devotion, and charity which cannot be attributed to war psychosis alone. Good qualities need not be denied. Pope Pius XII praises many of them in his Encyclical to the Americans. But what makes matters more complicated is the undeniable fact that great errors of mind are often found in the same persons who manifest exterior Christianity. Some, and their number is increasing, practise the works of faith and retain radical and even anti-Christian ideas. They are very zealous in keeping some Commandments but are entirely indifferent to the spirit of the Counsels and Beatitudes which is to a certain extent binding upon all Christians. Such people might be classed among the lukewarm, who are the most difficult to convert. Certain things they do not like to hear, read, or be reminded of, and these are frequently the very truths they ought to know and put into practice. Many examples could be given but this is not necessary.

At first sight, all this may appear to be an accusation and a judgment of others. This would be against the principle stated by Christ and, therefore, a weakness in Christian mentality. But these things were written like an examination of conscience, printed for the use of individuals and those entrusted with the guidance of souls, without accusing or judging any reader. Some zealous Christians may become upset by conditions but find consolation in the thought that sin always was and always will remain with us, although one kind or the other will predominate during different periods. Salvation must be assured personally. Some others may take matters less seriously and say: "Well, God will provide!" He certainly could do so by different kinds of miracles, but will He do so for those He has abundantly rewarded in cash? This is doubtful. History shows that miracles wrought in Lourdes and other famous places are almost exclusively in favor of the believing poor and helpless, or those on a lower standard of living.

It is the duty of the Church, ever optimistic, and of those who have a share in the care and guidance of others, to teach and encourage people to a nobler life. All must work for the reconstruction of a truly Christian mentality. Only a clear mind and willing heart will remain immune to false doctrines and unwarranted temporal considerations and thus be receptive of divine truth and heavenly grace. All Christians should "hunger and thirst after justice" by endeavoring to obtain a deeper knowledge of God's plan in creation and man's place in it. It is a most interesting and also a very practical study.

The clergy and the instructors in religion will find a constant challange and inspiration to greater efforts in the words of St. Paul: "I charge thee, before God and Jesus Christ, Who shall judge the living and the dead by His coming and His kingdom: Preach the word, be instant in season, out of season: reprove, entreat, rebuke in all patience and doctrine. For there shall be a time, when they will not endure sound doctrine; but, according to their own desires, they will heap to themselves teachers having itching ears: And will indeed turn away their hearing from the truth, but will be turned unto fables. But be thou vigilant, labor in all things, do the work of an evangelist, fulfill thy ministry" (II Tim., iv, 1-5).

For the purpose of creating and deepening the Christian mentality this book was written, and the intent is to do so in an interesting and a graphic manner.

A fine document giving a picture of the Catholic attitude to-

8   FORMING A CHRISTIAN MENTALITY

wards faith, or of Christian mentality, is the *Abjuration* demanded by the Church from adult converts. It is found in the Appendix to the Roman Ritual and reads in part:

"I believe the Holy Catholic Apostolic Roman Church to be the only and true Church established on earth by Jesus Christ, to which I submit myself with my whole heart. I believe all the articles that she proposes to my belief and I reject and condemn all that she rejects and condemns, and I am ready to observe all that she commands me. And especially I profess that I believe:

"One only God in three Divine Persons. . . .

"The Catholic doctrine of the Incarnation, Passion, Death, and Resurrection of our Lord Jesus Christ: and the personal union of the two Natures, the divine and the human: the divine Maternity of the most holy Mary, together with her most spotless Virginity;

"The true, real, and substantial presence of the Body and Blood, together with the Soul and Divinity of our Lord Jesus Christ, in the most holy Sacrament of the Eucharist;

"The seven Sacraments instituted by Jesus Christ for the salvation of mankind: that is to say, Baptism, Confirmation, Eucharist, Penance, Extreme Unction, Orders, Matrimony;

"Purgatory, the Resurrection of the dead, Everlasting life;

"The Primacy, not only of honour, but also of jurisdiction of the Roman Pontiff, successor of St. Peter, Prince of the Apostles, Vicar of Jesus Christ;

"The veneration of the Saints, and of their images;

"The authority of the Apostolic and Ecclesiastical Traditions, and of the Holy Scriptures, which we must interpret and understand only in the sense which our holy mother the Catholic Church has held, and does hold;

"And everything else that has been defined, and declared by the Sacred Canons, and by the General Councils, and particularly by the holy Council of Trent, and delivered, defined, and declared by the General Council of the Vatican, especially concerning the Primacy of the Roman Pontiff, and his infallible teaching authority."

After having considered the sources of faith more in detail in the next chapter, the reader will be prepared to ponder God's plan for man, and the place which man has to fill according to the divine ordination.

CHAPTER II

Fountains of Faith

THE TRUE SPIRITUAL LIFE of the soul consists in faith and morality. Faith, pertaining to the intellect, embraces also the worship and knowledge of God. Although the existence of God can be known by reason alone, a fuller knowledge about the nature of God—the mysteries of the Blessed Trinity, the Incarnation, etc.—comes to man only through Revelation.

Morality pertains chiefly to the will. It is life in harmony with the true faith, as St. Paul writes: "The just man liveth by faith" (Gal., iii, 11). In other words, it is the service and worship of God as taught to us by faith. This faith, and life by faith, has been made known to man in different ways.

The Bible

"God, Who, at sundry times and in divers manners, spoke in times past to the fathers by the prophets, last of all, in these days hath spoken to us by His Son, Whom He hath appointed heir of all things" (Heb., i, 1-2). The revelations made by God "to the fathers by the prophets" were laid down in the books of the Old Testament. All these truths leading up to Christ in prophecies, types, and symbols, as also moral laws, were accepted by Him and perfected. Jesus said: "One jot or one tittle shall not pass of the law" (Matt., v, 18). What God revealed by His Son and the Apostles is found in the books of the New Testament, which were not collected definitely before the third century. The complete collection of Sacred Writings is called the Bible, which means the Book of Books.

The Bible is, therefore, the main fountain of faith, but not the only one as we shall see presently. Nevertheless, for Christians, the New Testament is of the greatest importance. It contains not only the teachings of Christ but also their supplement and explanation by the Apostles, deacons (Luke, x, and Acts, vi), bishops and priests ordained by the Apostles (I Tim., i, 3, and iv, 14), together with the illuminating example of the first Christians (Acts, ii, 42-47). But even this wealth of doctrine did not cover everything as St. John the Evangelist expressly states at the end of the Gospel written by him.

It is evident in the Old Testament as in the New, that historians, teachers, and writers wrote about religious affairs without being appointed and empowered by God. The Church, the only divinely appointed teacher of mankind, did not accept books unless it could be firmly established that the writers were inspired by the Holy Ghost and that the writings had come down to the Church without substantial changes. In collecting the different books, the Church exercised her infallible teaching office and solemnly decided that all the books found in the complete Catholic Bible must be accepted as Divine Revelation, and that no one could add to it or eliminate any one book without separating from the community of the faithful. This decree of the Council of Trent [1] was especially directed against reformers who, in order to suit the Bible to their errors, made eliminations and falsely interpreted it.

From this it follows that passages from the Bible, interpreted according to the mind of the Church and quoted in confirmation of a certain doctrine, are incontrovertible proofs of a doctrine's correctness. This should be kept in mind whilst reading the following chapters. It also follows that the frequent and constant reading and study of the Bible with notes, are most effective means for deepening the faith and forming a Christian mentality or philosophy of life.

Newly revised editions of the Bible in different languages have created a new interest in Holy Scripture in many parts of the world. Americans bought many copies of the revision sponsored by the Confraternity of Christian Doctrine. This revision was

---

[1] Sess. IV, Denzinger, Bannwart, Umberg, "Enchiridion Symbolorum et Definitionum," 784, Ed. 15 et 16, Herder, Friburgi Brisgoviæ, 1922.

not published to counteract the sales of disapproved Bibles by the Bible Societies and "Bible Christians," but for the use of Catholics.

It is evident that the reading of the Bible is not necessary for salvation. In the first three centuries there was no New Testament generally available. In the following thousand years, Bibles were scarce. They had to be copied by hand and were seldom at the disposal of the unlettered. Nevertheless, Christians were strong in faith and died in it. The Bible was by no means neglected by the official teachers of religion.

The invention of the printing press brought a change in the availability of the Bible. The first book published by this new process was the Bible and this furnishes a definite proof of its popularity. On the other hand, the multiplication of Bibles made it possible for heretics to proclaim their adulterated Bible as the sole rule of faith. Having left the Church, the infallible interpreter of the Bible, they had no other choice than to leave the explanation of a book that could not interpret itself, to the mercy of the individual readers. Private interpretation is a purely human arrangement without a shadow of divine sanction. St. Jerome, whose translation and revision of the Bible is called the Vulgate Version, wrote: "Know ye that it is impossible to keep the right way in Holy Scripture without a leader and guide" (Epist. 53, 6).

The error of private interpretation of the Bible was an insult to the Word of God and had dire consequences. It submitted divine truths to human judgments, left the acceptance of a preacher's sermon to the audience, and facilitated the founding of hundreds of sects all giving the Bible, falsely interpreted, as a proof for their right to exist. Finally, it caused the complete rejection of the reliability of the Bible which can be guaranteed only by the Catholic Church, divinely appointed for this task.

The Holy Scriptures mean more and are of greater profit to Catholic readers. St. Paul writes: "What things soever were written [in the Scriptures], were written for our learning: that through patience and the comfort of the Scriptures, we might have hope" (Rom., xv, 4). And he adds: "All Scripture, inspired of God, is profitable to teach, to reprove, to correct, to instruct in justice, that the man of God may be perfect, furnished to every good work" (II Tim., iii, 16-17). St. John Chrysostom did not hesitate to call upon the laity: "Listen to me, please, all of you who live in the world: procure for yourselves Bibles as a medicine for your souls. Buy at least the New Testament . . . for your constant teacher" (In Col., 9-20).

These counsels extend in an unbroken line down to our own days. Our Holy Father, Pius XII, writes in his Encyclical on Bible Study (September 30, 1943):

> "Whosoever considers the immense labors undertaken by Catholic exegetes during well nigh two thousand years, so that the word of God, imparted to men, Holy Writ, might daily be more deeply and fully understood and more intensely loved, will easily be convinced that it is the serious duty of the faithful, and especially of priests, to make free and holy use of this treasure, accumulated throughout so many centuries by the greatest intellects. . . .
>
> "Let priests, therefore, who are bound by their office to procure the eternal salvation of the faithful, after they have themselves by diligent study perused the sacred pages and made them their own by prayer and meditation, assiduously distribute the heavenly treasures of the Divine Word by sermons, homilies and exhortations; let them confirm the Christian doctrine by sentences from the Sacred Books and illustrate it by outstanding examples from sacred history and in particular from the Gospel of Christ Our Lord. . . .
>
> "The same veneration [for the Sacred Scripture] the Bishops should endeavor daily to increase and perfect among the faithful committed to their care, encouraging all those initiatives by which men, with apostolic zeal, laudably strive to excite and foster among Catholics a greater knowledge of and love for the Sacred Books. Let them favor, therefore, and lend help to these pious associations whose aim it is to spread copies of Holy Writ, especially of the Gospels,[1] among the faithful, and to procure by every means that in Christian families the same be read daily with piety and devotion. . . ."

To forestall objections, it must be kept in mind that certainty and infallible truth are guaranteed only for the Catholic Bible

---

[1] Many portions of the Old Testament were not written for youth, and presuppose a morally and spiritually mature reader.

called the Vulgate and its approved translation. Furthermore, this guarantee pertains only to faith and morals and does not extend to history, science, sociology, and other things that have nothing to do with religious life. Practically all objections made against the Bible are of a nature that has nothing to do with religious life.

Tradition

The other great fountain or source of faith is Tradition which came to us indirectly from God through the Holy Spirit, Who guides and protects the Church against religious errors. Christ Himself assured us of this divine aid by saying: "I have yet many things to say to you: but you cannot bear them now. But when He, the Spirit of truth, is come, He will teach you all truth . . . and the things that are to come, He shall shew you" (John, xvi, 12-13). All that Christ taught, and the Apostles related, the Church guided by the Holy Spirit declares, explains, and develops in her progress to the end of time. This is covered by the term Tradition. This Tradition was the sole guide of true believers during the years before the Bible was written and while it was being written. In fact, without it we could not know the quality of the Scriptures, nor their importance, nor their true meaning, nor even their very existence. For these reasons Tradition was necessary and will remain of the greatest importance for all time to come.

What belongs to Tradition, this fountain of faith and inexhaustible treasure of truth, committed to the custodianship of the infallible Church? In general, all that the Church teaches or explains in matters of faith and morals that is not found in the Bible. In particular, Tradition embraces the ancient formulas of faith like the Apostolic, the **Nicene, and the Athanasian** Creeds. These are in accordance with the teachings of the Bible but are not found therein as we are wont to recite them. They were first spread by word of mouth.

Tradition is also found in the decisions and declarations of the infallible General Councils and dogmatic definitions of the Popes as teachers of the universal Church. This infallibility was given by Christ to Peter and his lawful successors when He said: "Thou art Peter; and upon this rock I will build My Church, and the gates of hell [i.e., all pernicious influences] shall not prevail against it" (Matt., xvi, 18). With these words, Christ gave to His Church stability, which necessarily includes infallibility. Moreover, He conferred personal infallibility upon Peter when He said to him: "I have prayed for thee, that thy faith fail not: and thou, being once converted, confirm thy brethren" (Luke, xxii, 32).

Tradition also embraces the writings and sermons of the Fathers and Doctors of the Church who explained the Scriptures, probed further into the articles and mysteries of faith, preserved the customs and regulations of the Church, and placed on record the heroic life of martyrs and confessors and other memorable events in the history of the Church.

A most important part of Tradition is the worship or Liturgy of the Church. It covers the official prayers exactly expressing the true faith, the forms of administering the Sacraments and celebrating Mass, sacred singing, exercises of faith, pictures, statues, and symbols used for generations in our churches, and similar features.

The Liturgy has also great educational value. The study of the Missal, Breviary, Ritual, and other liturgical books demonstrates to us how Holy Scripture is to be understood and how the texts are applied by the Church in the literal, symbolical, figurative, mystical, or any other approved sense. Some ceremonies, blessings, and consecrations could not be properly understood without the text accompanying them. Divine worship which began with the sacrifices offered by Cain and Abel, underwent constant changes and a development of its form, meaning, and splendor according to time and circumstances. Some of the changes were really substantial.

In the beginning of mankind faith was very simple. It merely covered the existence and justice of God and the duty of man to obey Him. Much more was added in the realm of faith and morals after God elected the Jews as the Chosen People and as the bearers of the promise of a Redeemer made by God after the

FOUNTAINS OF FAITH

fall of man. During this period of the Old Testament, divine worship was greatly developed, especially after the building of the Temple. Much of this Jewish worship was retained by the Church and the rest was changed or discarded.

The reality took the place of prophecies, types, and shadows. Christ became the sole eternal High-Priest and Sacrifice. The old ceremonial law was abrogated and the moral law was perfected. The Sabbath was changed to the Sunday in commemoration of the Resurrection and many houses of God took the place of the *one* Temple. Much of this was ordained by Christ Himself, most probably during the forty days before His Ascension into heaven. During these days, He also organized His Church in general, but left the neccessary details to the future. The Holy Spirit provides that this further development does not leave the right course.

In the early days of Christianity, faith and worship were very simple and confined to bare essentials. But as soon as circumstances permitted, the development was more rapid than in the early ages of mankind. Gradually Christian life became more in harmony with the better knowledge of faith and morals and the development of the Liturgy contributed much to the improvement of Christian living.

There is a difference and a similarity between Holy Scripture and Tradition. Holy Scripture is static. This source of Revelation was completed before the death of St. John, the last of the Apostles. It remains an inexhaustible mine of faith and morals, but nothing can be added to it. Tradition, however, is living and progressive. It also is a treasure trove of faith and morals, but its collection is not finished and its increase will continue until the end of time. Many things are found in the one that are not found in the other, but Tradition can never contradict Holy Scripture, when correctly interpreted. Where a contradiction or variation seems to exist, it is subjective rather than objective.

Although Tradition appears necessary to every true believer, there are others who reject it by declaring the Bible the only rule of faith. They demand and advocate a return to the simplicity of the earliest Christians. This is not only unwise but even foolish. The demand is a contradiction in itself, as all heresies are, because on the one hand it rejects Tradition, and on the other insists upon the Bible, which depends on the Church and Tradition for its canon, guarantee, and interpretation. It is even an impossibility to go back to the third or fourth century, because the Church is a living organism.

Christ told us that the kingdom of heaven, or the Church, is like a tiny seed, but grows into a tree (Matt., xiii, 31-33). A tree cannot become again a small plant or a still smaller seed. Nor can a tree be whittled down to its root and remain a tree. If it would not die in the process, it would at least be very crippled if another sprout should spring forth.

The one living Church founded by Christ (neither the Bible nor Tradition tells us that He founded more than one), must develop in size, must grow branches (the different rites), leaves, and blossoms, and must bring forth fruit. The tree itself cannot be reformed, nor can the Church, to which Christ guaranteed indefectibility in faith and morals, although individual members of this Church might need an improvement in both.

Both Holy Scripture and Tradition have the same validity and force when used as proofs for the confirmation of truths, provided both are applied according to the mind of the Church. The mind of the Church regarding both we find most clearly expressed in the texts used by the Church in her Liturgy. Moreover, the Liturgy accompanies us from the cradle to the grave.

It is well to keep this in mind whilst reading the following chapters. It is a great help in realizing their importance and it is a requisite for the formation of a Christian mentality that looks at things with the eyes of God.

CHAPTER III

Creation and Procreation

IN A STATEMENT to the 14,000 members of Italian Youth, Pope Pius XII has given the whole Church a three-point program that is as practical as it is fundamental. He said:

> "In the first place, human society must be re-placed upon a Christian foundation. Holy Scripture with its moral precepts must again be esteemed and honored.
> "The family must be re-elevated, and motherhood must again receive the halo of its sacramental dignity. The married must learn and understand their duties, and must fulfill their responsibilities conscientiously.
> "In every human society, authority, discipline, respect for the social order, mutual rights, and the realization of moral obligations must be restored." [1]

In this three-point program Pope Pius XII stresses, first, Holy Scripture as an excellent means to promote Christian living. He then desires that people should become better acquainted with the holy state and obligations of matrimony, and that all Christians, young and old, should better fulfill the duties essential to Christian living.

In considering this program from a pastoral viewpoint, the matter of an effective education in religion as the basis for the whole human life is naturally of prime importance. Many believe that a lack of religious knowledge is the principal cause of the deplorable worldliness we witness today. To a certain extent this may be true even among Catholics. But the knowledge of religion has not made all doctors of theology truly spiritual-minded. Fortunately, it is not necessary to be steeped in the sci-

---

[1] Address to Italian Youth, 1940 Cf. also the Pope's Christmas broadcast, 1942.

ence of religion in order to lead a very holy life. Average Catholics, not engaged in educational fields, do not need to know much more than the first principles of religion and their logical corollaries, because the gift of faith supplies more than we may be willing to concede. However, additional religious instruction can do no harm, although the good results of extended indoctrination are not clearly demonstrable, at least not in the matter of enhanced spirituality. Religious activities may have increased but this is not yet life *by* faith. It must not be forgotten that religious practice may be based on foundations other than faith

Nothing is so liable to produce an aversion to religion as over explanation and a wealth of details that are not brought into necessary connection with the foundation upon which they rest and the dogmas from which they flow.

In these chapters directed towards the re-spiritualization of our people we shall consider the fundamental facts of creation, regeneration, and procreation. For this purpose, Holy Scripture the Liturgy, and the pronouncements of the Church will be extensively utilized and applied to Christian living.

Before entering upon our task, it may be in order to say a few words about the Pope's expressed emphasis upon the Holy Scriptures. The reading of the Bible has practically disappeared among the majority of Catholics as well as among others, and among the clergy as well as the laity. What St. Paul wrote to Timothy can rarely be verified in men and women of our days "From thy infancy thou has known the Holy Scriptures, which can instruct thee to salvation by the faith which is in Christ Jesus." (II Tim., iii, 15). We priests have studied our theology in ponderous volumes, and have accepted the scriptural quotations as final; but we shall gradually lose all intimacy with the Word of God unless our meditations are made faithfully. Some oft-repeated portions we may remember, but perhaps we shall never realize their practical bearing on life. The laity, too, hear the Sunday Gospels, read the brief quotations in the Catechism or spiritual books, but, being disconnected from the body of Revelation, the passages cease to be overwhelming truths, and their lessons are not carried over into daily life. The conse

CREATION AND PROCREATION

quence is that the Bible is not read, because it is no longer appreciated, although it is the most important book existing. The reading of the Bible should again be promoted among the faithful, and this has lately been done with great success. Valuable suggestions on Scripture study are contained in the Introductions to many commentaries on Holy Scripture.[1]

After God had created heaven and earth and all the movable and immovable things they contained, He saw that all was good. To crown the work of His hands, God decided to create man. And He created man according to His own image and likeness. "Male and female He created them. And God blessed them saying: Increase and multiply, and fill the earth and subdue it, and rule over [it]. . . . And God saw all the things that He had made, and they were very good. . . . And He rested on the seventh day from all His work" (Gen., i, 27, 28, 31; ii, 2).

The creation of man is described in some detail in the second chapter of the Book of Genesis. "The Lord God formed man of the slime of the earth: and breathed into his face the breath of life, and man became a living soul. . . . And the Lord God took man, and put him into the paradise of pleasure . . . and He commanded him saying: Of every tree of paradise thou shalt eat: But of the tree of knowledge of good and evil thou shalt not eat. For in what day soever thou shalt eat of it, thou shalt die the death. And the Lord God said: It is not good for man to be alone: let us make him a help like unto himself. . . . Then the Lord God cast a deep sleep upon Adam: and when he was fast asleep, He took one of his ribs, and filled up flesh for it. And the Lord God built the rib which He took from Adam into a woman: and brought her [Eve] to Adam. And Adam said: This now is bone of my bones, and flesh of my flesh; she shall be called woman, because she was taken out of man. Wherefore a man shall leave father and mother, and shall cleave to his wife: and they shall be two in one flesh" (Gen., ii, 7-24). To this Jesus

---

[1] E.g.: John E. Steinmueller, "A Companion to Scripture Studies," 3 vols. (Wagner, New York, 1942, 1943); Archconfraternity of Christian Doctrine, "A Commentary on the New Testament" (Paterson, 1941); John Laux, "An Introduction to the Bible" (New York, 1934).

added: "What therefore God hath joined together, let no man put asunder" (Matt., xix, 6).

The creation of man endowed with intellect, free will, and immortality, according to the likeness of God, was necessarily a work of love, since it was an act of the will of God. It was pure and unselfish love, because it could not bring about any essential increase in God's happiness, honor, and glory. The essence and nature of God became reflected in man. He was a creation of love animated with the love of his Creator Whom he knew. The human soul was to love this God and all His creatures according to their rank for the sake of the Creator. This love was indicated by Adam's exclamation: "This now is bone of my bones, and flesh of my flesh . . . two in one flesh." This love before the fall of man differed from the carnal and often sinful love prevailing thereafter.

The original love of our first parents was an **outflow of God's** love that unites the Blessed Trinity and made man a partaker in the likeness of God. This bond of love between God and man and among men themselves had to undergo a test of the free will of man before it should become permanent as it was intended to be. The all-wise Creator ordained a test that was in conformity with the nature of the Creator and the nature of the creature. Adam, made to God's own image, had the faculties of the soul to know and love God. Faith and obedience had to be tested. Man had to prove in a practical manner that he loved above all things God, Whom he recognized as the highest good, and that he loved other things for the love of God. The Great Commandment founded in the nature of the image of God had to be kept.

For the purpose of testing obedience to this general and comprehensive law, a specific order and act was chosen by God. Adam must not prefer the fruit of a specified tree to the expressed will of his Creator, to Whom he was indebted for everything he had received and to Whom he was bound by love. Moreover, Adam's will was strengthened also by the threat of certain death in the event of disobedience.

Being in the possession of an unclouded intellect, our first parents knew fully what the punishment for disobedience would

CREATION AND PROCREATION

mean to mankind. But they failed miserably. The bonds of love uniting the Creator with man, and man with the Creator, were severed. Man separated himself from the Creator by his own free will. The consequences of this first and decisive failure against the Great Commandment are well recalled by Moses in his Canticle (Deut., xxxii): "The works of God are perfect. . . . He is just and right. . . . Is He not thy father, that hath possessed thee, and made thee, and created thee? . . . Thou hast forsaken the God that begot thee, and hast forgotten the Lord that created thee. The Lord saw, and was moved to wrath: because His own sons and daughters provoked Him. And He said: I will hide My face from them, and will consider what their last end shall be: for it is a perverse generation, and unfaithful children. . . . I will heap evils upon them, and will spend My arrows among them. They shall be consumed with famine, and birds shall devour them with a most bitter bite: I will send the teeth of beasts upon them, with the fury of creatures that trail upon the ground, and of serpents. Without, the sword shall lay them waste, and terror within, both the young man and the virgin, the sucking child with the man in years. . . . O that they would be wise and would understand, and would provide for their last end. How should one pursue after a thousand, and two chase ten thousand? Was it not, because their God had sold them, and the Lord had shut them up?" These words of Moses are prophetic; for they refer to the future as well as to the past. They indicate the conditions of our own days.

Many were the evils that came upon the first family on account of its failure to love God above all. To Adam God said: "Because thou hast hearkened to the voice of thy wife, and hast eaten of the tree, . . . cursed is the earth in thy work, with labor and toil shalt thou eat thereof all the days of thy life. Thorns and thistles shall it bring forth to thee. . . . In the sweat of thy face shalt thou eat bread till thou return to the earth, . . . for dust thou art and into dust thou shalt return" (Gen., iii, 17-19). And to Eve He said: "I will multiply thy sorrows, and thy conceptions: in sorrow shalt thou bring forth children, and thou shalt be under thy husband's power, and he shall have dominion over thee" (ibid. 16). And both were cast out of the Paradise of pleasure, to till the earth from which Adam was taken (ibid. 24). With the gates of Paradise, heaven too was closed.

However, the blessing of the Creator, to "grow and multiply," was not taken from man. After having left Paradise, "Adam knew Eve his wife: who conceived and brought forth Cain, saying: I have gotten a man *through* God" (Gen., iv, 1). And Adam "begot sons and daughters" (Gen., v, 4).

The words spoken by God to Adam and Eve were addressed to them as the representatives of mankind, and retain the same value for all their descendants until the day of judgment. But the exercise of the justice of God and the expression of His hatred for sin did not diminish His love for His creatures. He left them the hope for a betterment in the future. Adam had lost the first opportunity to prove himself worthy of immortality and blessedness; a second chance was to be given mankind to regain what had been lost. This hope was expressed by the words God spoke to the serpent: "I will put enmities between thee [Satan] and the woman, and thy seed and her seed: she shall crush thy head" (Gen., iii, 15). Here a regeneration of mankind was foretold.

The history of creation, as found in Divine Revelation, clearly teaches the holiness and unity of matrimony from the very beginning. This true concept of matrimony was never completely lost throughout the ages. It was preserved in the earliest times and during the history of the Chosen People, and was not confined to those who kept the faith in the Creator. All peoples who had not lost every vestige of an inborn morality continued to consider marriage as something mysterious and holy. It was something in which their Deity or deities had a hand. Shame or modesty did not cease to accompany the sex urge, and safeguarded sex to a considerable extent. It was nourished and kept alive by the laws and regulations imposed upon women after childbirth. Weddings were always accompanied by religious rites, sacrifices, and mystic ceremonies, and these ceremonies were considered natural by the people.

Nor was the unity of matrimony ever generally denied, either

CREATION AND PROCREATION

by peoples or by religious groups. Promiscuity or the unrestricted procreation by individuals never became a rule among peoples or tribes. Naturally, there were men who were degraded in this respect, and perhaps many of them; but they knew that they were doing wrong, as the excuses found in ancient documents clearly establish. There have been also teachers, ancient and modern, who claimed that the unity of matrimony evolved gradually and was not the rule among uncivilized peoples. These assertions, however, have not only never been proved, but they have been demonstrated to be utterly unfounded. Some have likewise entertained the idea that immorality reigned from the beginning of mankind, and that culture and civilization brought with it a decrease of immorality. However, it is more true and more solidly established that early mankind, although perhaps low in civilization, was truly moral, and that in many cases a degraded brand of culture brought about immorality. The farther people drifted away from God, the more was monogamy endangered.

The Jewish people, with their belief in the one true God, also preserved as a nation the original concepts of the sanctity and unity of matrimony. Jewish history as found in the Bible leaves no doubt about this. Regarding the sanctity of matrimony, the **Jews were** convinced that marriage was a union established by God for the very definite purpose of propagating and increasing the human race. They considered it holy, because it was according to the holy will of God, Who Himself cooperated in the propagation of man by creating the soul that was to impart to the material prepared by the parents the rational nature of a human being. Moreover, out of matrimony was to come the promised Redeemer. The children were considered the property of God, as well as of the parents, and were to be redeemed by offerings made to Him (Lev., xii, 8). Circumcision was ordained by God as the sign of the Covenant and, no doubt, also as a constant reminder to the Jews to control and mortify the sexual passion. The separate sexes were created for the purpose of complementing each other, and this purpose was reached perfectly by the permanent union between two persons, one of each sex.

This union was regulated by God Himself through the Mosaic Law. The Jews realized that matrimony was an instrument subject to God its Creator, and that its essence could not be subject to man or any human authority.

The unity of matrimony, a union between one man and one woman for life, remained the rule among the Hebrews, although they had their letter of dismissal and used it on certain occasions. Monogamy was universally the rule; polygamy was the exception, and never considered to be the ideal. Polygamy was tolerated by God, for reasons of His own. He tolerated it without giving His approval. Abraham took Agar in addition to his legitimate wife, Sarah, who was without child, but the children of Agar or other concubines were never considered legitimate nor held as bearers of the Promise. Jacob is mentioned as having had four women, but it seems that they were taken for more or less ideal reasons and not to satisfy lust. The disturbances created by this polygamy among the princes of the land clearly indicate that God's pleasure was absent (Gen., xxxv, 22).

The Mosaic laws regulating marriages among relatives are found in Leviticus, xviii, 6-18, and in Deuteronomy, xxv, 5-10. The punishments for irregular marriages are stated in Leviticus, xx, 20-21. Sexual delinquencies and crimes are treated in the same chapter. The main idea and objective was that the Jews should lead a chaste life (Deut., xxii, 19). There were other regulations prescribing abstinence from matrimonial acts at certain times and periods, and with regard to heredity. But all tended to the same end, and the end was realized to a great extent. Instead of degenerating deeper and deeper into sexual perversion, the original idea of matrimony became clearer and clearer among the Hebrews. Consequently, they differed greatly from the pagans surrounding them, among whom the process was reversed. The real and most prevailing form was undoubtedly monogamy, and this form is eulogized in the Psalms and by the prophets and historical writers.[1]

---

[1] It is not practical to cite all pertinent passages found in Holy Scripture. A large number of them are quoted in "Das sexuelle Leben der Voelker," by Dr. Joseph Mueller, to whom the writer is otherwise indebted (Schoening, Paderborn, 1934).

CREATION AND PROCREATION

The sexual disorders among the ancient cultured peoples (e.g., the Egyptians, Chaldeans, Asiatic Indians, Persians, Chinese, Greeks, and Romans) were much more numerous, but it must be kept in mind that these disorders advanced in numbers as well as gravity as the nations receded from God and religion. The people knew and appreciated chastity when they met with it, and their conscience did not leave them at rest when they acted against the laws of nature. Among all these peoples the idea of the holiness and unity of matrimony was never completely lost, although they may have failed to grasp its importance and to live up to the natural standards. There are numerous old pagan writers who bear witness to this fact, and clearly indicate that the true concept of matrimony among all had the same common foundation and origin. Many modern writers have tried to disprove this fact, but without success.

The following summary may serve as a conclusion to this chapter. An increase of religious knowledge does not always promote a truly Christian behavior. It does so only if it is constantly brought into connection with the essence of religion. For this purpose, Holy Scripture should again become the common property of the people as well as of the preachers. The Word of God tells us in what manner and why man was created according to God's image and likeness. Like God, man was endowed with intellect and free will. He should exercise these faculties to know and love God, thereby imitating the operations of God, knowledge and love. "Now this is eternal life: that they may know Thee, the only true God" (John, xvii, 3). "Thou shalt love the Lord thy God with thy whole heart, and with thy whole soul, and with thy whole mind, and with thy whole strength" (Deut., vi, 5), and you shall show it in a practical manner by loving "thy friend as thyself" (Lev., xix, 18), "that all may be one" (John, xvii, 21). For this man was created and life everlasting promised. Ethical perfection would be but a natural consequence. Unless there is oneness in love, there is discord by hatred. There is no intermediate condition. Man was so made that he is either for or against in faith and morals, no matter how fickle his conduct may be. Where there is holy love, there all Commandments are observed. Sex is by its very nature a strong urge and, as history shows, difficult to dominate. However, it is fundamental, and passion, unless it is regulated by faith, becomes an endless source of great disorders in the field of religion and of social life.

To preserve the flow of divine love through His creatures and back to Himself, God created man male and female, and sanctified the union of man and woman. This union should be real and permanent; the partners become of the same flesh and bone. God appointed that one of each sex by their union with each other should be the lawful propagators of mankind, and they should share as progenitors a mutual love. But "man when he was in honor did not understand" (Ps. xlviii, 21), although he could have done so. He lost faith in God and broke the bond of love with God by acting freely against His will. This was the beginning of all evils, including sexual and matrimonial irregularities. The drifting away from God made peoples miserable and intensified their wickedness. The Chosen People of old preserved the original concept of matrimony, and with it retained the honor of being the bearers of the Promise. "Charity is, therefore, also our fruit which, as the Apostle writes, springs from a pure heart, a good conscience, and an unfeigned faith" (St. Augustine).

CHAPTER IV

Regeneration and Sanctification

THE BOND OF LOVE between God and man, disrupted by original sin, was to be restored in the manner promised. The Emmanuel, God-with-us, our King and Lawgiver, the expectation and Saviour of the nations, was to come and reunite mankind with its Creator (Ant., December 23). "Behold a virgin shall conceive, and bear a Son, and His name shall be called Emmanuel" (Is., vii, 14). Eve had been made by God from a rib of Adam, but the new Adam was to be given to us by the woman prophesied in Paradise. The first woman, the mother of mankind, had a large share in the fall of man; the second mother, the mother of the children of God, would have a conspicuous part in the regeneration of mankind.

When the fullness of time appointed by the Creator had arrived, the Angel Gabriel was sent to Mary with the glad tidings that she had been chosen and prepared to become the Mother of God. Mary asked: "How shall this be done, because I know not man?" (Luke, i, 34). The Angel answered with the significant words: "The Holy Ghost shall come upon thee, and the power of the Most High shall overshadow thee. And therefore also the Holy which shall be born of thee shall be called the Son of God" (ibid., 35).

According to St. John (i, 1-14), this Son was the Word, the Second Person of the Blessed Trinity: "The Word was God. . . . All things were made by Him. . . . That was the true light, which enlighteneth every man that cometh into this world. He was in the world, and the world was made by Him, and the world knew Him not. . . . But as many as received Him, he gave them power to be made the sons of God, to them that believe in His name: who are born . . . of God. And the Word was made flesh, and dwelt among us . . . full of grace and truth." He taught mankind by word and example how to observe the Great Commandment, and as a pledge of His infinite love He died for us and assumed us into His Mystical Body, the Church. "Behold I do new things. . . . This people have I formed for Myself; they shall show forth My praise" (Is., xliii, 19-21). "Assemble yourselves, and come, and draw near together, ye that are saved of the Gentiles" (Is., xlv, 20).

The Incarnation and Redemption were acts of love. The exterior form of the union with God is the Church, a communion of the faithful believers in Christ, governed on earth by a visible Vicar appointed by Him. This communion is to be a permanent bond of love between the Creator and man, and between man and man. Men are to be so closely knitted together that they will form but one body in Christ the Lord. Therefore, the Church has to be indestructible, for it is to outlive the ages and to enter triumphantly into eternity: "Thou art Peter; and upon this rock I will build My Church, and the gates of hell shall not prevail against it" (Matt., xvi, 18). Outside of this Church salvation is impossible, but an invitation to membership is extended to all: "Teach ye all nations, . . . teaching them to observe all things whatsoever I have commanded you" (Matt., xxviii, 19-20). But fallen mankind could not enter into this intimate union with God until it was rescued from its miserable condition and restored, in so far as was necessary, to the state in which man was created. The holy image and likeness of God had to be restored by infusing anew into man the divine virtues of faith, hope, and charity.

To communicate the effects of the Redemption Christ instituted Baptism: "Teach ye all nations: baptizing them in the name of the Father, and of the Son, and of the Holy Ghost" (Matt., xxviii, 19). Baptism would reconcile God with man by the Holy Ghost, the Spirit of Love taking possession of man. This process of regeneration and adoption would bring with it membership in the Church—Christ's Mystical Body: "I live, now not I; but Christ liveth in me" (Gal., ii, 20). "The charity of

REGENERATION AND SANCTIFICATION

God appeared towards us, because God hath sent His only begotten Son ... that we may live by Him" (I John, iv, 9).

All this is wonderfully expressed in the Liturgy of Holy Saturday. As an introduction to the blessing of the baptismal water intended to bring about the transition from the death of sin to a life of grace, the deacon sings the *Exultet*. He calls upon the Angels, the earth, and the Church to sing a hymn of praise to the risen King of, Kings, Who reigns forever and has expelled all darkness. He continues: "It is meet and just that we praise Him Who with His blood paid on our behalf to the Eternal Father the debt of Adam. For it would profit us nothing to be born, had not we had the blessing of redemption. O priceless boon of boundless love, that Thou, O God, shouldst give Thine only Son to free a slave! His resurrection drives sin away and cleanses away all guilt; it gives innocence anew to them that are fallen and gladness to them that are in sorrow. Hatred it puts down; and makes smooth the ways of peace" (summarized).

Then follow twelve prophecies taken from the Old Testament which were formerly used for the instruction of the catechumens. They refer to important events in the life of mankind, beginning with the fall of man and continuing with the punishment of the Deluge, the election of the Chosen People, the passage through the Red Sea, the call of Isaias to the people to return to Jehovah and serve Him, the paschal lamb in Egypt, the destruction of Ninive, the promised land, and the three youths in the furnace. The orations following each Prophecy indicate the truths that were emphasized in the instructions.

After this preparation of the catechumens the ceremonies of blessing the baptismal water begin. On the way to the font the celebrant prays for the catechumens, beseeching God to grant mercifully "that the very thirsting of their faith may, through Baptism, sanctify them both in body and soul, through Jesus Christ": "O almighty and eternal God, ... send the Spirit of adoption to quicken with newness of life those whom Baptism brings forth."

The blessing of water is in the form of a Preface. It starts with rendering thanks to God Who with His invisible powers wonderfully imparts to the Sacraments their effects. Referring to Baptism in particular, it relates that in the very beginning the Spirit of God moving over the waters gave them sanctifying power, and used water in washing away the sins of a guilty world by the Flood, prefiguring the Sacrament of regeneration, that in one and the same element and its mystery wickedness should cease and holiness begin. Then some petitions are inserted for the increase in membership of the Church, and that the heavenly offspring born of the spotless womb of this divine font may issue unto new life. And howbeit in sex or age one differs from another, let grace, the mother of all, bring them forth all alike—all children of the Spirit, all in perfect purity.

The ceremony in which the celebrant touches the water with his hand is followed by the threefold blessing of God, Who in the beginning divided the water from the dry land, made it flow in four rivers, sweetened it in the wilderness, and brought it forth from a rock to slake the thirst of His people. Jesus Christ, Who changed water into wine, walked upon the waves, and was Himself baptized in the Jordan, is invoked. Water came forth from His side, together with His precious blood, and He gave His Apostles the command to baptize all who should believe.

After breathing thrice upon the water in the form of a cross and immersing the Paschal Candle in the water, the priest sings thrice: "May the power of the Holy Ghost descend upon this font into all its depths, and endue the whole substance of the water with the power of regeneration!" He concludes with the prayer: "In this font may every stain of sin be washed away; and may the nature of man, made after God's own image and made anew for the glory of its Creator, be cleansed from its former defilement; that everyone who shall come unto this Sacrament of regeneration may be born again and verily be, in pureness and innocence, a child. Through our Lord Jesus Christ Thy Son: Who shall come to judge the living and the dead, and the world by fire" (the fire being doubtless symbolized by the Paschal Candle).

In this summary of the solemn blessing of the baptismal water, the allusions to the prophecies and the life of Christ should not be overlooked. They furnish beautiful thoughts for illustrating sermons or instructions to converts. Some expressions like "born of the spotless womb," "children of the Spirit . . . in pureness and innocence," should be remembered for future reference.

The final part of the blessing of baptismal water includes the mixture of the oil of catechumens and holy chrism with the water in the name of the Blessed Trinity. In the early days of Christianity and for several centuries thereafter, the catechumens who had completed their instructions were baptized at this point.

The rite of Baptism for adults as well as for infants is very old. The latter is a limitation to the essentials. It was already in use in the fifth century, and received a permanent form in the Gregorian Sacramentary whence it was taken over into the *Rituale Romanum*. After the sixteenth century, Baptism by infusion was gradually substituted for immersion, but some of the ceremonies for the catechumens were retained.

Near the vestibule of the church an examination took place and after the personalia of the candidate had been registered, the priest asked: "What dost thou ask of the Church of God?" The answer is: "Faith." From this answer it is quite evident that an instruction on the Creed preceded the ceremonies that now follow. In the case of infants this instruction was to follow later. To impart it is an obligation that binds in conscience, not only the pastors, but even more so the parents and the sponsors. To ask for faith is an act of the will motivated by an earnest desire to live up to this faith. The elect asks for faith, because it will bring him to life everlasting. But to dispel any idea that the grace of Baptism and the gift of faith will bring salvation without the cooperation of Christians having the use of reason, the priest expressly states under what conditions heaven is granted to those who are baptized. The Commandments must be kept. They are summed up in one: "Thou shalt love the Lord thy God . . . and thy neighbor as thyself." It brings us back to creation when man was tested in this love. This again presupposes that the elect knows the Great Commandment and its corollaries as found in the Decalogue and the laws of the Church. The subsequent signing with the cross, imposing of the hand, and the exorcisms are ancient rites by which the Church expresses the acceptance of the candidate for membership, and the destruction of all bonds of Satan that may still exist. The giving of blessed salt signifies purification and preservation.

Led by the priest to the font, all recite together the Apostles' Creed and the Our Father. This again presupposes that the candidate has become acquainted with prayer, and has been instructed about the means of grace. All the instructions given before Baptism correspond with the three parts of the Catechism. The instruction for converts might, therefore, well be given with reference to this preparatory part of the rite of Baptism. In sermons, too, the close relation between religious truths and Baptism might be definitely and repeatedly emphasized. Then follow the touching of the nostrils and ears with saliva and the solemn tripartite oath of allegiance to Christ. Having renounced Satan and all his works and all his pomps, the candidate is anointed with oil to signify his complete loyalty to Christ the Anointed.

At the baptismal font there follows a more detailed examination about the belief as found in the Creed, and the elect must declare his willingness to be baptized. Only after Peter had declared his belief, "Thou art Christ, the Son of the living God" (Matt., xvi, 16), was he made the foundation of the indestructible Church (ibid. 18); and only after the elect has declared his belief is he baptized. The last command of Jesus to His Apostles found in the Gospel according to St. Matthew (xxviii, 19) is carried out: "Baptizing them [the instructed] in the name of the Father, and of the Son, and of the Holy Ghost." Baptism is conferred by the pouring of water accompanied by the identical formula enunciated by Christ.

The child of God is now anointed with chrism,[1] "wherewith Thou, O Lord, anointest priests, kings, prophets and martyrs" (Blessing of Oils). The presentation of the white gar-

---

[1] In ancient Roman use, when adults were baptized there were two anointings, one by a priest (which we still have) and the other by the Pope himself. The latter was the Sacrament of Confirmation. Cf. Ildephonso Schuster, "The Sacramentary," 5 vols. (London, 1925), vol. II, p. 307.

ment and the lighted candle is a symbolic expression of the never-to-be-forgotten truth that the preservation of sanctifying grace and the retention of the faith by the observance of the Commandments are absolutely necessary for the attainment of life everlasting. With the expression of the good wish that the baptized will remain in the peace of the Lord (which can be destroyed by sin only) the baptismal rite is concluded.

The Mass for Holy Saturday following Baptism brings out some beautiful truths. The Collect prays that God may preserve in the new offspring of His family the spirit of adoption which He conferred, and that, renewed in mind and body, they may render to God a pure service. In the Epistle St. Paul bids those who were baptized in the death of Christ and have risen with Him to a new life (Col., ii, 12): "Mind the things that are above, not the things that are upon the earth" (Col., iii, 2). The Gospel reminds those now risen with Christ that, like the Angel announcing the Resurrection, their countenances must be bright and their garments remain white. The Secret asks that Baptism and Holy Communion may profit them unto everlasting salvation. After the First Communion which the newly baptized were wont to receive at this Mass, the Church ends the Pre-Easter Liturgy with the prayer: "Pour down upon us, O Lord, the Spirit of Thy love; and of Thy goodness, make them to be of one mind . . . through Christ, Thy Son our Lord." The whole is summed up in two words: faith and love.

The Liturgy of the Church is not only effective and dramatic, but doctrinal as well. The rite of Baptism is not only the beginning but also the foundation and the reason for the entire Christian life. All the other Sacraments are complementary and additional to Baptism, but none of them is so absolutely necessary for salvation as the Sacrament of regeneration and spiritualization. All other Sacraments build upon the foundation of faith and love laid by Baptism. The life given to the baptized is a spiritual and supernatural life; it is nothing less than a participation in the divine life itself (I John, i). It is a life in union with God (John, xiv, 23). It is life originating in the death of Christ (John, vi, 48). It is a life in faith and love that brings with it hope and confidence in the final outcome, a trust in God, and the humility of the Saints. "I confess to thee, O Father, Lord of heaven and earth, because Thou hast hid these things from the wise and prudent, and hast revealed them to little ones" (Matt., xi, 25).

Our regeneration is truly wonderful, and effected in a manner which reminds us strongly of the Incarnation of God's only Son. As Mary was prepared by the Holy Ghost Who formed Jesus in her immaculate womb, so the Holy Ghost, the power of the Most High, enters the "spotless womb" of the baptismal water, and the new man who comes forth from it is called and is a son of God through adoption. "The Holy Ghost shall come upon thee, and the power of the Most High shall overshadow thee. And therefore also the Holy which shall be born of thee shall be called the Son of God" (Luke, i, 35). "Behold what manner of charity the Father hath bestowed upon us, that we should be called, and should be the sons of God. . . . We are now the sons of God" (I John, iii, 1-2). The Apostle is not speaking figuratively. The world and the worldly minded do not know this, because they do not know the love of the Father (ibid.).

The spiritual force of Christianity has not been diminished. It is constantly nourished and increased by the grace of Confirmation and the Holy Eucharist. If the union with God has been disrupted and the flow of grace stopped, the effects of Baptism—the childship of God and living membership in Christ's Mystical Body—are easily restored by Penance. Like leaven in the meal, the Word of God is still capable of permeating the whole, of expanding it and making it rise. Spirituality, too, can still effect this in Christian living. But as leaven needs a certain degree of warmth and rest, so does grace require a certain quietude and loving reflection to spiritualize man. "With desolation is all the land made desolate, because there is no one that considereth in the heart" (Jer., xii, 11). The good seed is still sown, but worldliness often hinders its growth.

Today the most important truths are partly forgotten, underestimated, neglected, or not applied to life by a large number of Christians, especially in the English-speaking world. General interest centers in the news, radio, profane literature, economics, and sports. Editors regard religion as a relatively minor concern of their readers in comparison with sports, movies, politics, and other secular activities and interests.[1] Publishers are afraid to print books of a purely spiritual nature for fear of having no sale. Literary critics, carefully hiding their names, find little to commend in strongly spiritual books, in which they often pick imaginary flaws. The Bible, the Imitation of Christ, and other spiritual classics are no longer the daily companions of otherwise practical Catholics. The science of Liturgy is enjoyed, but as a doctrine it is commonly neglected. All this is unfortunate, and accounts for the tremendous lack of spirituality.

But the picture is not all darkness. Of late, the efforts to spiritualize the clergy and laity have increased. They are worthy of hearty support. Not all that is being done for spiritualizing the American Church can be enumerated here, but some of the efforts deserve special mention.

The Confraternity of Christian Doctrine has provided new and appealing material for the teaching of the Catechism and Bible History. It is preparing a revised and popular edition of the Bible. The Spiritual Book Associates are promoting the distribution of books of outstanding value. Books on daily meditation for the laity, on the Mystical Body of Christ, and on the Liturgy are multiplying in the market, and should be recommended to the faithful by their spiritual leaders. The idea that the bulk of the laity is less spiritually inclined than the clergy or religious, or is not interested in divine matters, may be dismissed as without solid foundation. The high price of some books cannot be lowered unless the size of the editions—that is, the sale—increases. The hierarchy is determined to do everything possible to improve the conditions deplored in the Encyclical, "Sertum lætitiæ," and to make Christians more and more Christ-like. The Laymen's Retreat Movement recruits larger numbers of participants in closed retreats year after year. The different sodalities, societies, and organizations established for the promotion of moral perfection rejoice in increasing memberships. Catholic

[1] See also *Catholic Digest*, July, 1940, p. 10.

Action is already well under way in the fields of accidentals. All this is encouraging, consoling, and prophetic of good results, if the activities are supported by prayer and good example. "Between heretics and bad Catholics there is this difference: heretics believe what is wrong; the latter, however, believe the truth, but do not live in accord with their belief" (St. Augustine, In Matt., xi).

A world devoid of spirituality will not seek it unless its attention is called to spiritual things. Their great interior void is indeed realized by many, and a quest for something to fill it is unceasingly made. "Quærunt quod quærunt, sed non est ubi quærunt" (St. Augustine). A re-direction must take place, beginning with the foundation, Baptism. All worldliness is but the logical consequence of not fulfilling the "abrenunciation" made by the baptismal vows. If we could discover some simple and fundamental method (one suitable for everybody) of inducing Catholics to live up to the obligations imposed by Baptism, it certainly ought to be tried. Of what avail is a great building erected on a crumbling foundation! It may look good, but its collapse is but a matter of time.

Throughout the ages men have looked for such a fundamental means to re-Christianize Christianity and to re-spiritualize a world grown cold. Such a formula was given to the Church by St. Francis, the truly apostolic man and the seraph having the sign of the living God, who signed the servants of God on their foreheads (Apoc., vii, 3). It was accepted by the Church as a singular and outstanding institution, and was fostered and recommended by a long series of Popes. It brought forth more abundant fruits of sanctity and exercized a more salutary influence on Christian living than any other organization in the Church. To all who live in the world, Francis revealed Tertiarism in a form entirely unknown before his time, and nothing faintly like it was given to Christianity in the following centuries.

This Tertiarism is a special mode of Christian life according to the Gospel, instituted for the sole purpose of rekindling faith and intensifying the love of God. It is intended to maintain and nourish the essential sanctity infused by Baptism, by following a simple and easy rule of life. All manifestations of ethical perfection should be the fruits of life in the Third Order. Many in every walk of life do not understand its nature and character. Many hold its evident other-worldliness against it. Many still look skeptically at the encomia bestowed by the Pontiffs upon the Third Order, and, notwithstanding the rich fruits of faith and charity it has brought forth, deem it of less value than other religious organizations and movements that have a greater appeal to worldly people. But all who know its essence and nature, and grasp the significance of Tertiarism, readily follow the Church by giving preference to it above all others. Most objections to the contrary are of little importance and have already been solved.[1]

Where there is no real spiritual life, God is not known and loved as He is, nor is His law obeyed as it should be. Knowledge alone is no substitute for spirituality. Self-abnegation is absolutely required, but it must be taken in its full meaning, namely, to do what is required to fulfill the Great Commandment and to atone for offenses against it. The first rule is expressed by Christ thus: "If any man will come after Me, let him deny himself" (Matt., xvi, 24); and the second in His words: "Except you do penance, you shall all likewise perish" (Luke, xiii, 5).

It was not senility nor natural simplicity that made the aged Disciple of Love constantly refer to the Great Commandment. It was rather infused and tested wisdom that made him do so. He intended to lead his followers again and again to the law governing creation and generation, redemption and regeneration. In this matter modern preachers might perhaps learn from him. "Fides et Caritas!"

---

[1] This is more fully explained by the writer in "The Better Life" (Wagner, New York, 1942.)

CHAPTER V

Rearing Children in Faith and Piety

THE CHILD MAKES a family complete. It is born, baptized, and raised to exercise in time its natural and general vocation to increase and multiply, although some may select a supernatural or special vocation to which comparatively few are called. Hence, the education and training of children, so far as the home is concerned, is but a general one and the same for all.

The Liturgy, at the beginning of each new year, gives us some thoughts that can be applied to the beginning of a human life. It is St. Paul who writes to Titus thus: "When the goodness and kindness of God our Saviour appeared, . . . He saved us by the laver of regeneration, and renovation of the Holy Ghost: . . . that, being justified by His grace, we may be heirs, according to hope of life everlasting" (iii, 4-7). And in another place he states that "the grace of God . . . appeared to all men; instructing us, that, denying ungodliness, . . . we should live . . . godly in this world, looking for the blessed hope and coming of . . . our Saviour Jesus Christ. . . . These things speak, and exhort" (Tit., ii, 11 sqq.).

In these words the Apostle outlines a simple but comprehensive program for the religious education and training of children. It is at once positive and negative: rear the child in the hope of life everlasting and train it to deny ungodliness and worldly desires. Piety and innocence are the qualities that should be implanted and fostered from the very moment reason awakens. We know that this is done in truly religious families by parents who actually realize that the child given to them by God must again be returned to Him, and that they who were instrumental in bringing the child into this world are also bound to do what is in their power to bring it into heaven. But, unfortunately, as

Archbishop McNicholas stated: "The very atmosphere of the home is frequently irreligious or indifferent to religion." This is one of the great evils of our time and the root of many other ills which we meet.

A catechist who has been engaged with the little ones coming to our schools during the past several years, cannot fail to observe the change that has taken place among them. Not so long ago it was unusual to meet a new scholar who could not bless himself, could not recite a short prayer, and knew nothing about God and heaven. Such youngsters are now numerous. Another experience frequently met with is that children attending secular schools may have learned the whole small Catechism by heart, and yet the religious duties and truths it contains mean nothing to them. The realization of these truths is rapidly disappearing.

These two facts allow us to draw a whole series of well-founded conclusions. The fact that a child comes to school without knowing anything about God and ignorant of all religious signs or prayer, clearly indicates that there is in the home no religious expression that captivates a child. There are no religious pictures or statues, no family prayers in common, and there is not much talk of the right kind about religious truths and exercises. The festive spirit of the celebration of the great mysteries has never entered the home in an attractive form. Nothing about them is ever told the child.

It is true that young children do not understand much, but even before their understanding is fully developed they love much. The regular recitation of the Our Father and Hail Mary, and the making of the sign of the cross, afford fine opportunities for telling them about our Father in Heaven, about Jesus Who loves us, and about our Heavenly Mother. To tell the child that God is a Spirit infinitely perfect, eternal, and omnipotent, Who created us to obey, love, and serve Him for an eternal reward, means little or nothing to a very young child. There are divine perfections that are more suitable to inculcate love and piety. The child will understand if told that God made him because He loves him, and this will engender a corresponding love. To stress that God loves the child even if it is wayward, and never ceases to love and to long for the return of even the naughty and disobedient child, will bring better results than to threaten future punishments. After all, the love of God is the reason for our existence, and all else is but subservient to this.

Children, being naturally inquisitive, are especially interested in the why and wherefore of everything, religion included. But the answers to these questions are not given in the Catechism in such a way that a child could deduce them. Hence the aversion of so many children towards the study of the Catechism. It is different with Bible History, and it is a pity that this is so much neglected nowadays. The Bible is the most important of all books, not excluding the Catechism. Bible stories are certainly the best means to explain, dramatize, and vitalize religion. Mothers do not need to urge children to listen to stories from the Bible; they are only too eager to hear them repeatedly. This is about all that can be and should be done for the pre-school child.

Training must be added to education. In this regard, it may be helpful to consider how the Infant Jesus was brought up. His first religious act was a sacrifice, the circumcision. "A body Thou hast fitted to Me" (Heb., x, 5). And St. Paul writes: "I beseech you, therefore, brethren, by the mercy of God, that you present your bodies a living sacrifice, holy, pleasing unto God, your reasonable service"—that is, in conformity with the will of God (Rom., xii, 1). The second act of religion of the Boy Jesus recorded in the Gospel was His visit to the Temple in Jerusalem, to be in the house of His Father. There and then He dedicated Himself to His work. He inaugurated it by being subject to Mary and Joseph. "Behold I come: . . . that I should do Thy will, O God" (Heb., x, 7).

Much deserving care is bestowed upon the body of the child, but the relation between body and soul is not always correctly conceived. Some consider the body as most important during the time of infancy and youth. They think that, if the body is well provided for, the rest will follow naturally. This is, however, not always the case. The body may be coddled to the detriment of the soul, and this may produce evil effects in later years.

Body and soul must be considered as a unit with a supernatural end in view. The body is not to be despised; it is not merely the prison of the soul, nor the seat of the passions, nor the material cause of many sins. It has the honor and destiny of being a pleasing sacrifice to God through Christ in union with His Mystical Body. Its objective is a future resurrection in glory. This objective intended by the Creator and Redeemer, and the preparation for it effected by Baptism, are frequently overlooked in the training of the younger children. Of many a child the words of the Evangelist about Jesus might be reversed so as to read: "Johnny went home with his parents (after Baptism), and they were subject to him." Naturally Johnny soon goes his own ways, unless the very important habit of self-denial is inculcated from the beginning. Moral training should be begun in early infancy and must be continued for many years if a solid character capable of resisting the various temptations of later years is to result.

During the grammar school years, the religious instruction is the same for all children, irrespective of sex or future state in life. Attention will be called to the higher vocations, but a special preparation for them is deferred until the child enters an institution established for this purpose. Children are not forced nor urged to embrace a supernatural state of life; God calls them if He wants them, and this call should be fostered if there are signs indicating its presence.

A general religious training suitable for any form of Christian life is given. What pertains to the imparting of religious instruction in our schools does not concern us at present.[1] The pastor, however, will do all he possibly can to induce the parents to send their children to a Catholic school, wherever this is not impossible. But the mere enrollment of a child in a parochial school does not relieve the parents from all their educational duties. In fact, most of them remain. After all, the school attendance covers about one-sixth of the time of school age. The par-

---

[1] Cf. the author's article, "Teaching the Catechism," in *The Homiletic and Pastoral Review*, June, 1934.

ents and the home have definite and grave duties to fulfill during the remaining time, averaging about twenty hours per day.

The home must support the school and cooperate with it by reinforcing the religious instruction and by upholding the authority and dignity of the teacher. The habit which some parents have of criticizing teachers or their work before a child, never does any good, and may destroy all the good influence a teacher might otherwise exercise over a child. Children are by nature distracted and forgetful; they are good or naughty, and may even act wickedly several times a day without much scruple. It is important that the parents utilize these shortcomings of the child to remind him of what he is being told in school about faith, morals, and religious practices. Seemingly indifferent though the children may be, they nevertheless have tender consciences, and unless certain things are explained to them they are easily scandalized. This should be considered not only by the parents but also by all who constitute the family or the home.

Furthermore, opportunities must be provided for the children to carry out what they are taught or admonished to do by the teacher. It should not be forgotten that virtues are habits that can be acquired only by constant practice and exercise. Virtues must be fostered, and obstacles to their practice must be removed, so far as this is possible. Moreover, opportunities should be provided. Children forget and neglect, but that should not make parents give up their efforts. In the homily on the Feast of St. Don Bosco, St. John Chrysostom writes (freely translated): "You must continue to admonish in order to bring about a change and a virtuous life. You may retort: 'I have done this so often!' But if you did so all your life, you should not grow tired and must not despair. Do we not read how God Himself kept on admonishing mankind through the Prophets, the Apostles, the Evangelists (and their successors)? Do adults always heed admonitions? By no means. Did God cease to admonish us? No! Nothing is as valuable as a human soul." [1]

The religious life of children needs the constant supervision of the parents, especially in so far as the reception of the Sacraments

---
[1] Hom. lx in Matt., xviii.

REARING CHILDREN IN FAITH AND PIETY

and the observance of religious duties are concerned. The regular or frequent reception of the Sacraments is praiseworthy but not sufficient. All graces received will remain sterile unless they are used.

Why does it happen that so many of the children give up frequent reception of the Sacraments as soon as they leave the parochial school? Inconvenience or impossibility is rarely the reason for this default. Undoubtedly, the Sacraments worthily received were efficient, but little or no cooperation was extended to the grace they conferred. In order to be efficient and influential the Sacraments must be lived, they must result in a truly Christian life. A Christian life necessarily leads to sanctity. This thought is well expressed in the Postcommunion on the First Sunday after Epiphany: "We humbly beseech thee, Almighty God, that Thou wouldst grant to all whom Thou refreshest with Thy Sacraments, to serve Thee worthily by a life well pleasing to Thee." To this the Postcommunion on the following Sunday adds: ". . . that we may receive what they assure." If the Sacraments are not lived, their neglect after school-days will be just a matter of fact without much regret.

In such a case, supernatural life originated in Baptism has never been realized to be a participation in the divine life. The Sacraments have not brought about a life closely united with God, interiorly as well as exteriorly. After the world, Satan, and the passions have attained a greater hold on the soul of youth, it is more difficult to apply effective remedies. The penitential life needed for a change for the better may not be accepted. This, of course, is a concept of Christian living entirely different from that ordinarily prevailing. Nevertheless, it is the only concept that is correct and in harmony with the plan of God: "Seek ye first the kingdom of God . . . and all these [temporal] things shall be added unto you" (Luke, xii, 31). This holds true for children as well as for adults.

The soul and the body of the child need protection. Parents should know who and what enter the home, and who and what leave it. Not just everybody should be allowed contact with growing children. Some persons might be definitely told what is expected of visitors or to stay out. It is remarkable that some parents are more concerned about their material property than about the immortal souls of their children. The former they safeguard in every way, but they are not half so watchful of their children.

Besides persons who come in contact with the children in the home, there are many things, such as books, papers, and radio, which require the watchfulness of parents. No committees for decency in this or that field can relieve them of this duty. In reality, these committees will not become effective so far as children are concerned unless parents and other members of the family keep their eyes and ears open.

It is equally important that parents should know the whereabouts of their children when they leave the home, the companionship they cultivate, the places they visit, and what they engage in. Under certain conditions it may be necessary to assist them to enjoy whatever recreation is needed in the home or elsewhere.

Although occasions of sin and external temptations should be kept from children because they are as yet not sufficiently strong in character, it is impossible to remove all temptations. Nor is this desirable. St. James, writing to adults, states: "Blessed is the man that endureth temptation" (i, 12); and although we pray "lead us not into temptation" through our own neglect or by others, temptations that do arise may be very beneficial if properly resisted. If we do not give way to them, they serve to increase our virtue, to strengthen our loyalty to God, and to multiply our reward. Temptations may fill us with an aversion for the spirit and things of the world, may open our eyes, reveal our weaknesses, and thus prepare the way for self-knowledge and humility. Temptations endured with fortitude may shorten our purgatory, make us more careful and watchful, and be a strong incentive to prayer and penitential acts. Hence, the potential value of temptations is not small. But this cannot be said about the occasions of sin, unless they arise against our will and are not brought about by indifference or other sinful tendencies.[1]

---

[1] Baur, "Werde Licht," vol. I, p. 378.

As to sex instruction during childhood, not much need be said; in fact, too much is being talked about it already. Parents who have the correct idea about creation, procreation, regeneration, and the final end of man to be reached by the observance of the Commandments, and who are otherwise spiritually minded, will live up to the dignity conferred and the grace bestowed upon them by Matrimony. They will find the right words and sense the correct time to give the pertinent information a child needs to possess about sex life.[1] What is needed for the guidance and protection of adolescents will be considered in the proper place.

Of much greater importance for the character training of children and youth is the fostering of a true love and devotion to Mary, the Immaculate Virgin Mother of Jesus. Mary is much more than an historical figure holding an important place in the work of Redemption by bringing us Jesus and becoming the distributor of all graces. She is also a type representing the Church, the Mother of Christians, in whose womb Christ is reborn through Baptism and Confirmation. She is a symbol of Christianity in the state of sanctifying grace. Being our heavenly and spiritual Mother through Christ, Mary is naturally our most powerful and successful advocate before the throne of God, and by her simple life in union with Jesus she is for us a model without equal. Hence, Mary can never be too much loved and honored. In fact, a great devotion and attachment to her is a special sign of election, as the holy Doctors teach us.

Finally, of equal importance as a lasting contribution to the formation and training of children is the giving of good example in the home. It is here where religion must be lived continuously, and where virtues must be practised until they become a second nature. There must be something in the home that directs the mind and actions of all to another life that is not of this world. There was a time, not so long ago, when a Catholic home could be distinguished immediately from all other homes by its crucifix, pictures, statues, and other articles including books like the Lives of the Saints and the Bible. Especially the living room

---

[1] This topic has been fully dealt with by the writer in "Watchful Elders" (Bruce, Milwaukee, 1945).

was something like a sanctuary where the father was the guide, ruler, and provider, the mother the heart, and the children the conscience, of the family. In this sanctuary sacrifices demanded by common life were rendered charitably and family prayers were offered. Great changes took place in the American home during the last few decades. Spirituality and all that promoted it have gone out of fashion. May God grant that going to heaven will not become equally old-fashioned! There is no substitute for spirituality, except perhaps martyrdom.

A few years ago, the present writer had the opportunity to visit many countries in the Old World, and had access to homes of many nationalities. What astonished him most was the religious atmosphere found in these homes of Catholics, Orthodox, Protestants, and others, and how they differed in this respect from most of the American homes, completely devoid as the latter are of religious signs or activities. Meanwhile, several of the nations visited were found worthy of martyrdom. It is true that in many American country homes family prayers including the Rosary are still being said, but this can hardly be said of most of the homes in our cities. It is also true that attention has been called to these defects during missions (at least in connection with the sale of religious articles), but very much more will have to be done if the general standard of spirituality is to be raised to a higher level.[1]

At the age of thirteen or fourteen years, the child enters a new and decisive period of life. At that time, as a rule, a future vocation is chosen that determines the form and content of the subsequent education. Some of the boys and girls will be heroic in their choice, and will renounce the world to embrace a special and supernatural state of life. As these will receive their training in institutions away from the home and parish, they are of no further concern to us at present, except in so far as we aid them by prayers and encouragements to persevere in their chosen vocation. By far the majority of adolescents will continue on their

---

[1] Joseph Will and Kilian J. Hennrich, "Catholic Action Handbook" (Wagner, New York, 1936).

REARING CHILDREN IN FAITH AND PIETY 47

way to the general and natural vocation to grow and multiply, and to these we shall direct our special attention later.

A few corollaries and hints may conclude this chapter.

(1) The religious education and training of children must begin long before they enter school. To lay such a foundation for life is a duty placed by God upon all parents. Baptism demands it. The mother being in continual contact with small children has naturally the greatest responsibility in this matter. This fact should be impressed upon future mothers.

(2) This education and training of children must be based upon the supernatural status which the child has received in Baptism, and on the high dignity conferred upon parents by the Sacrament of Matrimony. All are members of the same Mystical Body of Christ.

(3) The training of children must insist upon the greatest respect due to God and to the parents as His representatives, and must foster a love for God, the saints, and all members of the family. Small sacrifices and little acts of self-denial must be demanded as being perfectly natural, and a strict regard for the truth must be insisted upon. The natural sense of shame and modesty must be protected and strengthened on account of their great protective value for the future. In this, all members of the home must cooperate in word and deed.

(4) Strangers entering the home as guests or employees must be carefully selected and observed. Later on, the school must be conscientiously chosen because it is an auxiliary to the home in educating the children. Hence, on the one hand, the parents have the right to select the school that cooperates best with the home regarding faith and morals, and, on the other hand, the parents have the duty to support the school in forming the child of God and the good citizen.

(5) Parents must absolutely refuse to surrender the supervision of the child to anyone so long as they can exercise this duty themselves. They must resist the separation of the child from the home, either by persons or organizations, clubs, etc., whenever they consider this detrimental or dangerous to the spiritual wel-

fare of the child. There are things that parents know about their children which others do not know.

If parents keep all these things in mind and act accordingly, both parents and children will live up to their status as ordained by God, and thus uphold the dignity of the Christian family.

CHAPTER VI

Spiritual Guidance towards Manhood

ADOLESCENTS ADVANCING in age should, like Christ, also grow in grace and wisdom with God and man. The only words spoken by Christ as a youth, that are recorded in the Gospel, were: "How is it that you sought me? Did you not know that I must be about My Father's business?" (Luke, ii, 49). And after He had finished His work, the last words He uttered were: "Father, into Thy hands I commend My spirit" (Luke, xxiii, 46). Living for and with God is the best preparation for any state of life which is to conclude with a happy death.

Young people entering high school or going to work are beginning to stand on their own feet; they think, draw conclusions, and formulate their plans for the future. This transitional period in education is also the time when passions awaken and grow stronger. Problems brought about by Satan, the world, and the flesh arise more frequently, because contact with the world and its views, ideas, and temptations has been widened. The young mind may be filled by divine knowledge but, as it is not yet trained by experience to make sound decisions, it cannot serve as a safe guide. Conflicts arise in which only the strong will be victorious.

Among the causes of these conflicts the following were mentioned by the late Bishop John A. Duffy, of Buffalo: the rush of modern life, contacts that are not congenial, lowered public opinion with regard to morality, too great a desire for good times, the degenerate tone of the stage, screen, and literature, economic pressure, the vanishing influence of the home, the decline of religion, etc.[1] Our public education cannot produce a better generation, and slowly but surely leads our people to atheism. Under

---
[1] *The Tablet* (Brooklyn, N. Y.), December 21, 1940.

these circumstances, spirituality declines and diminishes from generation to generation. Clerics, too, are children of the times. A new orientation in the guidance of youth is without doubt a necessity.

About this guidance much has been written and much has been done. A great variety of preventive and protective means has been proposed, encouraged, and inaugurated. All of these measures may be good in themselves, but, if we inquire deeply, we cannot fail to see the futility and ineffectiveness of many of them in practice. Nearly all past endeavors have been in the form of an *external* guidance, which is often not needed, although it does no harm. What is almost completely lacking is the foundation, the *interior* guidance, without which exterior guidance will not reform youth. Hence, both interior as well as exterior guidance should be extended—especially and primarily, the cultivation of the interior life. Moreover, at present too much stress is laid on minor evils as preventatives of bigger ones, instead of following what is known to be the expressed will of God and the Church. It is true that often seemingly plausible reasons are given for such a procedure, but one feels somehow that the blessing of God is absent. Youth simply does not improve.

Catholic Action in our country has engaged in the task of improving public opinion and morality by the Legion of Decency, Literature Committees, and propaganda to establish the justice and rights of religious education, etc. For our Catholic youth, in particular, organizations are formed to promote innocent recreation and Christian practices. All these attempts are good and may lessen or prevent many evils, but they may become futile unless the sanctity of youth is raised. Unless this is done, not only will many not be reached by these movements, but those who are reached will, when the temptation presents itself, do as they please. Here is where the difficulty lies. It is the consent of the will to sin that determines morality, and nothing else.

In this predicament a good Christian home life would be a great aid in saving the spirituality of youth. But the question may be asked: "What is a good Christian family?" Would a

SPIRITUAL GUIDANCE TOWARDS MANHOOD

definition based on the teachings of Christ as applied by spiritual leaders be accepted by a majority? This is doubtful, and many will say: "Times have changed." Not even the signs formerly believed to indicate a pious home and family are such today. Not even higher vocations are such signs unless the quality of those who embrace them is higher than prevailing standards and opinions.

In this work we must again start with fundamentals. What we are now doing will not make Christianity more influential in the affairs of the world, because the individual Christians are not completely dominated by it. Children trained in Christianity as outlined must continue to "walk in the spirit" (Gal., v, 16). According to the teaching of the Apostle this must be possible; how it can be brought about, will be considered here from a pastoral viewpoint.

Owing to the extent of the field to be covered we must group our endeavors and focus them upon definitive objectives. According to Pius XII, the most practical and also most necessary objectives are the preservation and increase of the faith, the improvement and stabilization of morals, and the proximate preparation for Matrimony. This seems to cover the nature and essence of Christianity in the individual and in society. "What dost thou ask of the Church of God?" "Faith." "What does faith bring to thee?" "Life everlasting, if thou keep the Commandments" (Rite of Baptism). "We are the children of saints, and we must not be joined together like heathens that know not God" (Tob., viii, 5). We must provide for the baptized what they asked for, must assist them to keep the promises they have made, and must guide them through this valley of tears to the happiness of eternal life with God. The means at our disposal are the Scriptures, the means of grace (Sacraments and prayer), and the guideposts of the Commandments of God and of the Church.

The preservation of the faith that was received in Baptism is one of the principal objectives of Confirmation. It is intended to complement Baptism by increasing the divine virtues and by giving a special power and strength to retain them. "If we live in the Spirit, let us also walk in the Spirit" (Gal., v, 25). Youth must learn more about this Sacrament, must develop a higher appreciation for it, and must cooperate more fully with its sacramental graces.

What is the Sacrament of Confirmation? The Catechism answers: "Confirmation is a Sacrament by which we [infallibly] receive the Holy Ghost, in order to become strong and perfect Christians." It is given to meet the greater demands created by stronger passions, more difficult struggles, and more frequent and violent temptations. "Command Thy strength, O God: confirm, O God, what Thou hast wrought in us" (Ps. lxvii, 29). Confirmation presupposes Baptism, and, although it is not absolutely necessary for salvation like Baptism, its wilful neglect may well cause the loss of the baptismal grace and gifts—faith, hope, and charity.

The spiritual but nevertheless real effects of Confirmation may be learned from the rite of the blessing of chrism, the material used in its administration. The Roman Pontifical says: "Holy Lord, bring about that all anointed with it may be adopted as Thy children through the Holy Ghost. While Baptism removes all stains, this holy unction beautifies our face. Sanctify this creature, chrism, wherefrom Thou anointest priests, kings, prophets, and martyrs." Baptism produces interior sanctity; Confirmation should bring about the "beauty of our face," an ethical perfection that is visible to others. The confirmed receive the chrism and its grace for the manifestation of all the four offices mentioned. "Chrism is the visible matter through which Thou constitutest it [Confirmation] a Sacrament of perfect salvation and full life" (Preface of the Blessing of Holy Oils).

But the exterior manifestation of perfection must be based on interior justice and sanctity. To this the gifts of the Holy Ghost forcefully contribute. They are directly opposed to the seven capital sins of pride, covetousness, lust, anger, gluttony, envy, and sloth. The gift of understanding exchanges natural cravings for supernatural aspirations towards things of lasting value. Counsel imparts advice on piety and charity, and makes men willing to lead the better life. Knowledge brings about a true evaluation of Christian living. Fortitude supports the doing of what is right

SPIRITUAL GUIDANCE TOWARDS MANHOOD

without regard to human respect and other obstacles. Piety disposes one to serve God faithfully, and the fear of God is the beginning of sanctity that finally culminates in the endless love and possession of God. Wisdom gives us the enjoyment of God even in this life.

The fruits of the Holy Ghost administered in Confirmation are twelve, as enumerated by St. Paul (Gal., v, 22). Three relate to God: charity, joy, and peace. Six concern our neighbor: patience, benignity, goodness, longanimity, faith, and mildness. The last three pertain to ourselves: modesty, continency, and chastity. Undoubtedly they refer to the baptismal *Abrenuncio* and the promise to keep the Great Commandment, because all these fruits are directly opposed to Satan, his works and pomps, the concupiscence of the eyes, the world, and the flesh. Aided by the Holy Ghost, to love God above all and our neighbor as ourselves can become a reality in faith and life.

With the basis of such an interior disposition, we must try by all means at our command to cultivate in youth, the "beauty of the face" or ethical perfection which will show itself in the fulfillment of the four offices mentioned above, spiritually interpreted.

(1) Christians should be *priests*. "You are ... a kingly priesthood" (I Peter, ii, 9). "Be you also ... a holy priesthood" (ibid. 5). Although not members of the hierarchical priesthood, we should bring sacrifices, pray, teach by word and example, and so bring others nearer to God by exemplifying the life of Christ.

(2) Christians should also be *kings*. The reign of Christ is one "of truth and light, of justice, love and peace—eternal and universal" (Preface of Christ the King). Christians should use the treasures of grace and rule over their passions. They should be leaders for others in peace and in war against the enemies of God.

(3) The Christian should be a *prophet*, seeing beyond earthly life and looking for the substance of things hoped for and promised by faith (Heb., xi, 1). In other words, he should have a lively faith.

(4) Finally, the Christian should be a *martyr*, a witness for Christ, not shirking the things that are necessary to reach salva-

tion even if they are arduous. Young people are heroic in so many things that are less profitable, but through cooperation with the grace of God and guided by faith youth's heroism and good will might be led into the proper channels. The Holy Ghost once renewed the face of the earth, because those who had received Him lived by faith and gave testimony of Christ. "The Spirit of truth . . . shall give testimony of Me. And you shall give testimony" (John, xv, 26-27). No one but the Holy Ghost can produce again such a change in the modern world.

The cultivation of the Christian spirit of youth based on Confirmation should be our foremost endeavor. It is the best means **to preserve, deepen,** and activate faith. How this can be done has been only partly indicated.[1]

The second step in the spiritualization of youth is the stabilization and improvement of morality. For this God also provided a Sacrament, Penance. There is no need to repeat what is found in every Catechism about the nature and effects of Penance. It will be more useful for our purpose to mention some thoughts that might impress our youth more deeply. .

A very progressive educator writes in *School and Society:*[2] "All guidance should aim towards self-analysis, coordination and motivation." For this purpose he recommends graded tests. He may not know it, but it is a fact that Penance demands self-analysis, coordination, and motivation. Confession demands an examination of conscience, and millions of young people would not otherwise know their condition or try to improve it. A coordination must take place between God's will and human behavior. One must judge oneself by the divine standard expressed by the Commandments. The world no longer does this. Confession provides for the lack of sound judgment, and demands sorrow for sins and true humility in telling them. None of the rules of the world require this. Confession demands a purpose of amendment which must be carried out. It is the best antidote

---

[1] Cf. the author's article, "Renovating the Spirit of Youth," in *The Homiletic and Pastoral Review*, May, 1935, p. 826.

[2] February 28, 1941, p. 250.

SPIRITUAL GUIDANCE TOWARDS MANHOOD

against all disorders and a strong motivation to shun what is wrong.

The Commandments serving as a basis for the examination of conscience are guide-posts to preserve the love of God and of neighbor. They indicate that love is rather a social virtue, because it requires at least two persons in order to become possible. Likewise, there is no true morality unless it is more than personal. It must be social also.

The primary objective of Penance is the remission of mortal sin. The special sacramental grace is given for moral improvement. Why is such an improvement often not noticed? To remain good or not to fall deeper into sin is a benefit that may escape our notice. In order to make greater progress possible, it may be necessary to remove obstacles hitherto overlooked.

Such are the venial sins knowingly and freely committed. It is true that they do not destroy the life of the soul and the love of God, but they act like lead on the feet of a swimmer, depressing the will, clouding the spirit, and dragging the soul away from loving God. Because it is a disregard of God, venial sin is clearly against His will and, therefore, a preferment of our own will for the sake of enjoyment of material benefits and other less desirable things. For this reason venial sin hinders the increase of grace and obstructs our cooperation with it. The will becomes averse to sacrifices, and forms a habit of surrendering; the judgment grows unreliable, and faith is weakened. There always is the proximate danger of the venial sinner falling seriously and becoming hardened in sin. The good seed sown by education, reading, and the Sacraments fall by the wayside and are trodden down (Luke, viii, 5).

There are many seemingly pious young people who detest mortal sin, but do not hesitate to commit a venial sin and make no earnest endeavor to overcome sinful habits. This creates a situation truly abhorrent to God, who said: "I know thy works, that thou art neither cold, nor hot. I would thou wert cold, or hot. But because thou art lukewarm, . . . I will begin to vomit thee out of My mouth" (Apoc., iii, 15-16). Much of the current lukewarmness and spiritual laziness is unwittingly promoted by guides who leave out of account the inherent heroism in so many of our good young people. The simplest things are often made too complicated.[1] "Perfect Thou my goings in Thy paths: . . . as for me, I shall appear before Thy sight in justice" (Ps. xvi, 5, 15).

The love based on faith, the foundation of hope and its fulfillment—given to us in Baptism, increased by Confirmation, restored after loss by Penance—needs constant nourishment if we are to persevere and bring abundant fruit. Christ provided this nourishment by instituting the Holy Eucharist: "Without Me you can do nothing" (John, xv, 5). But with Him we can do everything conducive to salvation. We are with Him in a special and most fruitful manner when we participate fully in the Holy Liturgy, the Mass including Holy Communion.

Much could be said about the Holy Eucharist as our sacrifice and food for our souls, but this is sufficiently explained in every handbook of religion. The Eucharist in the light of the doctrine of the Mystical Body would be interesting but would lead us from a simple method of spiritualization. However, the connection between Baptism and the liturgical sacrifice may be pointed out in a few words. At the foot of the altar, priest and people already in the state of grace ask for the restoration of baptismal innocence, to which the following prayers, including the Kyrie, are potent aids. The instructional part of the Mass is intended to increase the faith, and in the Offertory the divine and human are mixed to constitute a perfect sacrifice by Consecration. Communion brings about the most intimate union with Christ that is possible on earth, and it should culminate in an everlasting possession of God through love in heaven. The blessings of the Mass implored by the official and always effective prayers accompany Christians on their way through daily life.

If adolescents could be led to attend Mass daily, much would be gained. It is not necessary to enumerate the obstacles or invent additional ones. The few that are real and worthy of consideration are enough, and some of them might be overcome by a greater amount of good will. This does not mean that all could

---
[1] Cf. Baur, "Werde Licht," vol. II, pp. 43, 56.

attend Mass daily, but merely that many more could do so despite some inconveniences. However, difficulties will always remain.

The Liturgical Movement is doing what it can to promote increased attendance at daily Mass, and has already achieved remarkable success in places where it is actively promoted. The greatest obstacle preventing a full participation by the laity in the Liturgy seems to be the Latin language, especially in countries with a language not of Roman origin. The Latin Church may come to a time when it sees its way clear to remove this obstacle as far as it is possible and prudent. This language question, important as it is, is nevertheless but a disciplinary matter without basis in Revelation, and should not be insurmountable.

The exclusive use of Latin in the Liturgy undoubtedly furthered the ignorance of our people with regard to the holy mysteries. Translations and explanations may overcome some ignorance, but this is not sufficient for a full-hearted cooperation. People simply do not appreciate what is more or less foreign to them. Translations from an ancient and dead language do not always appeal to a people having a different background, symbolism, culture, and way of expression. So long as the faithful do not really know and experience what they are supposed to do in the Liturgy, they will not actively and most profitably participate in the Mass or any other liturgical function.

Furthermore, the greater part of the Mass (all but the Canon), as also certain parts in the administration of the Sacraments and other rites, are certainly intended to be understood by the faithful and the recipients. There can be no doubt about that. Hence it becomes partly apparent why in some countries where the language of the Liturgy was not akin to the language of the people Protestantism spread rapidly, whereas in the Latin countries and in the East where the Liturgy was understood by the people it had less chance to penetrate.

This does not mean that the Latin language should be entirely discarded in the Liturgy. It is too valuable in many respects. It only means that sufficient valid reasons should be found to permit the laity a greater participation in the Liturgy by allowing the use of the vernacular in some parts. The final judgment rests, of course, with the Church, but, this presupposed, a discussion of the matter is perfectly legitimate.[1]

However, whilst the discussions are going on and until the results are published, our young people should become better acquainted with what the Mass really is and means. No doubt, the pupils in our Catholic high schools receive such instructions, but others should also be reached by special means. The most hopeful means, in addition to talks in sodality or fraternity meetings, is undoubtedly the study club with the objective of understanding the Liturgy. For this purpose the substantial pamphlet, "Study the Mass," [2] is one of the best that has come to the notice of the present writer. Will this activity appeal to youth of high school age? To some it will not, but the majority, if correctly approached, will be really enthusiastic about it, as proved by experience. The invitations to form or join such a study circle should emphasize the profits the participants will gain for themselves. Spiritual gains still have some power to draw youth.

Certain readers might expect some mention here of sex instruction. It is the fashion at present. But having been occupied with this matter for a generation, the writer concludes that what has been said in the preceding pages will also take care of youth of high school age. His only specific instruction to this group is, as all spiritual writers insist, to keep away from the opposite sex, and to limit social life between the two sexes as much as possible. No valid objection can be brought against this rule, and a refutation of the many other suggested rules is not necessary. Moreover, most of the sex problems of this age can very well be solved by the confessor. Not more instruction about the mechanics of sex, but a prudent protection of youth, is needed, as well as the building of a stronger character.

Of the greatest importance for youth, as also for all others, is prayer—a means that is always available, always possible, and

---

[1] See the article of Dr. Pius Parsch in *Bibel und Liturgie*, October, 1940. Also various articles in *Orate Fratres* in recent years.

[2] Liturgical Press, Collegeville, Minn.

always beneficial. The raising of his mind and heart to God necessarily lifts man from the material and temporal to the spiritual and eternal. Moreover, it is necessary for salvation. St. Alphonsus Liguori writes: "All [adults] who are saved, are saved because they prayed; and all who are lost, are damned because they did not pray." Christ made practically the same declaration in the Garden of Gethsemani, but somehow it does not seem to make much impression upon many adolescents. Maybe a layman and great scientist will be listened to more eagerly.

Dr. Alexis Carrel asserted [1] that prayer is not only worship, but also a most powerful form of energy that is clearly demonstrable. It is, therefore, a builder of personality and character: "Its results can be measured in terms of increased physical buoyancy, greater intellectual vigor, moral stamina, and a deeper understanding of the relations underlying human relationships." Many moderns, and not merely the laity, look for these effects from sports, scouting, and similar activities, but in vain. Dr. Carrel put the question: "How does prayer fortify with such dynamic powers?" He answered: "When we pray, we link ourselves with God, the inexhaustible power that spins the universe." Dr. Carrel thought that we derive most power from prayer when we use it as a supplication that we may become more like God. Prayer should be regarded as a practice of the presence of God. Undoubtedly the doctor spoke from experience when he described prayer as being "the effort of man to reach God and to commune with the Creator, supreme wisdom, truth, beauty and strength, Father and Redeemer of each man. . . . Whenever we pray, we change body and soul for the better; prayer is never without good results." We can use any words of our own choice, no special form is needed; but the Our Father, the Psalms, and liturgical prayers are undoubtedly the best and most efficient.

But Dr. Carrel thought that an occasional prayer will not be so effective. Like Epictetus, he was of the opinion that man should think of God more often than he breathes, and concluded: "In order really to mold personality, prayer must become a habit.

---
[1] *Reader's Digest,* March, 1941 (used with permission of the publisher).

It is meaningless to pray in the morning and to live like a barbarian the remainder of the day. True prayer is a way of life. . . . Today, as never before, prayer is a binding necessity in the lives of men and nations. . . . For if the power of prayer is again released and used; if the spirit declares its aims clearly and boldly, there is yet hope that our prayers for [more spiritual Christians and] a better world will be answered." This is well said and it is in complete harmony with the oft-expressed sentiments of the recent Popes.

The spirit of prayer can be fruitfully promoted only by the Holy Ghost, but His action will manifest itself more efficaciously in prepared ground. At present the popular trend is towards novenas, and this trend may well be utilized for our purpose. It is not necessary to look for a specially attractive, well-known, or well-advertised saint; rather let us look for a definite, urgent, and important intention to attract the multitudes. Such intentions might be the founding of happy, religious, and prosperous families; invocation of the blessing of God upon our homes, or schools, or vocations, or professions, or businesses, etc.; the triumph of the Church over her enemies in the hearts of men; a truly penitential spirit (in Lent). More suggestions may be found in the petitions of the Litany of All Saints with the response, "We beseech Thee to hear us," and in the Orations in the Missal for Sundays and feasts. The glory of God and the Saints is thereby not diminished but enhanced when we engage in these public supplications. Suitable prayers for these devotions in a liturgical spirit may be found in the booklet, "Parish Devotions." [1]

---
[1] Our Sunday Visitor Press, Huntington, Ind.

CHAPTER VII

Holy Preparation for Chaste Wedlock

"ADOLESCENS VIR—virgo adulta, lux et crux animarum curæ."[1] These words of a prominent ecclesiastical writer may well serve as an introduction to the consideration of this important but critical period of human life. This age is accompanied by ever-increasing temptations, passions, and urges and doubts from within and without. Unless the adolescent, the natural man, is fortified by a supernatural spirit and outlook, falls—serious falls —may be expected.

Our young people approaching marriageable age are the children of their time. A new type of young men and young women confronts us.

The young man of today is no longer filled with respect and awe for the greatness of the change that is coming over him in preparation for the married state. He is no longer a St. Paul who can do all things in God Who strengthens him, but rather resembles Pelagius who did not appreciate nor need the grace of God. Nor is he willing like St. Christopher to carry the weight coming from God, no matter how high the floods of tribulation may rise. He is rather one who has figured it all out according to the wisdom of the world and the urges and demands of the flesh. It is difficult to advise him.

The young woman is no longer a hidden flower spreading the good odor of modesty and true womanhood, ennobling all with whom she comes into contact. She has left the shelter by which previous generations lovingly and prudently surrounded and protected her. She has become an integral unit in her own right, and does not intend to change her status for the position in mar-

---

[1] "The young man and the unmarried woman are the light and the cross of the care of souls."

ried life that God commands. She has become the full-fledged partner of the male in sports, on beaches, in business, education, and more undesirable things. Permanency of this state is demanded even in married life. Often, her indiscriminate reading has destroyed the last remnants of what made virgins respected and esteemed.

With not many exceptions, our young men and young women alike suffer from what St. Paul deplores, and for what he gives the only effective remedy: "There was given me a sting of my flesh, an angel of Satan, to buffet me, for which thing thrice I besought the Lord, that it might depart from me" (II Cor., xii, 7-8). The Lord could not take away the desires of the flesh because they were needed in the plan for propagating mankind, but He said: "My grace is sufficient for thee: for power is made manifest in infirmity" (ibid., 9). The neglect of the use of the means of grace has inflamed the passions to a degree unknown several decades ago. Seemingly, other means so lavishly recommended have not brought the desired results. The disorder has become greater than one would like to acknowledge, but such an acknowledgment is a prerequisite for a salutary improvement of conditions. Many of our young people come from families that could not well be called "a holy root," and but very few of these parents will aid their offspring in bringing about a Christian and truly holy wedlock. And even if they should try to influence their children, the whole mental attitude of youth is such that it does not make them inclined to listen to their elders and more experienced friends.

Notwithstanding all this, there is no reason to despair. Similar conditions have existed before in many places. "Where sin abounded, grace did more abound" (Rom., v, 20). What has been said about creation, regeneration, and the Sacrament of propagation will form a solid basis for further pastoral labors among youth. While others may base their hope on human wisdom and conclusions, the pastor will say with the Psalmist: "Behold they that go far from Thee shall perish: . . . it is good for me to adhere to my God, to put my hope in the Lord God" (Ps. lxxii, 27-28).

PREPARATION FOR CHASTE WEDLOCK

Seemingly, many of the modern candidates for Matrimony are not anxious to know what Christian marriage implies and requires from them in the realm of faith and sacrifices. Many of them are most interested in finding out all about how to get rid of undesirable partners, about birth control, etc. (and Catholics are among them in ever-increasing numbers), instead of learning how to enter matrimony holily with a good and congenial partner, and how to live with him or her peacefully, loyally, and godly until the end. But this does not excuse the representative of Christ for failing to tell them in and out of season, publicly and privately, all they ought to know about these matters.

Although not all sins lend themselves to treatment in the pulpit, especially before a mixed congregation, all that is positive, virtuous, and ordained by God can after a careful preparation be preached chastely and impressively. Pope Pius XI is a more recent example and authentic teacher of the guidance to be extended to young people of marriageable age. In this he followed in the footsteps of St. Paul and the Fathers and Doctors of the Church. They all spoke plainly, simply, definitely, without any appreciable fear of giving scandal. There need be no fear of scandalizing the "little ones," although a harvest of pharisaical scandal may be reaped. Fortunately, this type of scandal need not be avoided at a great cost.

In the preparation for Matrimony the choice of a partner or the acceptance of one evidently holds the first place. In his Encyclical, "Casti Connubii," [1] Pius XI writes: "On choosing a partner depends a great deal whether the forthcoming marriage will be happy or not, . . . whether it will be a help . . . or hindrance to Christian life." Hence, candidates should consider beforehand "so that they will not deplore for the rest of their lives the sorrows arising from an indiscreet marriage." The Pope also gives excellent advice on how to avoid unhappy marriages. In deliberating about taking a partner, a young person should consider: (1) God and the true religion; (2) himself or herself; (3) his or her partner; (4) the children to be expected; (5) civil society of which marriage is the fountain-head. During the de-

---
[1] All quotations unless otherwise specified are taken from this Encyclical.

liberations and as a preparation for family life, candidates for Matrimony should: (a) pray diligently, and (b) ask the advice of their parents or those who hold their place, and regard it seriously: "Honor thy father and thy mother, that it may be well with thee, and thou mayest be long-lived upon earth." This definite promise on the part of God is certainly worth striving for. These suggestions of the Pontiff deserve a more detailed consideration.

(1) Those intending to marry must, first of all, consider God and religion. Unless the Lord builds the house, all human labor is in vain. Past and more godly generations held it as an axiom that good marriages are made in heaven, provided they are entered into in the right manner and disposition. From Holy Scripture as gathered in the matrimonial laws of the Church we know the will of God with regard to selecting a partner. No one can neglect the observance of these laws of God without suffering the consequences. The impediments to matrimony, formulated by the Church but unquestionably based on the laws of God, may well serve as guide-posts in selecting a partner. All of them should be avoided under ordinary circumstances, since, when dispensations are demanded, they may turn out to be punishments for unruly children rather than particular favors.

If these impediments are to serve as guide-posts, as they are intended to be, it is quite evident that young people should be sufficiently acquainted with them before they become finally engaged. It is true that the more important impediments are found in the larger Catechisms, but it is also true that much is forgotten that is not of interest to children in their Catechism days; furthermore, grammar-school days are not the suitable time to enter into the real reasons for avoiding these impediments. When he has called the attention of a young couple to a real impediment, the present writer has more than once received the retort: "Does not the Church dispense from that?" In other words: "It amounts to nothing!" If this attitude is manifested only at the bridal examination or, what is worse, at the time of setting the day and time for the ceremony, it will then be too late to impart information and to rectify erroneous opinions with good results.

Among the more frequently met impediments are *disparitas cultus,* mixed religion, a previous matrimonial bond, public sin, and diverse relationships. All these, like the other impediments, are intended for the welfare of man and the promotion of the plan of salvation as willed by God. Evidently, God's will should prevail under all circumstances; otherwise there is little hope of abundant graces and special blessings. Canonists explain the meaning and juridical aspects of the diriment and prohibitive impediments. These are necessary for and of interest to pastors, but are not of interest to others. What are of importance and interest to young people are the spiritual implications that concern God and also themselves. These should be explained to them. Not every impediment can be treated here in this light, but a practical example may illustrate what is meant.

The unbaptized cannot receive the Sacrament of Matrimony, nor can the Christian who marries an unbaptized person, because the bridegroom and bride administer the Sacrament to each other in consequence of Baptism. The baptized partner cannot administer it to the unbaptized, because the latter is incapable of receiving the Sacrament; on the other hand, the unbaptized person cannot administer it to the baptized partner, because the source of the power needed for such administration, Baptism, is absent. A dispensation does not remedy this deficiency, although under certain conditions it makes the natural union lawful. Now, where there is no Sacrament, there are no sacramental graces, nor is there the intimate relation to the Mystical Body of Christ as far as the couple is concerned.

Such unions, being against the revealed will of God, are constantly displeasing to God. To remove this displeasure and for other spiritual effects, the law of the Church demands constant efforts on the part of the Catholic to bring about his or her partner's conversion, in order that a valid Baptism may elevate the natural union to a Sacrament. Evidently this duty is very serious, but unfortunately it is very commonly neglected—"for the sake of peace." But there is no peace with God so long as efforts to change irregular conditions are not continued. More of these spiritual implications may be deduced from what has been said about the Sacraments of Baptism and Matrimony. Here the question may be asked: "Will these spiritual considerations influence worldly Catholics intending to ask for major dispensations?" The present writer can state that, in two cases within his own experience, the plain statement that there would be no Sacrament and no blessing of God changed the intention completely.

Some other pertinent thoughts are expressed by Pius XI. "Whence [from such forbidden marriages] it comes about not unfrequently, as experience shows, that deplorable defections from religion occur (in addition to the falling away of the Catholic partner) among the offspring, or at least a headlong descent into religious indifference.... It becomes much more difficult to imitate by a lively conformity of spirit the mystery of . . . that close union between Christ and His Church." There are many more fine thoughts in the same Encyclical worth quoting, but only a statement of the old Roman law will presently be added: "Marriage is . . . a sharing of life and the communication of divine and human rights."

Similar spiritual considerations and effects may be found in the case of all marriages for which major dispensations are required. All the impediments are primarily intended to safeguard the rights of God and religion. The spiritual reasons will have more effect upon candidates, because usually all the secular consequences of the irregular marriages have been already considered and dismissed as unimportant.

If a disastrous ending of marriage is to be forestalled, wrong beginnings must be resisted. There must be no intimate familiarity with those not of the Faith, no company keeping with such persons; it is sinful and must be confessed. No desire for forbidden fruit should be aroused, although Satan may suggest that everything will turn out all right. A discreet question in time may prevent disaster. Unfortunately many of those who contemplate irregular marriages give up the reception of the Sacraments, and these must be reached by other means, to which we shall return later.

Of more than ordinary importance is the certainty that the prospective partner exercises his or her religion faithfully. One who does not live up to religious obligations and practices may be more dangerous to the peace of a family and the welfare of the children than the unbaptized or heretical. "Now we, brethren, as Isaac was, are the children of promise. But as then he, that was born according to the flesh, persecuted him that was after the spirit; so also is it now. . . . Cast out the bondwoman . . ." (Gal., iv, 28-30).

(2) The second obligation of those intending to marry is to consider themselves. They must examine themselves as to whether both are determined to enter a permanent union and to face the consequences of this step according to the will of God. This is especially necessary with regard to the children God may deign to send them. Simply to say, "We will abstain for some time" or "We will see to that when the time comes," does not express a Christian attitude. It would amount to taking the ordering of creation out of the hands of the Creator, as far as it is possible for men to do so.

Against contraception Pope Pius XI declares in his Encyclical on Christian Marriage:

> "No reason, however grave, may be put forward by which anything intrinsically against nature may become conformable to nature and morally good. Since, therefore, the conjugal act is destined primarily by nature for the begetting of children, those who in exercising it deliberately frustrate its natural power and purpose, sin against nature and commit a deed which is shameful and intrinsically vicious. Small wonder, therefore, if Holy Writ bears witness that the Divine Majesty regards with greatest detestation this horrible crime and at times has punished it with death. As St. Augustine notes: 'Intercourse even with one's legitimate wife is unlawful and wicked where the conception of the offspring is prevented. Onan, the son of Juda, did this and the Lord killed him for it' (St. August. 'De conjug. adult.' lib. II, n. 12; Gen. xxxviii, 8-10). . . . The Catholic Church . . . in order that she preserve the chastity of the nuptial union from being defiled by this foul stain, raises her voice in token of her divine ambassadorship and through Our mouth proclaims anew: any use whatsoever of matrimony exercised in such a way that the act is deliberately frustrated in its natural power to generate life is an offense against the law of God and of nature, and those who indulge in such are branded with the guilt of grave sin. . . .

> "Holy Church knows well that not infrequently one of the parties is sinned against rather than sinning, when for a grave cause he or she reluctantly allows the perversion of the right order. In such a case, there is no sin, provided that, mindful of the law of charity, he or she does not neglect to seek to dissuade and to deter the partner from sin. Nor are those considered as acting against nature who in the married state use their right in the proper manner, although on account of natural reasons either of time or of certain defects, new life cannot be brought forth. For in matrimony as well as in the use of the matrimonial rights there are secondary ends such as mutual aid, the cultivating of mutual love, and the quieting of concupiscence which husband and wife are not forbidden to consider so long as they are subordinated to the primary end and so long as the intrinsic nature of the act is preserved.
>
> ". . . There are no possible circumstances in which husband and wife cannot, strengthened by the grace of God, faithfully fulfill their duties and preserve in wedlock their chastity unspotted. This truth of Christian Faith is expressed by the teaching of the Council of Trent; 'Let no one be so rash as to assert that which the Fathers of the Council have placed under anathema, namely, that there are precepts of God impossible for the just to observe. God does not ask the impossible, but by His commands, instructs you to do what you are able, and to pray for what you are not able that He may help you' (Conc. Trid. Sess. VI, cap. 11)."

If either or both parties marry with a condition against the substance of marriage, and this condition enters into their contract, such a marriage is null and void and is a sacrilege. Such a condition or act against the substance of matrimony could be against the generation of offspring (contraception and abortion); against the mutual corporal rights of the parties (adultery); or against the indissolubility of marriage (thinking that divorces and adultery sever the marriage bond). Even the internal act of the will excluding some essential quality of matrimony would render the consent invalid and the contract null and void. Mutual agreement on the part of the parties to exclude some essential quality of marriage is not needed to invalidate the contract. If such an agreement takes place before consent the marriage could be proved to be invalid. But without such an expressed and mutual agreement the presumption of law holds that the marriage is true and valid, even though the marriage may be null and void before God on account of an internal act on the part of one or both parties excluding some essential quality of marriage.

If one or both parties have the intention of not fulfilling the duties of marriage, such a contract is valid provided the parties do not make that intention a condition entering into the marriage contract itself. Such parties undertake the married state absolutely but do not intend to fulfill all its obligations. Here we distinguish between the essence of marriage and its use. Such intentions are wrong but the contract of marriage would be valid.

If the contracting parties agree to preserve continence, and make this a condition of the marriage contract, such a marriage is valid because we distinguish between a right and its use. The agreement of not using the marital right does not nullify the transference of that right by marital consent.[1] This should be stated to candidates plainly, and not in a roundabout way which may unknowingly leave loopholes for misunderstanding.

Other considerations are whether the partners have the ability to care for a home, and the strength and courage to carry a cross if it should be laid upon them; also whether they have some physical incapacity that is regulated by the diriment impediments. Incurable or hereditary diseases (or dispositions towards disorders) may make matrimony highly inadvisable.

(3) Each partner should reasonably consider the other. At the age of mating when passions are naturally very strong, young people are liable to forget the time when they will be normally together. What the blindness of passion may have overlooked, will then appear as it really is. "Let not sin . . . reign in your mortal body, so as to obey the lusts thereof" (Rom., vi, 12). Hence, before the time arrives for being bound together, partners should consider each other. Character, social life, and health must be taken into consideration. Not all characters harmonize,

---
[1] Arturus Vermeersch, "Theologiæ Moralis Principia—Responsa—Consilia" (Altera Editio, Università Gregoriana, Roma, 1927), vol. III, p. 680. H. Noldin and A. Schmitt, "Summa Theologiæ Moralis" (Editio XX, Rauch, Oeniponte, 1930), vol. III, pp. 634-36. Henry Davis, "Moral and Pastoral Theology" (Sheed & Ward, New York, 1935), vol. IV, pp. 185-6. E. J. Mahoney, "Christian Marriage" (Macmillan, New York, 1928), p. 30.

and not all are adapted to happy and intimate living. Precarious health is not necessarily, but nevertheless is often, a cause of many worries and of the cooling of conjugal love and attachment. The past conduct of a partner offers a good indication of what the future may bring. A change for the better is possible, but not very probable.

(4) Partners must think of the offspring that may be expected. They should ask themselves: "Can I support them, raise them, care for them as I should, and sacrifice for them? Can I guide them to God from Whom they come and to Whom they must be returned? Is there at least good hope that I can perform these duties if they should devolve upon me?" Each partner should ask these questions, since death may leave one alone. These questions are not really answered by saying that the other partner will attend to that, one can engage help, everything can be had for money. This is merely shifting one's personal responsibilities to others. Money and health are not necessarily permanent. They may be lost as quickly as life itself. God is not bound to provide us with all we like or desire, although He has promised to give us what we need. Moreover, where personal service is not rendered, the charity and love so necessary for the formation of the character of children are lacking. It is not necessaray to enlarge upon this, since so many children of the wealthy show the ruinous effects of parental neglect.

(5) Civic obligations must also be considered. The civil laws about licenses and other regulations which the State may lawfully impose must be observed. The State is interested in the civil effects of matrimony, and endeavors to make social life happy and orderly. For this reason, the Encyclical insists upon the observance of civic ordinances.

(6) Finally, Pius XI recommends strongly that young people should pray incessantly and ask the advice of their parents in matrimonial matters. In fact, he makes it obligatory. If the advice of the parents seems unreasonable, it may be disregarded, but in most cases parents have the true welfare of their children at heart and are undoubtedly more experienced than they. It makes little difference that parents belong to another generation,

PREPARATION FOR CHASTE WEDLOCK 71

because the things that really matter are irrevocably fixed and not subject to periodical changes. The blessing of the parents builds the houses of children.

So far not much has been said about the economic aspects of matrimony. The main reason for this is that we are at present concerned about the spiritualization of young people, and therefore finances (in so far as they reflect covetousness) need not be mentioned, as St. Paul admonishes (Eph., v, 3). Generally speaking, people never have all they want, nor what they consider necessary. Even wealthy people must sometimes do without things. Really poor people place more confidence in God than in all else, and with them economics does not play the most important rôle. It is rather those of the middle-class that do not want to be without a number of things which are by no means necessary. Those who would marry must accommodate themselves to circumstances or lead a chaste life as celibates. The continuation of the human race does not depend upon them. This does not mean that young people should not be helped to get a good start in life; it merely emphasizes the fact that economic factors are not the most important, although they deserve some consideration from a Christian viewpoint. Thrift is recommended to young couples as a means of providing something for a day when it may be greatly needed.

After this predominantly theoretical exposition, a few practical pastoral thoughts may be added about courtship and what it implies. This courtship, like what precedes and follows it, must be holy. Its predominant features must be piety, chastity, and prudence. The piety inaugurated in childhood and extended during youth must be intensified in the period before marriage. The grace of God and light from above are needed if the young couple are to conquer the temptations that increase in number as well as in force, and if they wish to see things in a true light. This strength and ability God will not grant unless He is asked for it by prayer, and unless the means He instituted for this purpose are used. Among these means frequent Holy Communion, the seed of virginity, is of the greatest importance in our time.

The preservation of chastity should be strongly inculcated, not only from a spiritual but also from a human and practical viewpoint. By prohibiting unchaste thoughts, desires, words, and actions, God does not wish to eliminate natural pleasures connected with sex, but He demands that they be postponed until they become legitimate in lawful wedlock or are exchanged for the higher values of the state of virginity.

Sexual powers and the pleasures accompanying them were not created by God for the benefit and pleasure of the individual, but for the welfare and increase of the human race at large, and finally for His own greater glory. The postponement of these pleasures may demand self-restraint and necessitate fierce struggles, but in return for the observance of His will God grants great life-values which accompany and reward a chaste youth. The victory over sexual temptation brings with it ever-increasing joy, happiness, and self-restraint so necessary in many vicissitudes of life. It brings about natural development of the creative powers, preserves the health and freshness of the body, etherealizes the beauty of the countenance, attracts similar characters, and makes one well liked. Chastity also safeguards social life by precluding grave scandals and by ensuring the unity of the family to be established. Therefore, a chaste youth is the best guarantee for a happy married life.

This becomes still more obvious when we consider what losses, immediate and future, follow the disregard of the angelic virtue. An unchaste life always brings with it a defilement of the mind and a string of evil habits that are very difficult to eradicate. Social disgrace, the degradation of women, venereal diseases, and the murder of innocents and their exclusion from heaven are some of unchastity's evil fruits. Equally great are the evil consequences of an unchaste youth witnessed in married life. Among these are infidelity, divorce, bigamy, destruction of home and family life, and often self-destruction in time and eternity. These things are not duly feared by our generation, not because they may not come to pass nor because they are not so evil in themselves, but because the prevalent standards of the world at large, opposed diametrically to the standards of God, are deceiving young and old. Nevertheless, some of these evils will overtake all of our youth who are not prepared and trained by chastity.

Courtship presumes the intention to marry. All other particular friendships between persons of the different sexes are, as a rule, sexual and sinful. However, a friendship or brief engagement preceding marriage is not only not sinful in itself but is even necessary. But during the time of courtship or steady engagement the sixth and ninth Commandments retain their full force, and do not permit any of the familiarities that will be legitimate and good after the marriage has been contracted.

Courtship, being the proximate preparation and also the laying of the foundation for married life, requires great prudence from the start, since remedies attempted later may be unsuccessful. The importance of the issue at stake requires prayer for light and guidance so that the right partner may be selected and accepted. The right partner for a good Catholic is obviously another practical Catholic. God did not intend any other for His beloved children. Evidently the identity in nature should be accompanied by a similarity in grace (Gen., ii, 23). This partner must also have a good character corresponding to the character of the other, if future peace and happiness are to result. Physical and social advantages, desirable as they may be, are not always permanent, and hence should be estimated accordingly. They should never be determining factors, because they really are of less importance than spiritual or moral qualities. Persons known to neglect God, their parents, and other important duties will most probably also neglect their partners in marriage. Those who indicate that they live above their means, or who are drinkers or otherwise extravagant in their mode of life, will most probably continue to remain so when married.

Love at first sight furnishes a precarious foundation for marriage. If one wishes to avoid an error, one should not look for a partner where good young people are unlikely to be found. Truly good, serious, and careful youngsters do not frequent public dance-halls, dubious resorts, drinking places, etc. Such places are often the sources of evils that are deplored when it is too late. They should be avoided by matrimonial candidates.

Youth should not be in too great a hurry in the choice of a partner. The young man or woman should investigate before any steps towards matrimony are taken. On the other hand, it is not advisable that these investigations be prolonged for years and years. Because of congested living conditions, especially in our larger cities, the first serious approach between lovers unfortunately seldom begins in the family circle. Nevertheless, undue deliberations and unnecessary delays should be avoided. After all, it does not require a long time to find out about the nobility of character, desirable qualities, habits, etc., of an intended partner. The presence of firm religious principles, an earnest will to serve God, serious views of life, moderate demands, courage, decent family relations free from grave stigmas, good physical conditions, and sound economic prospects can soon be ascertained. Here it should be remembered that a happy young pair arouses the envy and hatred of Satan, who will leave no wheel unturned to bring about serious falls, especially if engagements are prolonged beyond a reasonable space of time.[1]

---

[1] More material on this subject can be found in the author's book, "Seraphic Youth" (Third Order Bureau, 1936).

CHAPTER VIII

The Great Sacrament

CHRIST, HAVING COME into this world to save it, naturally applied His redeeming work first to the family. After having lived for thirty years hidden in His own family, He began His public career by manifesting His divine power at the marriage feast in Cana. He had special reasons for attending the feast with His disciples, because what He intended to do was contributory to His office as the Saviour. Like His priests after Him, He was there to witness the marriage contract and to confirm it on the part of God. The Apostles also were present to receive an increase in faith and to solemnize the occasion in the home, which was the ordinary place of Jewish family worship. Mary had preceded them, no doubt, to assist the family in preparing for the festivities.

It was she who noticed the deficiency of wine, the usual and common drink at practically all Eastern meals. She approached Jesus, saying: "They have no wine." Jesus, conscious of His messianic character, indicates in His reply that the will of His Father was the determining factor in this case. He said to her: "Woman, what is that to Me and to thee? My hour is not yet come" (John, ii, 4). He evidently could not act before the time appointed by His Father had arrived. In His answer, Jesus calls His mother "woman," not only to indicate that His public life would be a source of separation between them, but principally to bring Mary into connection with the prophecy and promise made to Eve that the seed of "the woman" should crush the head of Satan (Gen., iii, 15).

Mary, enlightened from above, understood that something extraordinary was going to take place, when He ordered the water pots to be filled so that no more fluid could be added. Without any further urging and without adding any explanation, Jesus said: "Draw out now, and carry to the chief steward," (John, ii, 8). In that very moment, the water turned into such excellent wine that the tasting steward said to the bridegroom: "Thou hast kept the good wine until now" (ibid., 10). The Evangelist adds that this was the first miracle Jesus wrought, and that His disciples believed in Him.

No further incidents of this occasion are related, nor is any additional explanation given. However, it is highly significant that Jesus wrought His first public miracle at a marriage, by changing water into a superior wine in the presence of His disciples. The marriage feast at Cana would have been a fine occasion for some statement about the nature of matrimony under the new dispensation; yet for reasons of His own Jesus kept silence. But the circumstances surrounding the miracle clearly point to the two great states of life, matrimony and the priesthood, both to be inaugurated by Sacraments on account of their singular importance as instruments to provide for the existence, growth, and welfare of the human race and the Church, the Mystical Body of Christ. The new wine provided by the miracle was better than the wine served to the guests from the beginning. Wine is often used in Holy Scripture to signify or indicate charity or love. The bride in the Canticle (ii, 4) exclaims: "He [the beloved] brought me into the cellar of wine, he set in order charity in me."

As far as the effect of the miracle upon the disciples is concerned, it is expressly stated that it strengthened their faith in the power of Christ. This was important with regard to the divine banquet and nuptials of the Holy Eucharist. From what happened at Cana, Christ's disciples present and future could deduce that one who can change water into wine can also change wine into His blood and bread into His flesh. The same divine power is needed and suffices for all this. Moreover, this power could elevate matrimony to the dignity and efficiency of a Sacrament.

The Evangelists do not tell us exactly on what occasion the Sacrament of Matrimony was instituted by Christ. His words

THE GREAT SACRAMENT 77

regarding matrimony as related by St. Mark (x, 6-12) and St. Matthew (xix, 6) are but restatements of the original concept of matrimony. St. Luke (xvi, 18) adds something that had seemingly been forgotten by most of the Jews, although it was ancient truth: "Every one that putteth away his wife, and marrieth another, committeth adultery; and he that marrieth her that is put away from her husband, committeth adultery." It was not necessary to say more about it. Matrimony, the instrument for human generation, jointly operated by God and man, existed from the beginning. Its natural effects had not been lost by the fall of man. All that was necessary was to adapt it to the new supernatural order brought about by the Redemption. It had to be elevated to the condition in which it existed at the moment of creation when it was permeated by the love of God. The elevation to a grace-conferring union was willed by Christ and takes place as a result of Baptism. Hence, among the baptized there is no valid matrimony that is not at the same time a Sacrament. Holy Scripture and the teaching of the infallible Church leave no doubt about this.

Since all the words spoken by Christ about matrimony were uttered before He instituted the Sacrament of Baptism after His Resurrection, we must turn to the writings of the Apostles as explained by the Councils in order to find the mind of Christ and to understand the full significance of the sacramental or grace-giving character of Matrimony.

St. Paul calls the marital union a great Sacrament in Christ and in the Church (Eph., v, 32). He distinguishes it clearly from pagan marriages and unions that are not effected in Christ and in His Church. In fact, he compares the supernatural union between husband and wife with the mystical union between Christ, the head, and the Church, His body, for which He gave Himself unsparingly and completely. Christ brings forth in the Church by means of Matrimony a holy offspring, "cleansing it by the laver of water in the word of life" (ibid., 26). The spiritual paternity of Holy Orders exercised in Baptism is added to the natural paternity of the parents. As God cooperates in the production of a child by creating its soul, so Christ brings about its rebirth in the supernatural order. This is clearly stated in the rite of Ordination in which it is asked from God "that the priest (*alter Christus*) may show forth an abundance of paternity."

In this way the Church and her members grow together in a living organism unto the full stature of Christ. The fruit of Matrimony, the child of man, is made a member of Christ, is intimately united with Christ, and is made similar to Christ. Children are born into a natural family; the paternity exercised in Baptism makes them members of the family of God by inserting them into the supernatural and mystical but truly real body of Christ, which is His Church. St. Paul writes: "I admonish you as my dearest children. . . . For in Christ Jesus, by the Gospel [through Baptism], I have begotten you" (I Cor., iv, 14-15). The incorporation of the fruit of Matrimony into the Church is absolutely demanded by the plan of salvation. On this depends the last end of man, which is an eternal union with God and the possession of all it implies.

The Sacrament of Matrimony is not effected or administered by the priest, who as representative of the Church examines and witnesses the contract. At the time the couple declare their consent to the mutual contract, the natural union is raised to the supernatural sphere of a Sacrament by the very fact that they are validly baptized. This power to elevate the natural union resides in no one else. Hence, marriage among the unbaptized remains in the natural order, but is nevertheless subject to the natural and divine laws. Persons living in a natural union lack the sacramental graces, and this lack will make it very difficult for them to preserve the holiness, unity, and indissolubility that is required also in natural marriages. The matrimonial disorders confronting us so frequently in natural marriages must be ascribed not only to human sinfulness, but also to the absence of special graces that permanently accompany married Christians.

The Sacrament of Matrimony is far superior to the natural marriage. The Roman Catechism says: "For as marriage, as a natural union, was instituted from the beginning to propagate the human race, so was the sacramental dignity subsequently conferred upon it in order that a people might be begotten and

THE GREAT SACRAMENT

brought up for the service and worship of the true God and of Christ our Saviour." For this purpose the Sacrament bestows grace, as the Council of Trent teaches: "By His passion Christ . . . merited for us the grace that perfects the natural love of husband and wife, confirms the indissoluble union existing between them, and sanctifies them," that their marriage may be "honorable in all, and the bed undefiled" (Heb., xiii, 4).[1]

Here it may be observed that, although the Jews and Gentiles were convinced that there was something divine in marriage (as clearly evidenced by their abhorrence of infidelity and other sexual vices, and by their respect for matrimonial regulations existing before the Redemption), their unions fell short of the real nature of a Sacrament, as already explained.

The graces bestowed upon the married are intended for the good of the whole subsequent family to come, for the preservation of conjugal fidelity and unity, and for the perseverance of the couple unto the end. Raineri-Hagan [2] enumerate three great blessings flowing from the Sacrament of Matrimony based upon the Roman Catechism.[3] (1) There is the blessing of the family, that is to say, of the children born of a lawful wife: "The woman shall be saved through child-bearing, if she continue in faith" (I Tim., ii, 15). This pertains to bearing children and also to bringing them up and training them in the practice of piety: "Hast thou children? Instruct them, and bow down their neck from their childhood" (Eccles., vii, 25). (2). The second blessing of marriage is mutual fidelity or faith in each other. This is the result of a special, holy, and pure love—not such as adulterers or fornicators have for each other, but a love such as Christ has for His Church: "Husbands, love your wives, as Christ also loved the Church" (Eph., v, 25). (3) The third blessing is the indissoluble bond of matrimony: "The Lord commandeth that the wife depart not from her husband. And if she depart, that she remain

---

[1] Sess. XXIV, Denzinger, 969.
[2] "Catechetical Instruction" (Benziger, New York, 1909), vol. II.
[3] Conc. Flor., "Dec. pro Armenis," Denzinger, 702; Conc. Trid., Sess. XXIV, Denzinger, 969 sq.

unmarried, or be reconciled to her husband. And let not the husband put away his wife" (I Cor., vii, 10-11).

Turning to the rite of Matrimony, which is the form of the sacramental contract, we find that it is short and confined to essentials. Each of the partners signifies twice by words and signs acceptance of the other for a lawful partner "to have and to hold from this day forward . . . till death do us part." The priest confirms the union with the blessing of God. The consent is given before at least two witnesses, who also sign the documents. Marriage being a public contract with civil implications, the State is interested in it and can prescribe legal requirements; but the State has no power with regard to the matrimonial bonds. The blessing of the ring which now follows asks God "that she who is to wear it, being true to her husband in all things, may abide in peace . . . , and live with him in well-requited affection." Whilst placing the ring on the finger of his wife, the husband once more pledges to her his fidelity. After the recitation of several invocations imploring God's grace and aid, the rite concludes with a prayer in which special stress is laid on the welfare of the expected offspring. The rite for a mixed marriage is the same, except that the ring is not blessed nor is any other blessing given.

In view of the great importance of the Sacrament of Matrimony, its rite may seem rather short. However, in days of deeper faith and more leisure to attend to spiritual affairs, marriage was regularly followed by the Divine Liturgy of the Mass. This was the rule and not an exception. The rubric in the Roman Ritual states: "This [the contract] having been completed, if the nuptials are to be solemnized, the pastor celebrates the Mass 'For Bridegroom and Bride,' according to the rubrics of the Missal." The Proper of this Mass is very beautiful, dogmatic, and inspiring, and might well form the subject of a lecture or instruction to young people.

The Mass begins with the Introit: "May the God of Israel join you together; and may He be with you, who took pity upon two only children; and now, O Lord, make them bless Thee more fully" (Tob., viii, 17-19). These words refer to the marriage of young Tobias and Sara so wonderfully arranged by God, Who granted this favor in answer to their prayers and righteousness. The Church adopts the prayer of the pious parents of Sara, and asks God that henceforth the newly wed may "bless the Lord more fully," by loving God in keeping His Commandments. "Blessed are all they that fear the Lord; that walk in His ways" (Introit, Ps. cxxvii, 1).

The continuation of this Psalm, used in the Gradual, adds cogent reasons why the married should live more justly: "For [doing so] thou shalt eat the labors of thy hand. . . . It shall be well with thee. Thy wife shall be as a fruitful vine, on the sides of thy house, and thy children as olive plants, round about thy table. Behold, thus shall the man be blessed that feareth the Lord" (Ps. cxxvii, 2-4). Tobias and Sara were such a God-fearing pair. Tobias confessed: "Lord, Thou knowest that not for fleshly love do I take my sister to wife, but only for the love of posterity, in which Thy name may be blessed for ever and ever" (Tob. viii, 9). Sara imbued by the same sentiments asked: "Have mercy on us, O Lord . . . and let us grow old together in health" (ibid., 10). To this Raguel and Anna added: "Make them, O Lord, . . . offer up to Thee a sacrifice of Thy praise, and of their health, that all nations may know that Thou alone art God in all the earth" (ibid., 19).

The Collect prays "that what is administered by our service may be more effectually fulfilled by God's blessing."

In the Epistle St. Paul admonishes women to be subject to their husbands, and commands the husbands to love their wives as their own bodies—all for the love of Christ Who loved the Church, and in imitation of Christ Who sacrificed Himself for the Church in order to cleanse and sanctify it. The Apostle recalls the original unity and indissolubility of matrimony, and pronounces the New Testament nuptials to be a great Sacrament in Christ and in the Church (Eph., v, 22-32). To the other doctrines contained in this Epistle we shall return later.

The Gradual consists of several verses of Psalm cxxvii quoted above. But since the blessing of a numerous posterity has been solicited by the Church, strong encouragement is added lest its fulfillment and the accompanying labors and worries might frighten the newly wed: "The Lord will send thee help from the sanctuary, and strengthen thee out of Sion" (Ps. xix, 3). The use of prayer and the Sacraments is implied here. Occasionally the Tract is added: "The Lord bless thee out of Sion; and mayest thou see the good of Jerusalem all the days of thy life!" Temporal prosperity is asked for in this invocation. During Easter time, for the Tract is substituted: "The Lord that made heaven and earth, bless thee out of Sion" (Ps. cxxxiii, 3). What man might not expect to accomplish, God can bring to pass.

It is strange that this plain and fully accepted truth does not arouse in man more confidence and a faith that transplants mountains. After all, what can man alone do without the supporting blessing of God? How far would the five loaves of bread and the few dried fishes have reached among the multitude of five thousand, without His blessing? But these being multiplied by the blessing of Christ, all the multitude were filled and much food was left over. Day after day this miracle is repeated in many poor families, but, like everything else in life, it depends upon obedience to the will of God, especially with regard to the number of offspring. This fact is repeatedly stressed in the words of the Mass. Nothing is added about prudence, carefulness, etc. God is faithful. Man cannot outsmart Him.

The Gospel (Matt., xix, 3-6) contains the words of Christ quoted from Genesis: "For this cause shall a man leave father and mother, and shall cleave to his wife, and they two shall be in one flesh." To this Christ adds: "Now they are not two, but one flesh. What therefore God hath joined together, let no man put asunder." Notwithstanding the fact that God foreknows all that accompanies married life, He did not grant for any cause whatever a release from the bonds of matrimony—from a burden which He Himself intended to help His children carry until death.

Confident in the goodness and power of God, the Offertory expresses the sentiment that should prevail in the soul of bridegroom and bride, alike: "I trusted in Thee, O Lord. I said: Thou art my God, my times are in Thy hands" (Ps. xxx, 15-16).

THE GREAT SACRAMENT 83

The Secret adds: "Be Thou, O Lord, the ruler of this institution [of matrimony] of which Thou art the author." Whatever may happen, God will provide for His faithful servants. It may not be all that they desire, but it will be all they need.

The same thought is taken up again in the first prayer of the Bridal Blessing: ". . . Lord, graciously favor Thy institution, by which Thou hast provided for the propagation of mankind; that the union made by Thy authority may be preserved by Thy assistance."

The second part of this special Blessing is a prayer, a dogmatic exposition, an exhortation, and an intercession. It is directly addressed to the bride, but is indirectly intended for both partners. This part, one of the most beautiful documents found in the Liturgy, unfolds the history of matrimony from the beginning until its elevation by Christ to a great Sacrament in His Church. Although perhaps often read by the pastor, it may be useful to quote and explain the parts as we go along, for there are priests and layfolk that have rarely or never given their full attention to this Blessing.

It begins: "O God, who by the power of Thy might didst make all things of nothing and having ordained the beginning of the universe and made man to the image of God, didst so appoint for him the inseparable help of woman as to give the body of the woman its beginning from the flesh of the man, teaching us thereby that what it pleased Thee to form from one could never lawfully be put asunder. O God, who hast consecrated the conjugal union by so excellent a mystery as to presignify the sacred union of Christ and the Church by the nuptial contract: O God, by whom woman is united with man, and that alliance ordained in the beginning is gifted with that blessing which alone was not taken away either by the punishment of original sin, or by the sentence of the deluge: look down favorably upon this Thy handmaid, who . . . prays to be shielded by Thy protection. May there be upon her a yoke of charity and peace!"

Nothing but the wickedness of man can take away the blessing "to increase and multiply" from those to whom God gave this faculty. "There are eunuchs, who were born so . . . and . . .

who were made so by men; and . . . who have made themselves eunuchs for the kingdom of heaven" (Matt., xix, 12). Christ declares it lawful to abstain from marriage for higher and legitimate motives. Prudential reasons for abstaining from lawful intercourse are frequently rather imprudent. A couple who assumed the burden and honor of providing for the growth and continued existence of Christ's Mystical Body, will not say with the disciples: "If the case of a man with his wife be so, it is not expedient to marry" (ibid., 10). They will follow the counsel of Christ and confess: God has given this glorious task to us and we will accept it with all it entails. God will provide! Ask and you shall receive.

The Church prays: "May there be upon the bride a yoke of charity!" The whole moral life of man is governed by love—either by a love that unites him with God, or a love that draws away from Him. The charity asked for the bride is the love of God, the charity about which St. Paul writes that it is patient, kind, envieth not, dealeth not perversely; is not puffed up, nor ambitious, nor provoked to anger; thinketh no evil, beareth all things, endureth all things, and remains in peace (I Cor., xiii, 4-7).

The Blessing continues as an instruction as well as a prayer: "Faithful and chaste may she marry in Christ, and ever follow the example of holy women! May she be pleasing to her husband, as Rachel; prudent, as Rebecca; long-lived and faithful, as Sara! May the author of evil have no share in any of her actions." Satan stands for the unholy love that separates from God. His actions are his works and his pomps which all Christians have renounced at Baptism. He draws towards the world that is antagonistic to Christ. "For all that is in the world, is the concupiscence of the flesh, and the concupiscence of the eyes, and the pride of life, which is not of the Father" (I John, ii, 16). Thus the rite refers to Baptism in which the sacramental dignity of Matrimony originates, and having emphasized the necessity of constant essential sanctity, points out the moral perfection that should be based upon it and should be its fruit.

The Blessing continues: "May she remain constant in faith"—

in the faith for which she asked in Baptism as a necessary means for obtaining life everlasting—and "keep the Commandments" (which is equally necessary for salvation). Based upon this faith is the fact of "being united to one," and the observance of the Commandments demands that "she may shun unlawful relations." Should temptation arise, "may she protect her weakness by the strength of discipline!" This discipline she should exercise by being "serious and reserved, revered for modesty, instructed in heavenly doctrine," and living accordingly. After these personal good qualities have been mentioned, reference is made to some social perfections. "May she be fruitful in children, and well liked and innocent; and may she arrive at the repose of the blessed; and the kingdom of heaven," as a reward for the faithful performance of the duties that her state of life imposes upon her!

Turning to both, the Blessing concludes: "May they both see their children's children to the third and fourth generation, and attain desired old age," with the help of God!

In the Communion the Church refers to the Eucharistic Banquet and the presence of Christ in the bride and groom, as a foretaste of heaven and the permanent union with God. Allusion is also made to the special temporal reward asked for in the Bridal Blessing that precedes and that which soon follows: "Behold, thus shall every man be blessed that feareth the Lord; and mayest thou see thy children's children, and peace upon Israel" (Ps. cxxvii, 4, 6).

This peace upon Israel, the family of God's predilection, is of such importance in married life that God is especially asked for it in the Postcommunion: "We beseech Thee, Almighty God, accompany the institution of Thy providence with gracious favor; that Thou mayest preserve with lasting peace those whom Thou unitest in lawful union."

Before the blessing of the congregation, the concluding part of the Bridal Blessing is repeated as the special good wish of the Church, the pastor, and his parish: "May the God of Abraham, the God of Isaac and the God of Jacob be with you, and may He fulfill His blessing in you; that you may see your children's children even to the third and fourth generation and afterwards possess life everlasting, by the assistance of our Lord Jesus Christ."

Very few Catholics, including the better educated, have such a concept of matrimony as is contained in the prayers and ceremonies of the Liturgy. Hence, they lack the best and most solid foundation upon which a holy and happy family life can rest. Happiness and holiness are not exclusive; they rather complement each other. At present much is being done to lead our young people to ethical perfection, and some truly remarkable results have been attained. But looking at the manner in which virtues are promoted and vices combatted, it seems that the foundations of spiritual life are being neglected. Expressions, ideas, and views seem to negate the good works. The question arises how a structure can weather severe storms if it has not a solid foundation. The edifice above the surface may occasion no apprehension; it may look strong and be beautifully designed and ornamented, but all this cannot compensate for the fundamental weakness of the structure. Let us humbly and frankly acknowledge that the collapse of seemingly well-constructed families and homes must have been caused by a lack of a basic religion. Inadequately prepared, their members could not withstand the temptations of the world, and succumbed to the ravages of scandals and material evils surrounding them.

Such catastrophes are rapidly increasing in number, and the cure of a social plague is necessarily a slow process. The social structure has to be rebuilt. A beginning might be made by preaching more dogmatic sermons and by linking morals with the truths from which they flow, or by which they are demanded. Mere scriptural quotations or references to the Gospel do not strongly influence hearers who are not convinced of the paramount importance of the Bible, and who know neither the divine sanction of Holy Writ nor the explanation of the texts and their application to Christian living. Nor are illustrations sufficient proofs for the rationality of the moral demands of Christianity, unless the opposing claims are clearly demonstrated as untenable. This is not a defense of rationalism, but a plea for the creation of an understanding capable of moving the will.

THE GREAT SACRAMENT 87

Although necessary for teaching what must be believed and done or omitted, catechetical and moral sermons do not as a rule bring out the beauty, symmetry, and coherence of religion and its place in life. Nor do they create that enthusiasm for religion which contributes so much towards the strengthening of faith. For assistance in this respect the faithful are now clamoring, and quite rightfully. Some recent radio sermons have catered to this need, and have been very well received.

Much profit might accrue from interesting and practical study clubs, since pearls discovered by one's own efforts usually appear to be more precious and more worthy of preservation. Lectures in popular form might also be useful for spiritualization, but, like study clubs, they reach but a fraction of the number of people that regularly crowd the Sunday Masses.

CHAPTER IX

The Christian Family in Faith

THERE CAN BE no domestic, national, or international unity without truly religious families which inculcate the love of God and neighbor, and aspire to higher values than natural and material things. This is also true and important in view of the last end of man. By way of the family man enters legitimately into this world, and it is also the family that should imbue him with such principles of life as will make happy entry into the next world at once possible and probable. This requires a special type of family, entirely different from the worldly type of family now prevailing. Unless this requirement is kept in mind and acted upon, the welfare of the State and of the Kingdom of God on earth is endangered. In his Encyclical on the Mystical Body the present Holy Father writes:

> "For the social needs of the Church, Christ has provided in a particular manner by two sacraments which He instituted. Through Matrimony, when the contracting parties are ministers of grace to each other, provision is made for the external and properly regulated increase of Christian society and, what is of greater importance, for the correct religious education of the offspring without which this Mystical Body would be in grave danger. . . . We cannot pass over in silence the fathers and mothers of families, to whom Our Saviour has entrusted the most delicate members of His Mystical Body. We plead with them for the love of Christ and the Church to give the greatest possible care to the children confided to them, and to look to protecting them from the multiplicity of snares into which they can fall so easily today."

The family always was and still is the most important unit of mankind. As the families are, so the community will be. The whole cannot be better than its constituent parts. It is, therefore, but natural that Christ Who had come to save mankind should give His first attention to the sanctification of the home and family. He not only willed to be born in a family, but He also lived in the family for all but the last three years of His earthly life. His hidden life in Nazareth was to be the standard of Christian family life for all time to come. The Gospel outlines the family life of Christ by recording its more important episodes. St. Luke relates the annunciation, incarnation, nativity, presentation, flight to Egypt, and the return to Nazareth. As the only further event he describes the early visit to the Temple of Jerusalem and what happened there. About the years following until He left His home, we read nothing but that "Jesus advanced in wisdom and age, and grace with God and men" (Luke, ii, 52).

These last events about the home life of Jesus are read in the Gospel of the Feast of the Holy Family, and the Mass and Office for this day contain some beautiful lessons for Christian families to take to heart. In the Lessons of the First Nocturn of this feast, St. Paul, having explained that with Christ His followers have also risen to a new life, tells us to follow the teachings of Christ, because He is among us (in His Church) and instructs us. Thereafter, the Apostle states the teachings of Christ (Col., iii, 18-21):

> "*Wives*, be subject to your husbands, as it behoveth in the Lord.
> "*Husbands*, love your wives, and be not bitter towards them.
> "*Children*, obey your parents in all things. . . .
> "*Fathers*, provoke not your children to indignation. . . ."

To all—parents, children, servants and masters—he says: "Be instant in prayer" (Col., iv, 2).

Pope Leo XIII expands this instruction in the Lessons of the Second Nocturn: "The fathers of families have in Joseph a true model of vigilance, loyalty, and domestic care. . . . The mothers have in Mary an example of love, modesty, perfect submission, and conjugal fidelity. . . . The children see in Jesus a model of perfect obedience which they should admire, cultivate, and imitate." The learned Pope continues: "All may learn from the Holy Family. . . . Those of royal blood and rulers may learn from the royal family of David how to preserve their dignity and to rule with kindness. . . . The wealthy may learn to esteem virtues more than material possessions. . . . Laborers and the poor may learn from the humble family of Nazareth to work diligently, to be thrifty and satisfied with the will of God."

The Oration explains the objective of the feast beautifully: "O Lord Jesus Christ, who by subjecting Thyself unto Mary and Joseph hast sanctified domestic life with unspeakable virtues, do Thou grant that, by the help of Mary and Joseph, we may order our lives after the example of Thy Holy Family, and obtain everlasting fellowship with it." Prayer also determines our life and actions. Hence the final injunction of St. Paul: "Be instant in prayer."

No Christian way of life, including family life, can be successful without a religious spirit and practice. It may be prosperous, but this is not the final end. Within the home religion smoothes and tempers the different characters. It promotes a fuller understanding and a deeper appreciation of the sanctity and unity of matrimony. In the exercise of religion, prayer in all its forms must hold the first place. Speaking to the ladies of Rome, Pope Pius XII declared that the negation of God is the cause of the world's ills today, including those of the family. Where prayer is neglected, God is negated and often denied, at least in practice.

Prayer is the most hopeful, the most effective, and in truth the only medium to spiritualize the family as a unit and every man in particular. The spiritualizing of mankind must begin with the individual. There are spirits that draw man and society away from God. The Evil Spirit is one of them, but the most dangerous is the materialistic or earthly spirit of man himself. In spite of religious exercises, in spite of the reception of the Sacraments, in spite of prayer and extrovert Catholic Action, this purely human spirit may prevail. This spirit, if not combatted, is more dangerous than Satan, the world, and the flesh, because it delights in everything that pleases man without seriously considering the will of God. Against this widely prevailing natural spirit, St. Paul gives no other remedy but: "Be instant in prayer." Prayer lifts man from the earth to God.

Several good treatises on the Christian family have appeared recently. They all concern themselves with the virtues to be practised and the evils to be shunned. They enumerate the vices pointed out in the Encyclical on Chaste Wedlock (divorce, birth control, companionate and experimental marriages, etc.), but very few point out the outstanding value of prayer in avoiding them. Nevertheless, what an old missionary said remains ever true: "None of these evils and all the domestic virtues are found in families where prayers are said in common and where husbands and wives kneel down to pray before they retire." Unfortunately, the American way of life is not identical with the Christian way of life. Treating of holiness in the Church, Pope Pius XII states in his Encyclical on the Mystical Body:

> "When the Fathers of the Church sing the praises of this Mystical Body of Christ—with its ministries, its variety of ranks, its offices, its conditions, its orders, its duties—they are thinking not only of those who have received sacred orders, but of all those, too, who following the evangelical counsels, pass their lives either actively among men, or in the silence of the cloister, or who aim at combining the active and contemplative life according to their institute. They were thinking of those who, though living in the world, consecrate themselves wholeheartedly to spiritual or corporal works of mercy; as well as those who live in the state of Holy Matrimony. Indeed let this be clearly understood, especially in these our days: The fathers and mothers of families and those who are spiritual parents through Baptism, and in particular those members of the laity who assist the ecclesiastical Hierarchy in spreading the kingdom of the Divine Redeemer, occupy an honorable, even though often lowly, place in the Christian community. Under the impulse of God and with His help, they can reach the peak of holiness, and such holiness, Jesus Christ has promised, will never be wanting to the Church."

At present it is not necessary to add much more on the desirable domestic virtues already enumerated in this and preceding chapters. What has been said about the virtues to be practised by individuals ought to suffice, because domestic virtues are the sum-total of the virtues of the members coordinated for the welfare of the whole family. It may be more timely and practical to discuss some means that will strengthen the will of Catholics to lead a good family life and increase their confidence in the assistance of God. Pope Pius XI also suggested that means should be found and applied to make Christian married life possible and less burdensome. Of course, condoning existing crimes or perhaps excusing and justifying them by calling attention to the existing social and economic conditions is always wrong. It may also happen that information true in itself may seriously weaken the necessary confidence in God.

As an example, birth control may serve. Birth control in whatever way it is practised cannot be said to be pleasing to God, except by abstinence for a higher reason. A serious situation faces pastors of souls. Fully sixty per cent of the families in the United States have either no children at all or only one or two. Catholics must be among them. Such a situation is not remedied or improved by saying that the problem is ninety per cent economic. It is not, but it certainly may be ninety per cent criminal, because economic reasons are not as a rule sufficient to induce one to accept celibacy. Formerly, there was an unshakable belief in the providence of God, and there still is among people not heavily endowed with goods of this world. Many had a strong faith in the blessing of God, and were convinced that a curse of God invited by malpractice could not be staved off by material excuses. The believing poor still have the larger families, and they will become the lawful heirs of wealthy criminals.

Nor can absolution be granted lightly to habitual offenders against the laws of nature. A child with an immortal soul cannot be weighed against material or social standing. The soul prevented from coming into existence is of greater importance than the building of a church. The case is plain with those who minimize these matters: "I will strike the shepherd, and the sheep shall be dispersed" (Mark, xiv, 27). No real good can be expected unless God's will is done. "Two parts [of the sheep] shall be scattered, and shall perish: but the third part shall be left. . . . And I will bring the third part through the fire, and will refine them as silver is refined: and will try them as gold is tried. They shall call on My name, and I will hear them. I will say: Thou art My people" (Zach., xiii, 8-9). Who would not prefer the latter to the first, putting aside all worldly prudence?

THE CHRISTIAN FAMILY IN FAITH

While these pages were being written, a mother called upon a priest and complained bitterly that God had taken away to war the only two sons she wanted to have. Her story was very pathetic, and she wound up by saying: "It would be better for mothers to have no children at all!" The listener was so perplexed by the outburst of this socially prominent Catholic woman that he found no other words to say than that his own mother had lost two sons through war but had seven sons still left to her. Much more could not well be said under the circumstances. This case, tragic as it is, is by no means an isolated one, at least not in so far as the sentiments expressed are concerned.

There can be no doubt that with regard to family life in its more important phases Catholics are in troubled circumstances, but serious as many of these conditions are, the laws of God are very plain. However, all that is possible should be done to help and console needy families. Not only should spirituality be inculcated persistently, but also the forces opposing it must be weakened and if possible destroyed.

The Federation of Switzerland took an important step in this connection by forming a committee appointed by and representing the *Forum Helveticum*. The work assigned to this committee was to formulate a program for the preservation of the religious and ethical values of the family. During the year 1940 the problems were studied and recommendations were issued that were subsequently approved by the Catholic Action of Switzerland. The second part of the report concerns itself with the creation of a public opinion favorable to the upholding of Christian family life and principles. It contains much that is of great value for all countries. We intend to draw freely upon this document, which appeared in condensed form as a press release of the Central Verein.

In order to bring about a more favorable public opinion towards a truly Christian family life, Catholic Action supported by the pulpit must create an abhorrence of all theories, philosophies, ideologies, and customs militating against it. This is evident, but the question how this can be done in a practical manner needs a more detailed exposition.

(1) The first step is to arouse in everyone a personal sense of responsibility in restoring the family and keeping it as God intended it to be. There is no one who is not in one way or another interested in the family. It is the unit in which society originates, and taken in a cumulative sense it is more important than the State or any other organized body. Hence, what is detrimental to families hurts all mankind. When Catholic Action has taken root and operates in every diocese, at least the Catholic world will be safeguarded in this respect, since the Christian family is undoubtedly one of its first concerns.

(2) Although all Catholics should know the importance, nature, and essence of matrimonial life, the whole Catholic body could not well be moved to action in all the fields where action is required. What is the concern of all would likely prove of no special concern to any one in particular. Smaller groups must be selected from among the most promising material, and must be specially educated for advising on the formation and upholding of Christian marriage and the family. This education, preferably imparted by lectures or study courses, should bring about a full knowledge and a personal conviction of the religious significance and the ethical foundation of marriage and the family.

In addition to this, the group must be prepared for disseminating the truths and principles presented. The earlier chapters of this book will furnish much of the material needed for this task. But more must be done. The members of the group must preserve contact with each other for the purpose of solving certain problems and for concerted action, when necessary. Different groups striving for the same or similar ends should be combined or coordinated in order that every field influencing the family may be fully covered, and that all may labor according to the same principles. Unless this is done, too much power may be spent on social and economic problems, and too little emphasis may be placed on the more important religious implications. Moreover, there should be a balanced program covering positive and negative, preventive and remedial, work.

(3) These coordinated groups, when ready, must keep up a systematic propaganda for influencing the public in favor of a

THE CHRISTIAN FAMILY IN FAITH

religious-ethical concept of matrimony. Truths must be spread, errors corrected, and falsehoods exposed in such a way that there will remain no doubts in the mind of those who have the will to do what is right.

In this connection, personal contact may be the most successful in individual cases, but for the creation or preservation of a Christian public opinion many other means must be used. For spreading religious propaganda, the public press is of great importance. Although it is not always easy to get specifically Catholic articles or features into the newspapers, it is often possible to express one's surprise to the editor that important statements of Catholic authorities have not been published. Editors are sensitive to the demands of readers, and even more so to the expressed wishes of advertisers. Furthermore, it is easier for a group to get space for communications or corrections addressed to the editors. Catholic publications must enlighten their readers about books and important articles in widely read publications, whenever these spread errors about matrimony with the halo of authority.

Happily, our own press is not so dependent on advertisers that it cannot call a spade a spade. It is a good sign that our Catholic papers and magazines are becoming more and more educational and inspirational; for this they deserve the wholehearted support of Catholics, who should see that one or more of them enter every Catholic home. When Catholics support their press, they will also see that propaganda for the Christian family will receive increased attention therein. Some doctrines may offend certain readers, but that is a matter of minor importance in a case where so great values are at stake.

In addition to supporting and utilizing the press for propaganda in behalf of the Christian family, the distribution of good and practical pamphlets among individuals and of books through libraries is of no small importance. Groups should engage in this field. Publishers will not refuse responsible groups the aids to make the proper selection.

The radio has not as yet been extensively used in behalf of the family. The Catholic Hour addresses already published include but one series on this subject. A series on the essence, nature, and laws of Catholic marriage and their explanation would certainly be productive of good. Evidently, the mere recommendation of virtues would not move certain classes of people unless an explanation of the crimes against the family is added. This is one of the delicate tasks that must be undertaken if public opinion is to be reformed.

More has been done in censoring films, plays, and magazines, but methods could be improved. What is meant by "banned" or on the "forbidden list," is well enough understood by Catholics. "Spotted" or "objectionable in parts" clearly means partly not bad. Very few, however, will draw the conclusion that, since the bad is inseparable from the whole, the whole must be rejected and shunned. Worldly standards do not count if they are at variance with the divine standards, which are the only guides for Catholics. Any lowering of standards is especially wrong and dangerous in things concerning Christian matrimony and family life. Carrying water on both shoulders means that one is neither hot nor cold. After all, Catholics must safeguard their own, and they can guide others only by being outspokenly Catholic. In this connection Christ Himself must be our model. He spoke out even at the risk of offending others, including those in authority. Charity does not mean a complacency with everything.

Another public task for groups working to protect the Christian family is the cleansing of cabarets, dance halls, and other dangerous places of amusement. In smaller places this may not be so difficult, and in larger cities at least public sentiment against them should be aroused. Even if nothing more should be achieved than making entertainment under parish auspices irreproachable, much good will result. Young people cannot then speciously justify their attendance at questionable resorts by saying: "What is the difference?"

(4) As an auxiliary force to be drawn upon by groups, all parents should be interested in public education especially in higher institutions. This interest they should display in addition to sending their own children to Catholic schools. It is evident that our public education dominates the American people at large.

Catholic attention should be extended not only to what is taught, but also to the guiding educational principles. Parents cannot delegate the responsibility for their children to just any kind of teachers or systems. Public school teachers of all ranks and grades, being the paid servants of the parents, cannot afford to resist a strong public opinion. Academic freedom may retain the right to teach what is true, and to teach as probable what is actually such, but must not become dogmatic in what is wrong, speculative, or sheer humbug. Formerly all teaching was an honored profession; public teaching today is often a career or job in which novelties are used to deceive the masses and so gain material advantages. This makes it difficult for Catholics to influence public education, and nothing but a strong public opinion can repel some of the attacks upon Christian living. As long as public educators insist on acting as the representatives of a pagan or at least religiously indifferent State, they get away with anything and everything. Not watchful waiting but concerted action will avail us here.

(5) The making of laws that directly or indirectly influence the Catholic family should be watched, and, if necessary, strong action taken—either against them or in favor of them, as the case may require. Such laws may concern birth prevention, divorce, observance of the Lord's Day, economic support of poor families, venereal diseases, alcoholism, and many other matters. It is well known that the most abhorrent practices are commended under deceptive names. Today not everything that seems or sounds innocent is really such.

In many of the matters just enumerated action has already been taken by national, diocesan, or local units, but it must become a universal crusade. All these questions concern individuals as well as the famliy, Church, and State. Ways and means must be found and applied to interest all. Purely spiritual influences like missions and retreats, although of primary importance, are seemingly not sufficient under present conditions, and do not contribute much to improve public opinion. Other means must be added. Christ is the head of the natural, material, and secular order, as well as of the supernatural, spiritual, and moral order. Hence, His members must be guided according to His will, conniving with neither left nor right extremists.

As a means of arousing general interest in the Christian family, many countries have organized Home or Family Weeks (or Congresses), during which the home, school, press, recreation, etc., were considered in a series of sermons supported by a forum on selected topics. The sermons were of an educational and inspirational nature; the forum was intended to facilitate the drafting of practical conclusions. The special objectives of the Home Week were the preservation and sanctity of the family, the guidance and protection of youth, and the restoration or maintenance of public morality. There was some difference in minor objectives in different places. These Weeks proved to be very popular; although not spectacular, they attracted the press, and their resolutions were brought to the notice of many who did not attend the sessions. Moreover, they were fruitful in many ways, especially when they followed a mission or retreat. Much of the material needed for sermons during a Family Week held in a parish is found in the Encyclicals on Chaste Wedlock, on the Christian Education of Youth, on Christ the King, and on the Mystical Body, and in this book.

A few more thoughts that might serve to interest parishioners in a gathering in behalf of the Christian family, may be added.

The Liberals and other opponents of Christianity know very well the importance of the Christian family in the world. Although most of their attacks on the family are indirect, the results are devastating. They fully realize the natural and supernatural value of the family for the Kingdom of God. Parents and their children are always chosen first for moral destruction. After this has been accomplished to a certain extent, the rest of their program is comparatively easy. The knowledge of this should arouse Catholics to meet their opponents with increased zeal and confidence in God. They are not fighting for something indifferent or of small consequence. On the contrary, the values to be defended are really tremendous in the natural as well as the supernatural order.

Among the *natural* factors are the following:

THE CHRISTIAN FAMILY IN FAITH

(a) The family could not originate except by the will of God. He creates the soul and entrusts the living man to the care of the family. The soul, naturally Christian, finds in the Christian family its most congenial place. Grace can there produce fruit.

(b) The Christian family life makes young and old receptive for the teachings and demands of Christianity. The child naturally sees in its father "the image and glory of God" (I Cor., xi, 7). The child recognizes in him the ruler, protector, and provider of the home. Even the young child will find it easy to extend these concepts to Our Father in Heaven. Equally easy is the progression from a loving mother to the Mother of Christ. Later on, the child will extend fraternal love to other persons it may meet. This love might well be in proportion to the size of the family in which it grows up (Matt., v, 45; Luke, xv, 18 sqq.).

(c) The moral virtues will flourish best in the Christian home. The community life of the family is undoubtedly the best school for exercising charity, correcting faults, learning respect for authority, and implanting the Christian ideal of sex life.

(d) For the parents, the family is the foremost workshop of Christianity. Religion aids parents in the education, training, and guidance of children, and grace will enable both parents and children to bear the burdens of family life. Christianity creates in the whole family a peace, security, and receptiveness for all that is good, not to be found in any other human institution.

(e) The benefits of Christian families naturally redound to the State, not only biologically and morally, but also in the economic and industrial domains. Moral order, social tranquillity, healthy traditions, laws, science, art, and culture have risen to the highest level in countries predominantly populated by Christian families.

To preserve and increase these natural values, God raised the family to an institution accompanied by a Sacrament productive of additional supernatural values. St. Robert Bellarmine writes: "The Sacrament of Matrimony can be regarded in two ways: first in the making and then in its permanent state. For it is a Sacrament like that of the Eucharist, which, not only when it is being conferred but also whilst it remains, is a Sacrament; as long as the married partners are alive, so long is their union a Sacrament of Christ and the Church" (quoted in the Encyclical on Chaste Wedlock).

Since the married state is a reflection of the relation of Christ to the Church, the blessings of the family necessarily accrue to the Church of God and the salvation of man. Let us enumerate some of these *supernatural* blessings.

(a) The parents receive a constant stream of grace flowing over to the children, which gives the whole family life a religious foundation and spiritual background. Notice the behavior of members at home and away from it.

(b) The sacramental blessings are increased whenever the family increases, in order that the children too may become spiritually minded and may become increasingly willing to lead a good Christian life. Nothing—not even Catholic schools and institutions—can be a full substitute for the family influence.

(c) Parents who through the dispensation of a loving God have found their mutual love crowned in Christian marriage will also lead their children to a union in Christ. New and truly Christian families ordinarily originate in truly Christian homes.

(d) The truly Christian family is undoubtedly the only recruiting ground for higher vocations. Personal sanctity is found most frequently in the family. Hence the often recurring phrase in the biographies of saints in the Breviary: "Piis parentibus natus." [1]

The concept of the Christian family, which takes the place of the original sinless pair in Paradise, must be kept clearly in mind. God ordained all for His own greater honor and glory which cannot be taken away from Him nor substantially diminished. He created everything on earth for the service of man (the composite of all that exists outside of Him, including the spirits), and gave man and woman the faculty to increase and multiply. This gives a special meaning to sex in humanity. It makes man the co-creator not only of his offspring but of his own temporal and eternal happiness. This alone raises the human family, and more so the Christian family, incomparably above reproduction in the case of all other creatures.

---

[1] "Born of devout parents."

PART TWO: WORSHIP

"The annual celebrations of the sacred mysteries are far more efficacious for the instruction of the people in matters of faith and thereby leading them to the inner joys of life than any, even the most weighty, pronouncements of the teaching Church."

Pope Pius XI, in Encyclical on Christ the King, "Quas primas," December 11, 1925.

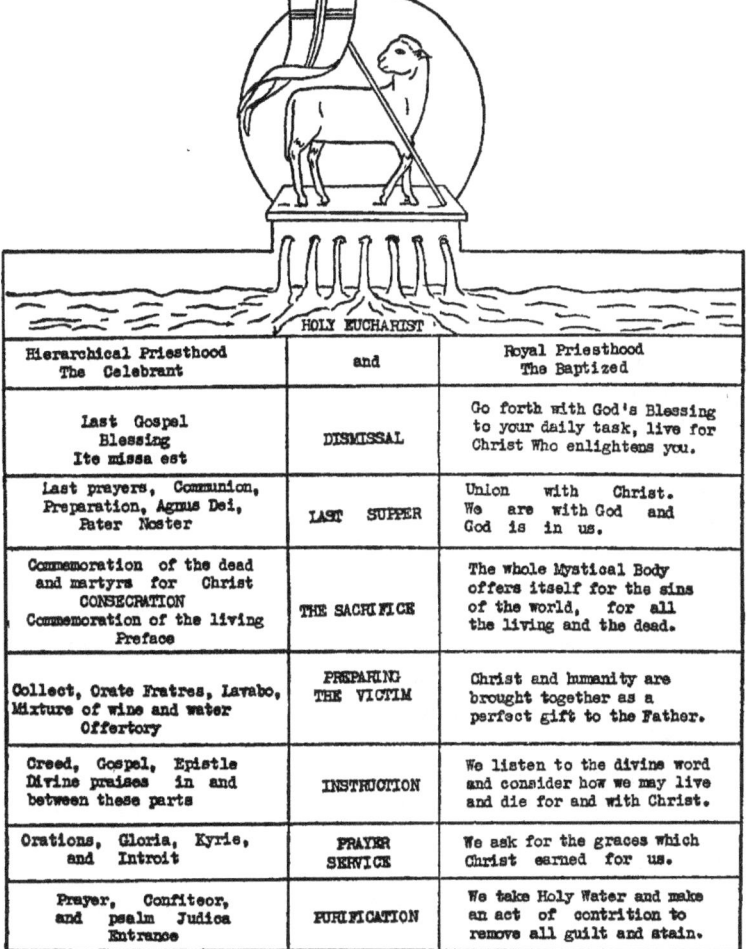

Hierarchical Priesthood The Celebrant	HOLY EUCHARIST and	Royal Priesthood The Baptized
Last Gospel Blessing Ite missa est	DISMISSAL	Go forth with God's Blessing to your daily task, live for Christ Who enlightens you.
Last prayers, Communion, Preparation, Agnus Dei, Pater Noster	LAST SUPPER	Union with Christ. We are with God and God is in us.
Commemoration of the dead and martyrs for Christ CONSECRATION Commemoration of the living Preface	THE SACRIFICE	The whole Mystical Body offers itself for the sins of the world, for all the living and the dead.
Collect, Orate Fratres, Lavabo, Mixture of wine and water Offertory	PREPARING THE VICTIM	Christ and humanity are brought together as a perfect gift to the Father.
Creed, Gospel, Epistle Divine praises in and between these parts	INSTRUCTION	We listen to the divine word and consider how we may live and die for and with Christ.
Orations, Gloria, Kyrie, and Introit	PRAYER SERVICE	We ask for the graces which Christ earned for us.
Prayer, Confiteor, and psalm Judica Entrance	PURIFICATION	We take Holy Water and make an act of contrition to remove all guilt and stain.

Herwer Kreilkamp

CHAPTER X

The Redemption in the Liturgy

IN THE FOLLOWING CHAPTERS we continue in our purpose of forming a true Christian mentality without which the three-point program of Pope Pius XII could not be realized. But here we proceed predominantly on the basis of the Liturgy in which the most important truths of Christianity are dramatized, illustrated, and adapted to induce the faithful to live and think with the Church.

The visible head of the Church, of the Mystical Body, has said it is necessary for the welfare of Christianity that: (1) human society be re-placed upon the Christian foundation; (2) the family be restored to the sacramental dignity to which Christ elevated it; (3) the social order again be made moral by creating a realization of its moral obligations through bringing Christ the King before individuals as well as before groups and rulers. It is evident, without further explanation, that if the members think differently or not in harmony with the head, a serious discord exists which makes salutary labor of the Church for the whole of mankind unfruitful.

This second part of the book is intended as a complement to the first part, with emphasis, however, on the Liturgy. It may seem that the following chapters repeat some of the subjects treated in Part One, but they are here considered from a liturgical pastoral angle and from new motives. When man beholds the care God bestowed upon him and the dignity and position to which He raised him in the Creation and Redemption, this should help him to realize the duties that accompany every honor and position.

The Fall of Man and Restoration to Grace

"God created man incorruptible [immortal], and to the image of His own likeness He made him. But by the envy of the devil, death came into the world" (Wis., ii, 23-24). The fall of Adam brought with it the consequences which are the causes of all the evils that have come upon mankind throughout the ages. "If one does not hold that the first man, Adam, when he transgressed the Commandment of God given in Paradise, immediately lost the holiness and justice in which he was created; and that through this sin of revolt he brought upon himself the anger and displeasure of God and in consequence his death with which God had threatened him, and with this death the servitude under the power of Satan who reigned thereafter in the realm of death; and that in consequence of this sin of revolt the whole Adam deteriorated in body and soul, *Anathema sit*" (Conc. Trid.).[1] Hence, our first parents became despoiled of all supernatural qualities and were weakened in their natural powers, but in such a manner that their free will and the faculty to judge between good and evil were not taken from them.

Humanly speaking, the most unfortunate consequence of original sin is that all the offspring of Adam, the Immaculate Virgin Mary excepted, are born in this state of sin and guilt. "By one man sin entered into this world, and by sin death; and so death passed upon all men, in whom all have sinned" (Rom., v, 12). But St. Paul adds: "As by the disobedience of one man many were made sinners, so also by the obedience of one, many shall be made just. . . . Where sin abounded, grace did more abound; that, as sin hath reigned to death, so also grace might reign unto life everlasting, through Jesus Christ our Lord" (ibid., 19-21). Christ was the Restorer promised after the fall of man, and about Him the Church sings in the *Exultet:* "O happy fall, that gained us such a Saviour, and so great! O priceless boon of boundless love, that Thou to free a slave shouldst give Thine only Son! O surely needed sin of Adam's fall, which Christ with His death has washed away!"

---

[1] Sess. V, Denzinger, 788.

THE REDEMPTION IN THE LITURGY

Awareness of Consequent Truths

It is usually taken for granted that these truths are so well known by Catholics that they need rarely be mentioned outside of catechetical instructions. But are they known to all? All may indeed have heard them in early childhood, but many have forgotten them. A majority may still remember them, but they no longer realize their importance as the basic facts upon which all human conduct rests, and by which all else is governed, and according to which all else must be judged.

This remark applies, not only to the life and conduct of individuals, but also to all social and political conduct. These truths simply represent the norm for God's dealing with mankind. Do non-Catholic Christians recognize these basic truths as underlying the life of mankind? Some do, but the majority of them look upon these principles as things of the past, and are content to take life as it appears to be without reflecting upon the causes of good and evil. By far the greatest number of men do not know or do not believe these truths, and either resist or try to discredit them by all means at their command, fair or foul. They speak, write, and act as if all people were as wrong as they are, and so form a public opinion that is destructive of the divine order.

What can be done about it? Not much unless Christians are persistently outspoken without offending individuals. The simple truths (1) that God created man in holiness, truth, and immortality, (2) that the sin of our first parents brought death, error, and sinfulness to all, and (3) that Christ redeemed all mankind in order to enable us to reach eternal happiness, can be and are taught in our grammar schools; but their bearing on daily life cannot be fully impressed during early years. Much explaining has been done in the past, and the explanations continued in sermons, but the synthesis has been lacking. A foundation was laid, but it was not cemented together with the superstructure. It was all piece-work, and the complete form was never seen. Hence, the importance of doing the will of God made but a small impression on people—an impression not strong enough to form the conscience and to fortify the will.

The constant repetition of fundamental truths may, indeed, rescue them from oblivion, but unless they are connected with life, they will irritate rather than create a spiritual and fruitful conviction. The short Sunday sermons are not very efficacious in presenting an integral picture of the fundamentals of Christian life. Longer sermons, where they are possible, are avoided by young people and by those who need them most. Why? Might it be because the short sermons (which are the most difficult to make solid and attractive) were considered by their preachers as being just a short talk, or the occasion for a few pious thoughts or a brief admonition, not needing much time to prepare? It seems that the movement for more fruitful preaching should extend to the preacher as well as to the flock. Preaching Sunday after Sunday without sufficient preparation and orderly planning may cause the loss of the habit of logical and effective preaching, because the orator may present a multitude of accidentals without referring to the substance of religion that must form the basis for the whole of Christian life.

A course of sermons, as prescribed in many dioceses for the Sundays throughout the year, is a useful plan for developing a picture of a good Christian in the course of time, but it is nothing more than an aid. As a rule, such a syllabus presents the topics without any coordination with the Gospel (except perhaps a mere reference to it) and without any integration. General as the outlines based on such syllabi must be, they offer a wealth of generalities without much in particular, unless the preacher makes them his own by selecting one or two points and applying them to the needs of his audience. This specific application may vary according to times and circumstances. It will certainly do no harm to go a little further than the contents of the small Catechism and insist on the practice of virtues as well as on the shunning of sin.

So long as our young people think that they do not lose much by missing sermons, they will use all kinds of excuses for absenting themselves. Of course, some people would not like to miss a

THE REDEMPTION IN THE LITURGY 107

sermon by Father Peter, but would not take the trouble to listen to Father Paul. However, it is not always the brilliancy of the preacher that attracts and bears fruit. In the case of the holy Curé d'Ars, it was personal sanctity and words from the heart that converted sinners and formed saints.

This is sufficient illustration that there exists a double problem that should not only be realized and deplored, but also courageously faced. The solution may seem to be difficult, but about the possibility of solving it there should not be much doubt.

An Ideal Means of Instruction

One way of solving the twofold problem, as the writer sees it, is to follow the method applied by the Church during the Liturgical Year. The Church teaches and dramatizes the Faith annually, and brings out the importance of the mysteries by so presenting them in her Liturgy that little explanation is needed to give the faithful a working knowledge of the content. The knowledge of the mere essentials of the Liturgy would make Catholics love and live their religion. Pope Sixtus V writes in this regard:

> "The sacred rites and ceremonies which the Church, taught by apostolic tradition, employs in the administration of the Sacraments, in the divine offices, and in all which pertains to the worship of God or of the saints, are a powerful means of instruction for the Christian people in the true faith; by them souls may easily be led to meditate on sublime truths and thus they will find their devotion enkindled." [1]

Bossuet did not hesitate to declare that the Liturgy of the Church is the main instrument of Tradition.[2] Fr. James O'Mahoney, O.F.M.Cap., has this telling passage:

> "What is the truth that is in the liturgy? Is it not the truth of Christ Himself? . . . The essential knowledge for religion and life is in the liturgy, and if the faithful but knew the liturgy, nothing would be wanting in that knowledge that leadeth to salvation." [3]

---
[1] Bull "Immensa," 1588.
[2] "Etats d'oraison," chap. vi.
[3] "Wherefore This Waste?" (Burns, Oates & Washbourne, London, 1936), p. 75.

108   FORMING A CHRISTIAN MENTALITY

We agree with this writer and with many Popes, bishops, and other writers, that if there be ignorance of religion in any person or community, it is due in large part, to ignorance of the Sacred Liturgy. In this matter Pope Pius XI lays down a general truth applicable to all liturgies:

> "The annual celebrations of the sacred mysteries are far more efficacious for the instruction of the people in matters of faith and thereby leading them to the inner joys of life than any, even the most weighty, pronouncements of the teaching Church. For the latter reach mainly the few more erudite men, while the former attain and teach all the faithful; the latter speak, so to say, once, the former daily and continuously; the latter have a salutary effect chiefly on the mind, the former on both mind and soul, i.e., on the entire man." [1]

The most suitable material for this purpose is found in Matins, the Proper of the Masses *de tempore*, and the Roman Ritual. Since all these sources have a biblical foundation, they provide a wonderful and effective plan for the making of a perfect Christian. How?

The Season of Advent and Christmas, and thence to Septuagesima Sunday exclusive, is dedicated to the preparation for and the birth and home life of the Redeemer. The extent and formation of Christ's Mystical Body are emphasized and illustrated on the Epiphany and the following Sundays.

On Septuagesima Sunday begins the history of the sinfulness of man, and the Liturgy illustrates the awful condition of mankind and every sinner in particular, which Christ came to remedy by His life, Passion, and death. This history culminates in the Resurrection on Easter Sunday. Parallel with this runs the admonition to penance, which results in the resurrection of the whole Church from the death of sin by Baptism or Penance. This makes the glorious resurrection of the Mystical Body complete, and the work of Christ effective for those of good will.

The season from Easter to Trinity Sunday serves to teach and illustrate the nature, effects, and demands of Baptism complemented by Confirmation. The rest of the Sundays enlarge on the

---

[1] "Quas primas," Encyclical on Christ the King, 1925.

life of the baptized, modelled on the life and teaching of Christ.

Hence, the Liturgical Year covers the Creed, the means of grace, and the Commandments in a psychological rather than a formally logical order. The latter method is the least effective for practical purposes. There can be little doubt that, if we follow the Church in her method and plan of instructions and use the material she places before us in the liturgical books, the explanation of Christian life will become more interesting and will produce more abundant fruit in life itself. To live with the Church in thought and action is the genuine Christian life. Unless life is based on truth, firm principles and facts, too much room is left for moods and fancies. But to confine teaching to the Catechism alone, is a departure from the method in vogue during the first half of the existence of the Church. It makes religion an abstract science, and neglects it as a way of life. Those who obtain the real idea of Christian life from the Liturgy of the great mysteries will also know the Catechism.

This, however, does not imply that the small Catechisms are superfluous for the teaching of the young. Indeed, these are necessary, because without them many would get no religious instruction whatever. Nevertheless, it must be repeated that the Catechism without a progressive additional instruction is insufficient. Who does the explaining beyond the etymological meaning of words? Who coordinates the truths? Who synthesizes all into the picture of a perfect Christian? The teacher or lay catechist cannot do all this, even if he had the knowledge, because the capacity of young pupils is limited. The greater part of the labor involved is left for the preacher. Anything that will aid in the performance of this pastoral duty will be welcomed by every good shepherd of souls.

CHAPTER XI

Advent and Christmas

Preparing for the Redeemer

IF WE LOOK at the Liturgy of the First Sunday in Advent, it might appear that the Ecclesiastical Year begins with the end of all things, and its first message is the same as that of the preceding Sunday. However, in all liturgical seasons, the Church combines the past, present, and future with emphasis on one leading thought. During Advent this thought is the coming of Christ.

Contemplating the Liturgy of Advent, we find that the present is introduced by consistently pointing out that Christ is daily reborn upon our altars during Holy Mass, and that He daily descends from heaven "for us men and for our salvation." Also that Christ lives and dwells among us in His Church, always ready to come to us, and that we should receive Him in Holy Communion; that He is the vine who gives life and fruitfulness to the branches as the Head of the Mystical Body, visibly represented by the Pope, bishops, priests, and all that are baptized. Hence, we must walk in the sight of God putting on the Lord Jesus Christ (First Sunday, Orations and Epistle).

The present is brought into connection with the future time when Christ will come again to judge the living and the dead. At what time this will happen, no one knows but the Father. All that we need to know is that with the birth of Christ the Kingdom of God came among us and is still at hand (Gospel). "None that wait on Thee, shall be ashamed. Show me Thy way, O Lord, . . . teach me Thy paths, extend to us Thy mercy . . . and grant us salvation" (Gradual). These thoughts recur in different forms throughout the Mass and Office of the First Sunday. All this is intended to stir up grace in our hearts that we may be

ADVENT AND CHRISTMAS 111

saved by His deliverance (Oration). We should become worthy of the blessings that the Redeemer brought and still brings.

The Mass of the Blessed Virgin on Saturdays during Advent is significantly celebrated in the Station Church of St. Mary Major, the present home of the Blessed Virgin in Rome. There the Church rejoices in the message brought by the Angel in answer to the prayer of the Chosen People: "Drop down dew, ye heavens, . . . let the earth bud forth a Saviour." Gabriel said to Mary: "Thou shalt conceive . . . and bring forth a Son . . . Jesus" (Gospel).

This sketchy outline of the Liturgy of the first week in Advent, together with the thoughts found in the Divine Office, will greatly facilitate the finding of practical topics based on a Gospel that is so similar to that of the preceding Sunday. By practical topics, the writer understands here topics that develop the Christian personality as a background for moral improvement.

Before proceeding any further, it might be useful to insert a few words about the Roman Stations noted in the Missal. Some knowledge about the Station churches may often supply an interesting introduction to a sermon or instruction.

When the Church was still in her infancy, Peter established his see in Rome as the head and mother of all churches; the title of Holy City accompanied the Church and was hence applied to Rome. Jerusalem (Judaism) refused to accept the Messiah, and thenceforth salvation was to be found in the Church of Rome located among the Gentiles. Historically and geographically Jerusalem remained what it was, as did every other place in Palestine; but spiritually and symbolically it became reconstructed on the banks of the Tiber. Thereafter, Sion—Jerusalem and the Sanctuary of the Old Testament—was transferred to the center of Christianity. Naturally, the localities connected with the life of Christ and other immovable things could not be transferred, but their memory was perpetuated in certain Roman churches or basilicas, and to these Christians flock to celebrate the holy mysteries even at the present time. The pictures, relics, and surroundings of these great basilicas, constructed after the Church emerged from the catacombs, enlivened the faith and warmed the hearts of the pious visitors. Some public rites were performed exclusively in Rome in one of these churches.

It would lead us too far at present to furnish a detailed description of these Station churches, of which some will be mentioned later. May it suffice to state that, after the Church spread far and wide, the mention of the Station in the Missal was to serve to unite in spirit and devotion all the scattered members of the universal Church with those who were on that very day celebrating with great solemnity the same feast or mystery in Rome, the see of the Vicar of Christ and visible head of the Kingdom of God on earth.

It is not without significance that the Liturgy of the Second Sunday of Advent is celebrated with a great concourse of people in the Church of the Holy Cross in Jerusalem at Rome. This fact gives a special meaning to the Introit of the Mass: "People of Sion, behold the Lord shall come to save the nations." The Gentiles who accepted Christ were likewise to be redeemed. Although this was announced by the prophets, the belief prevailed among the Jews that the Messiah would come to save Israel alone. Since the time for His coming as foretold by Daniel had now arrived, John the Baptist addressed to Jesus this question: "Art thou He that is to come?" Christ furnished the affirmative answer by pointing out the works that He did. Of course, John knew Jesus, and also knew that it was his own office to prepare the way for the coming Redeemer. In this, the Baptist is a type of the Church and every one of her members. All have the duty to lead souls to the Saviour, while simultaneously preparing themselves for His coming by grace.

The Mass of the Third Sunday develops these thoughts by singing at the Introit: "Rejoice in the Lord always: again I say rejoice, . . . for the Lord is nigh." The Gospel relates how St. John emphasized His nearness by saying: "There hath stood one in the midst of you, whom you know not." These words might well be addressed today to many who do not wish to know the Church and seek a salvation without Christ.

Between the First and Third Sundays the Church has inserted the Feast of the Immaculate Conception of the Blessed Virgin

ADVENT AND CHRISTMAS

Mary. On this day the Church reminds us of the preparation God made for the Incarnation of His Son, and thus laid the foundation for the Mystical Body that will be built up by Jesus. The "woman" promised in Paradise as the Mother of Him Who was to conquer Satan became mankind's "solitary boast" by being conceived without the stain of original sin. Owing to a special privilege bestowed upon her alone, the fruit of the Redemption was applied to her even before the Redeemer had been conceived. Originating in the fullness of grace, Mary continued to increase in grace until the end, and therefore was never under the power of Satan or under his dominion. In her immaculate womb took place the miracle and mystery of the Incarnation: the Word of God was made flesh by the overshadowing of the Holy Ghost. Mary the Virgin remained virginal before, during, and after the birth of her Son. This shows how the Heavenly Father prepared for the birth of Christ by grace and holiness.

It is appropriate to remember all this during Advent, because Mary, the Christ-bearer, presents another mystery of great importance to the brethren of Christ. This mystery is concerned with the foundation for Christ's Mystical Body, whose members we are. As soon as the Second Person of God assumed human nature, humanity became capable of participating in the divinity. Pope Pius X expressed this clearly when he wrote:

> "Is Mary not the mother of Christ? Consequently, she is also our mother. . . . As God-Man, the Redeemer had like all human beings a physical body; but as Restorer of our race [to the childship of God], He has also a spiritual and supernatural [mystical] body. This is the community of all who believe in Him: 'We being many, are one body in Christ' (Rom., xii, 5). Christ assumed His own body from the chaste flesh of His mother, but also formed Himself a body of all who followed Him. Therefore, it may be said that, when she bore the Son of God, the Saviour of the world, Mary enshrined all whose life was contained in the life of Christ, as St. Paul writes: 'We are members of His body, of His flesh, and of His bones' (Eph., v, 30). We originated in Mary in the form of a body connected with the Head.[1] For this reason we are in

[1] As the human race was potentially in our first parents, similarly the children of God were potentially in Christ and Mary.

a spiritual and mystical sense children of Mary, and she is really the mother of the members that we are." [1]

At the eve of the completion of the Redemption, "the disciple [representing all of us] took her to his own" (John, xix, 27). Pope Pius XII writes: "She [Mary], who corporally was the mother of our head, through the added title of pain and glory, became spiritually the mother of all His members." [2] But more about this later.

Returning to the Advent Liturgy, we notice that time is progressing and Christmas will soon be here. On the Third Sunday we were told that "the Lord is nigh" (Introit). This refers both to Christ's coming on the altar, and also at this time most appropriately to the celebration of His birthday. We pray "that by the grace of His visitation the darkness of our mind may be enlightened." The appeal of the voice calling in the wilderness and urging us to prepare by making straight the way of the Lord, should not pass unheeded. Everything that interferes with the coming of Christ into our hearts should be removed, and His future abode should be embellished by virtues. Our personal preparation by prayer and penance is facilitated by the following Ember Days.

The Liturgy on the Fourth Sunday continues this preparation and especially calls upon the dispensers of the mysteries to be faithful to their sacred calling.

In order that the clergy and the faithful may not forget the nearness of Christ in their preoccupation with earthly things, the Church recites the great antiphons before and after the Magnificat. They recall the nature and outstanding qualities of the God-Man and end with a petition. Based on the Scriptures, they contain a wealth of spiritualizing thoughts. Together with the Mass of the Vigil, they urge us to receive Christ with a lively faith. After all, what the eye beheld on the first Christmas at Bethlehem was not the most important thing. It is more important to realize that the Infant lying in the manger is also God,

---

[1] "Ad diem illum," Encyclical on the Immaculate Conception, February 2, 1904.
[2] "Mystici Corporis," June 29, 1943.

ADVENT AND CHRISTMAS

the Mediator between the Father and men; and that He is not weak, but the King, Ruler, and Judge of all creatures. This faith tells us that Christians, renewed by penance and enlivened in faith by the motives enumerated in the Epistles and Lessons, will undoubtedly celebrate a happy and joyful Christmas, and will also be "full of grace and truth."

Birth of the Redeemer

The birthday of the Redeemer is thus recorded in the Martyrology:

> "In the year 5199 after the creation of the world; in the year 2795 after the Deluge; in the year 2015 after the birth of Abraham; in the year 1510 after the Israelites left the Egyptian captivity; in the year 1032 after the anointing of King David; in the 65th year-week after the prophecy of Daniel; in the 194th Olympiad; in the year 752 after the founding of Rome; in the 42nd year of the empire of Augustus Octavianus, when the whole world was at peace; in the sixth age of the world: *Jesus Christ,* eternal God and Son of the Eternal Father, to sanctify the world by His most merciful coming, having been conceived by the Holy Ghost, and nine months having passed, was born in Bethlehem of Judea as man from Mary the Virgin. The celebration of the birth of Our Lord Jesus Christ."

It is the Nativity of Him Who was "full of grace and truth, . . . of Whose fullness we have all received" (John, i, 14, 16).

It is the feast of God's merciful love. "God so loved the world, as to give His only begotten Son; that whosoever believeth in Him, may not perish, but may have life everlasting" (John, iii, 16). The Child lying in the crib is lovely to contemplate, and as such already captivates the heart. But the Liturgy constantly points out that what we behold is far more than a human infant. The feast has essentially a dogmatic character; love and faith have equal rights at the crib. The Matins begin with the invitation: "The Anointed is born to us; come let us adore." All three Masses express this thought in different scriptural texts.

The Liturgy uses the historical fact as a basis for teaching, and thereby connects it with the present. Christ's coming in the flesh made the celebration of Mass possible. Every Consecration is a Christmas, a coming of Christ upon our altars. Both comings constitute the prelude for His final coming in glory. At the same time the Liturgy commemorates Christ's coming to our soul in Baptism, in Communion, and in grace that comes to us also by other means. This makes the Feast of the Nativity, not only an historical commemoration, but also a renewal full of grace, provided the significance of the mysteries is applied to our own lives.

The First Mass, celebrated since the beginning of the seventh century in the Basilica of St. Mary Major during the silent night, invites us to joy and oration: "Glory to God in the highest. . . . Let the earth be glad before the Lord. . . . The Lord hath said to Me: This day have I begotten Thee." Logically, the Church prays: "Grant . . . that we may enjoy in heaven His happiness the mystery of whose light we have known upon earth."

The Second Mass is appropriately celebrated in the Church of St. Anastasia. The Child born unto us to die for us, will rise and live forever. Having been born as God-Man, He will not cease to be God or Man. "A light shall shine upon us this day, for Our Lord is born to us, . . . the wonderful God, the Prince of peace, the Father of the world to come, of whose reign there shall be no end" (Introit). The faithful are urged to adhere to Him and to submit to His reign in mind and body. "Grant, . . . Almighty God, that, being filled with the new light of the Incarnate Word, what by faith shineth in our minds may be shown forth in our works" (Oration). Therefore, "let us see this word that has come to pass, which the Lord hath showed us. . . . And seeing they understood" (Gospel).

The Third Mass was formerly celebrated in St. Peter's but at present takes place in St. Mary Major's. Both basilicas are significant. In St. Peter's we behold the Mystical Body symbolized by the Vicar of Christ, surrounded by the faithful representing all members who live dispersed over the world. Mary, of course is the Mother of Christ, and in Him the Mother of Christians also. The whole Proper of the Mass celebrated at the peak of the day is dedicated to the eternal birth of the Second Person of God and to His human birth in time without interrupting Hi divine power and majesty. "A Child is born to us, and a Son is given to us; whose government is upon His shoulder. . . . O sing unto the Lord a new song; for He hath done marvellous things" (Introit). "Let all the angels of God adore Him. . . . His throne is for ever and ever, and His years shall not fail" (Epistle). "The world was made by Him. The Word was God. . . . The Word was made flesh and dwelt among us; and we saw His glory" (Gospel). Inspired by all this, the Church prays: "Grant, O Almighty God, that the new birth of Thine only begotten Son in the flesh may deliver us who are held by the old bondage under the yoke of sin. . . ." Freed from sin, we ask for a life with and in Christ by charity.

These thoughts are continued on the Feast of the Circumcision by calling upon us to change from a carnal to a spiritual mode of life.

The Meaning of Advent and Christmas

A summary of the meaning of Advent and Christmas for practical purposes may form our conclusion. After the fall of our first parents, mankind fell deeper and deeper into misery and sin. Only a small number of men kept the faith in the coming of a Restorer, who was promised in Paradise. In time, God chose Israel as the bearer of the promise. The rest of mankind almost completely fell away from the one true God. Patriarchs and prophets spoke again and again, laboring to keep Israel faithful by gradually enlightening the Jews about the coming of the Redeemer, and constantly admonishing them to live up to the laws of Jehovah. Finally, the Redeemer came, but Israel received Him not, and by rejecting Him caused their own rejection.

The Church replaced the Synagogue, and to forestall the rejection of her children at the final judgment, continues the work of the prophets. But instead of looking forward to a Redeemer to come, she places emphasis on the fact that He came. Conditions repeat themselves. Mankind has drifted more and more away from Christ. Many of those who once dwelt in the paradise of baptismal innocence, have become unfaithful by falling into schisms, heresies, and sin.

These situations the Advent Liturgy has in mind, since it emphasizes, illustrates, and proves three truths: (1) that the Redeemer Who came was truly God and truly Man; (2) that we shall have no share in the Redemption unless we are and remain united with Him by sanctifying grace; (3) that, if we have lost baptismal innocence, we must regain it and bring it with us to the judgment seat of God. Unless we do this, we shall have caused our own rejection as did the Jews of old. These demands the Church deduces from the preparations that God made for the coming of the Redeemer and from the nature of the Redeemer Himself.

In short, the Liturgy aims at an increase in faith and virtues. The Church has a right to demand this. The Baptist reminds us of our Baptism, when we asked for faith and promised to adhere to God alone by turning away from Satan, the world and its pomps. This faith must be kept pure, and the promises be fulfilled conscientiously. This alone will secure our final end. "This is eternal life: that they may know Thee, the only true God, and Jesus Christ, Whom Thou hast sent" (John, xvii, 3). "If thou wilt enter into life, keep the commandments" (Matt., xix, 17). Earthly life is but a prelude to the life to come, to our birth to everlasting **happiness.**

CHAPTER XII

The Epiphany of the Lord

"BEHOLD, I [CAME TO] MAKE all things new!" (Apoc., xxi, 5). This activity of the Redeemer, revealed to St. John on Patmos, began with His birth. The Old Dispensation that was intended to prepare for Christ and for the theocracy of Israel was to be changed into a New Dispensation in which Christ would reign as an invincible King. After His birth Jesus did not wait long to inaugurate this radical change. The Jews had been invited to the Crib in the persons of the shepherds; they came and saw what had come to pass, and "returned, glorifying and praising God" (Luke, ii, 20). But it is nowhere mentioned that the shepherds *adored* Him, nor are they venerated as saints. They simply vanished, and seemingly were the first ones of the many Jews who saw Him but received Him not. They wanted a Messiah according to their own ideas. The New Dispensation was offered to them first, but as a people they will be the last ones to accept it.

Judaism had fulfilled its mission as a carrier of the faith and the promise. When the Redeemer came, Juda's preference among nations ceased. The Synagogue received a few years of grace and then vanished without hope of a resurrection. After that, only individual Jews are called to merge themselves with the Mystical Body of Him Whom they rejected whilst He was living among them as God-Man. Christ turned to the Gentiles, to all who were not Jews, for the material to build His Kingdom on earth. He Himself did not personally go and preach to the Gentiles, but He called their representatives to Himself and manifested to them His person and divine nature.

The first manifestation of this kind described in the Gospel is the visit of the Magi, which is celebrated on one of the most solemn and oldest feasts in the Church, called the Epiphany

(Manifestation) of the Lord. The episode is related in the Gospel according to St. Matthew (ii, 1-12). A brief commentary on the pericope will enhance its significance.

"There came wise men from the East to Jerusalem," seeking the newly born King of the Jews. Holy Scripture does not give their number, names, or nationality. The traditional number of three was arrived at by the number of gifts offered to Jesus: gold, frankincense, and myrrh. Later on, the Magi were presumed to be descendants of the three sons of Noe (Sem, Cham, and Japhet), or representatives of the three continents known at that time (Asia, Africa, and Europe). Undoubtedly, they were Gentiles. Not all descendants of Sem became Jews, for the latter called Abraham their father.

These Wise Men were of some importance according to Oriental standards. They were learned, because they had knowledge of the prophecies which were not generally known outside of Jewish circles. They knew something about astronomy; otherwise they would not have discovered a new and special star. And they were wise; otherwise they could not have seen the connection between the prophecies and that particular star. A grace from above most probably enlightened them, but grace builds upon nature and is usually not a substitute for study, reading, and research. They also must have been men of some importance; their gifts and the fact that Herod received them and called a council to advise them, establish this sufficiently. Whether they were rulers or kings over their peoples is not certain, but the tradition that they were kings is very old. However, the fact that their bones are venerated as sacred relics proves that their visit to Bethlehem was not without good effects upon their whole life.

"Entering into the house, they found the Child with Mary His mother." It is natural to assume that after the departure of the crowd who had come to Bethlehem for the census registration the Holy Family moved out of the stable to a house. Joseph, although not mentioned in this passage, was also present, because soon after the departure of the Wise Men an Angel appeared to

Joseph telling him to leave immediately for Egypt with the Child and His Mother.

One special act of the Magi, not mentioned at the visit of the shepherds, was that "falling down they adored Him; and . . . offered Him gifts." The Wise Men adored Him as God, and they gave royal gifts to acknowledge Him as a King before whom they could not appear with empty hands.

Then they "went back another way into their country." The reason for taking a different way home was because Herod sought to kill the Child, but this text is also spiritually interpreted by saying that they followed another way of living after they had confirmed their faith, realized their hope, and demonstrated their love to the Infant Saviour.

Great Antiquity of the Feast

The Feast of the Epiphany, now celebrated on January 6, is not an anniversary, since the visit of the Magi must have taken place after the presentation of Jesus in the Temple on February 2; and after the visit of the Magi the flight into Egypt took place without delay. There are several reasons for this apparent chronological disorder. The Epiphany celebrates three principal manifestations of Christ's Divinity simultaneously because they have a close relation to one another, as we shall see later. These manifestations are: (1) His appearance to the Gentiles as Redeemer; (2) His manifestation as God-Man by the first miracle at Cana; and (3) the testimony of His being the Son of God given by His Father at the Baptism in the Jordan. All three are basic in the New Dispensation, but all three could not have happened in the same year and about the same date.

In addition to this, the birth of Christ was also celebrated on the Epiphany in the early centuries of the Latin Church, as is still the case in the Oriental Rites. The descendants of the Gentiles rejoiced more in the fact that the Redeemer had come for all than in the fact that He had come to the Jews. Later on, when the birth of Christ was fixed on December 25 and received a special celebration and Liturgy, the Feast of the Epiphany (celebrated long before the introduction of Christmas) was left on the original day.

A few historical remarks of no dogmatical importance but of some interest may be added here. The names given to the Wise Men, Caspar, Melchior, and Balthasar, appear for the first time in a manuscript of the sixth century. Whether there was a long earlier tradition regarding these names is not known. According to a tradition written down in the eleventh century, the relics of the Magi were brought to Constantinople by the Empress St. Helena, and thence were transferred in the fourth century to Milan in Italy. After the destruction of Milan by the Emperor Frederick Barbarossa in the year 1164, the conquerors took the reliquary to Cologne and built the famous cathedral for them in the thirteenth century.

The Divine Office

Of greater importance for us than the historical notes is the present liturgical or mystical meaning of the Epiphany. Its practical significance for Christianity is expressed by the Antiphon before and after the *Benedictus:* "Today the Church is espoused to the Heavenly Bridegroom, because Christ in the Jordan washed away her sins; the Magi came with gifts to the royal nuptials; and the wine changed from water rejoiced the feasters." It was the invisible preparation, expressed by visible events, for the Church that Christ was to establish upon Himself as the corner-stone and upon the Apostles as its foundation (Eph., ii, 20). The Liturgy dwells on the extent and scope of the Church that was to be consecrated on Pentecost.

The visit of the Magi who followed the star, revealed that the Messiah had come to save all men, and that His reign or Kingdom on earth was to embrace Gentiles (non-Jews), as well as the descendants of Abraham. Hence, the Church celebrating the mysteries of the Epiphany calls upon all men to enroll under Christ the King: "I am a king. For this was I born, and for this came I into the world" (John, xviii, 37). As a Bridegroom, He espouses all souls that believe in Him throughout the ages. Holy

THE EPIPHANY OF THE LORD 123

Communion is a manifestation of the hidden God-Man uniting Himself with the soul on earth, establishing a temporal union that will be consummated in eternity.

Let us enter a little deeper into the Liturgy and try to grasp some of its meaning. The Matins of the feast, omitting the usual Invitatory and hymn, begins abruptly with the First Nocturn. The Messianic Psalms are the call of the King to submit to His reign. "Bring to the Lord glory, honor and adoration," He calls, and "His voice is penetrating, powerful and majestic in works." Come to Him and "the Lord will give strength to His people and will bless them with peace" (Ps. xxviii, 10). The Church is the true home of peace, because "our God is our refuge and strength, a helper in troubles, which have found us exceedingly. . . . Be still and see that I am God. . . . The Lord of armies . . . is our protector" (Ps. xlv, 2, 11, 12). Therefore rejoice, all ye nations, because Christ is the King of all the earth and reigns over all the nations. "The princes of the peoples are gathered together, with the God of Abraham," in the Church of Christ (Ps. xlvi, 10).

In the Lessons Isaias foretells in spirit the grace that will come to those who enter the Church of Christ. All nations are invited: "All you that thirst, come to the waters [of grace]. . . . Incline your ear and come to Me. . . . Behold I have given Him [Christ the Redeemer] as a witness to the people; as a leader and a master to the Gentiles. . . . I will make an everlasting covenant with you, . . . a covenant of love and mercy. Hearken diligently to Me, and your soul shall live and you shall eat that which is good, and your souls shall be delighted. . . . Therefore, seek ye the Lord while He may be found: call upon Him while He is near" (Is., lv, 1-6).

At the end of the Lessons the Church adds a bridal hymn: "I will greatly rejoice in the Lord, and my soul shall be joyful in my God: for He hath clothed me with the garments of salvation [in Baptism], and with the robe of justice He has covered me [sanctifying grace], as a bridegroom decked with a crown, and as a bride adorned with her jewels [of divine virtues]" (Is., lxi, 10). Then the fruits of this bridal union are indicated: "For as the earth bringeth forth her bud, and as the garden causeth her seed to shoot forth, so shall the Lord God make justice [faith and charity] to spring forth, and praise [good works and virtues] before all the nations" (ibid., 11).

In the Second Nocturn the Church rejoices that her glorious King of heaven and earth is to reign over all men without exception. This is independent of the will of man, because He cannot be rejected. All the earth shall adore Christ as God and as Man, because He is terrific in His power and unlimited in strength. He will change everything for the better and will reign forever. Trials will come upon us, but He will listen to our prayers (Ps. lxv, 19-20). To Christ, the Father turned over justice and judgment. He will aid the poor and humiliate the oppressors. "In His days justice shall spring up, and an abundance of peace [of soul], . . . and He shall rule from sea to sea. . . . All the kings of the earth shall adore Him; all nations shall serve Him. . . . In Him shall all the tribes of the earth be blessed. All nations shall magnify Him" (Ps. lxxi).

Having inspired confidence in the Divine Ruler, the Liturgy prays with and for us: "Give joy to the soul of Thy servant, . . . for Thou, O Lord, art sweet and mild, and plenteous in mercy to all that call upon Thee. . . . Conduct me, O Lord, in Thy way, and I will walk in Thy truth; let my heart rejoice that it may fear Thy name. . . . Show me a token for good: that they who hate me [and Thy Church] may see, and be confounded . . ." (Ps. lxxxv).

In the Lessons Pope St. Leo the Great calls upon his congregation to rejoice in such a powerful and adorable Ruler, Whom the Jewish King Herod could not destroy, but to Whom the pagan Egypt gave shelter. From this St. Leo concludes that the Church passed from the Jews to the Gentiles, who adored and received Christ.

In the Third Nocturn Christ is announced and praised as the Founder and the Life of the Church: "The foundations thereof [of the Church] are in the holy mountains. . . . Glorious things are said of thee, O City of God. . . . Behold the foreigners were there, . . . and the Highest Himself hath founded her . . ."

(Ps. lxxxvi). "Praise and ·beauty are before Him; holiness and sanctity in His sanctuary. . . . Let all the earth be moved by His presence. . . . He shall judge the world with justice, and the people with His truth" (Ps. xcv). "The Lord preserveth the souls of His saints. . . . Light is risen to the just, and joy to the right of heart" (Ps. xcvi).

St. Gregory furnishes the Homily, and says that an Angel was sent to the Jewish shepherds but a star led the Gentile Magi. Why? He answers with St. Paul that prophets (angels) were sent to the believers and not to infidels; signs, however, were employed with Gentiles and not with the faithful. In the New Dispensation Christ Himself spoke personally to all and sent His Apostles to preach in His name to all nations. All elements have cooperated to make Christ known. The firmament sent the fiery star to announce His birth; the water of the sea became solid under His feet; the air and wind obeyed Him; and the earth trembled and was riven when He died. But all these testimonies, including the Resurrection, did not move the hearts of the Jews (and many others after them) to faith and penance. We the Gentiles did better, and from the fullness of our heart we intone the *Te Deum* and pray: "Rank us in glory with Thy Saints above, bless Thy people and rule them raised to glory from the grave."

The theme of Lauds is stated in the Chapter: "For Sion's sake I will not hold my peace, and for the sake of Jerusalem, I will not rest till her Just One come forth as brightness, and her Saviour be lighted as a lamp" (Is., lxii, 1). Beautiful thoughts and doctrines are presented in the antiphons and hymns of the Divine Office, but these must be left to private study.

The Mass

The Mass begins with the words: "Behold the Ruler is come; and a kingdom is in His hand, and power and dominion" (cf. Mal., iii, 1). "Give the King Thy judgment, O God, and Thy righteousness unto the King's Son" (Ps. lxxi, 1). The manifestation of the Lord to the Gentiles is the dominating thought in the Proper of the Mass. The Epistle is a part of the Lessons recited in the First Nocturn and the Gospel announces the fulfillment of the prophecy.

The Gradual and Offertory emphasize the thoughts: "Arise and be enlightened, O Jerusalem [Christian congregation or soul], for thy light is come, and the glory of the Lord is risen upon thee. . . . We have seen His star, . . . and are come with gifts." The Secret explains these gifts. Our offerings are no longer gold, frankincense, and myrrh, "but He who by these same offerings is signified, immolated, and received, Jesus Christ our Lord, Himself." The Preface inserts the words: "Thanks to Thee, Holy Lord, . . . because when Thine only begotten Son appeared in the substance of our mortal flesh, He made us anew by the new light of His immortality." What a change did the New Dispensation bring about, and how little is this realized! The Communion and the following prayer recount that we come with our gifts, bringing the gold of faith, the incense of love and devotion, and the myrrh of penance and sacrifice. To this the petition is added: ". . . that what we celebrate with a solemn office, we may attain by the understanding of a purified mind." The final Blessing assures us of God's favor.

So, we leave the Sacrifice with the final words of the Last Gospel ringing in our ears and echoing in our hearts: "The Word was made flesh and dwelt among us; and we saw His glory, as it were the glory of the Only Begotten of the Father, full of grace and truth (John, i, 14). Thanks be to God." Returning to our secular occupations, we foster the hope that all may be fulfilled in us for which the Divine Office and the Liturgy pray throughout the Octave: "O God, . . . mercifully grant that we who already know Thee by faith, may be led onward even to the beholding of the beauty of Thy Majesty" (in heaven).

In addition to glorifying God, the Divine Liturgy intends, as a secondary but no less important objective to us, to serve the sanctification of man. In this also God is glorified. To attain this objective, the drama of the Liturgy teaches, illustrates, excites, inflames, and moves the heart or will to live and act in harmony with the mysteries of Christ. Because we are members of Christ's Body, these mysteries are our very own. The Liturgy also furnishes the grace to make these mysteries fruitful. This is clearly established by the often-recurring phrases: *Deus, qui . . . docuisti . . . excitasti . . . inflammasti . . . etc.* Mysteries are not merely stories of the past, but facts that are still present. As such, they are still of the greatest importance to all mankind, since they decide our lot here and hereafter. It is, therefore, to the principal values for Christian life contained and expressed in the Liturgy of the feast, that we must now turn. These values are doctrinal and moral.

Doctrines Emphasized by the Epiphany

The outstanding and fundamental doctrines emphasized and illustrated by the celebration are:

(1) *Christ is the absolute Ruler and King over all visible creation.* St. Paul writes: "In that He has subjected all things to Him, He left nothing not subject to Him. But now we see not as yet all things subject to Him" (Heb., ii, 8). "He must reign until He hath put all His enemies under His feet" (I Cor., xv, 25). "And of His kingdom there shall be no end" (Luke, i, 33).

(2) *Christ must reign in our souls,* for souls cannot live without Him. "To every one of us is given grace, according to the measure of the giving of Christ" (Eph., iv, 7). He "is the image of the invisible God, . . . before all, . . . the head of the body, the Church, . . . that in all things He may hold the primacy" (Col., i, 15-18).

(3) *Christ alone can save us.* No one else can. Hence, we need Him. "And you, whereas you were some time alienated and enemies, . . . yet now He hath reconciled in the body of His flesh through death," writes St. Paul (ibid., 21-22). This reconciliation must be made perpetual, and, therefore, Christ Himself says: "Without Me you can do nothing." It was Christ Who sent the star to the Magi, and unless He sends actual grace to us we can neither accomplish nor even begin anything good.

Moral Lessons of the Feast

Having been enlightened by these doctrines and become convinced of their beauty and truth, we may profitably consider some important moral conclusions practical for everyday life.

(1) In the Magi we recognize the Gentiles of the past, present, and future, especially ourselves who, entirely without personal merit, were called to Christianity by the Saviour, to be His very own. "You have not chosen Me, but I have chosen you," said the Master (John, xv, 16). Day after day He reveals to us His goodness and the greatness of our calling. We have seen His star, and have recognized Him as the first-born among brethren. "For whom He foreknew, He also predestinated to be made conformable to the image of His Son" (Rom., viii, 29).

The Magi had their troubles until they reached Christ in Bethlehem. Christ came to us in Baptism, but we shall not reach Him in heaven without exertion. The prophet says: "For Thy sake we are put to death all the day long." St. Paul adds: "But in all these things [our troubles and trials] we overcome, because of Him that hath loved us; . . . [and nothing] can separate us from the love of God, which is in Christ Jesus our Lord" (Rom., viii, 37-39). If we love Christ as He loves us, we shall follow Him and also love the Church that is Christ. All this should inspire us to "walk worthy of the vocation" to Christianity (Eph., iv, 1).

(2) The Magi returned home by another way. On earth we have no permanent abode, and may follow different ways to arrive at earthly destinies. But we are also pilgrims to heaven, and to reach this final end there is but one way, the following of Christ, Who said: "I am the way, and the truth, and the life. No one comes to the Father but by Me" (John, xiv, 6). Hence, we must leave the ways of sin, human judgments, earthly aspirations, and worldliness that conflict with the teachings of Christ, because "we have seen the Lord" (John, xx, 25) and have vowed to follow His light. The vicissitudes of life are so many occasions to bring us nearer to Him. The destination we shall reach in eternity depends on the way we follow in life.

The stations on the way where the pilgrims may obtain encouragement and strength to overcome the obstacles and to correct their ways if they have erred, are the Holy Sacrifice of the Mass and the Sacraments and prayer. In the Mass we offer with Christ our little gifts—the gold of faith, the incense of adoration, and the myrrh of penance and sacrifice. We receive in turn from Christ graces of infinite value needed for conversion, improvement, and perseverance.

(3) The Magi after having returned to their people were not slow in making known the results of their trip. They spread the news that they had found Him for Whom mankind had been waiting. Did they change their secular occupations or professions? Most probably not, because there was no need for that. All they did was to make known the coming of the Redeemer to those with whom they came in contact. The visit to the Lord had filled them with the zeal of the apostolate. The Magi would have been forgotten in history like the shepherds, if they had not labored for the extension of the reign of Christ Whom they had recognized as God and as universal Ruler. This zeal for Christ was a baptism of desire by which they entered the Church then being formed. The founding of the Kingdom of God on earth was announced and its extension made known by the Epiphany of the Lord, and from that time on the construction progressed and is not yet completed.

Everyone who knows Christ and recognizes Him as the Head of the Church, can aid in its extension. To do this, it is not necessary to leave the world; on the cóntrary, unless the laity constitutes the largest unit in the missionary force, the progress of the Church must necessarily be slow. What are the several thousand ordained missionaries among so many millions of pagans? Nor is it necessary for people living in the world to change their way of living. All that is required for being successful as missionaries is the moral change necessary to make their lives truly Christian. This is not only necessary for converting others, but equally so for saving our own souls. St. Augustine says: "You who are called Christians because you are Christ's repudiate this name if you act differently from what you believe, especially by not showing your faith by good works" ("Ad catech.," IV, i, 9). Good example is the best method to spread the Faith and to increase the number of faithful. It is an effective means of preaching, because action speaks louder than words.

The first Christians employed this apostolate successfully. Not everyone can publicly announce the Faith from the pulpit, over the radio, on street corners, in lectures and writings; but all can give a good example. All the direct means of spreading the Faith will not be very effective unless the good life of Christians forms the background and also the proof. In addition to this, many may have an opportunity to spread the Faith privately among friends, acquaintances, companions in the office, store, factory, army, etc. In the biographies of converts we learn that the first impulse towards turning to the Church usually came from associates.

Opportunities for guiding and leading others to the right path are not lacking. St. Jude furnishes in his Epistle some very pertinent thoughts. His Epistle is called Catholic, because its content is of universal application and not limited as to time and circumstances. It is addressed "to them that are beloved in God the Father, and preserved in Jesus Christ, and called." To these Catholics he issues a warning against false prophets constantly arising: "Woe unto them, for they have gone in the way of Cain: and after the error of Balaam they have for reward poured out themselves, and have perished in the contradiction of Core. . . . Feasting together without fear . . . [they are] clouds without water, which are carried about by winds [of public opinion], trees of the autumn, unfruitful, twice dead, plucked up by the roots, raging waves of the sea, foaming out their own confusion, wandering stars, to whom the storm of darkness is reserved forever."

It does not need much explaining and adaptation to recognize among the false prophets so graphically described many prominent characters figuring in the public press, airing themselves in magazines, best-sellers, and professional or educational journals, "foaming out" their errors without blushing or shame. A good word in season addressed to our associates will do much to neutralize such obnoxious counsels and principles, and to retard or obviate the corruption of careless Christians.

If millions of Catholics would interest themselves in showing the fruits of Christianity in their everyday life, the words of Henoch, quoted by St. Jude, would come to pass: "Behold, the Lord cometh with thousands of His saints, to execute judgment upon all, and to reprove all the ungodly for all the works of their ungodliness . . . and of all the hard things which ungodly sinners have spoken against God." It is not necessary to defer this until the day of judgment. Many can be saved before that time by our kind words and prudent antagonism. The Apostle concludes his Epistle with the admonition: "But you, my beloved, building yourselves upon your most holy faith, . . . keep yourselves in the love of God, waiting for the mercy of our Lord Jesus Christ. . . . Some indeed reprove, . . . but others save; . . . and on others have mercy."

Conclusion

The effects of the Epiphany (Manifestation) of Our Lord were not the same in all who learned about it. As far as Herod was concerned, the effects were most deplorable. When he heard about the newly born King of the Jews, he was troubled, and, under the pretext of wishing to adore, he sought to kill the Child. God protected His Son and will protect the Church. But "why have the Gentiles raged, and the people devised vain things? The kings of the earth stood up . . . against . . . Christ" (Ps. ii, 1-2). Because of ignorance, jealousy, hatred, and malice. Herod and his people were the first who persecuted Christ on earth, but they could not have crucified Him against His will. Even after His death the persecutions did not cease, but continued in the form of persecutions of His Church.

As soon as Christ becomes visible in His followers, as soon as His Church extends her influence and her prestige increases—in one word, as soon as her divine authority becomes apparent, immediately the chorus of big and small rulers in government, politics, diplomacy, education, commerce, industry, and labor shouts: "We do not want the Church (Christ) to reign over us!" This is nothing new. Christ knew it, and assured us that the gates of hell would not prevail against His Church built upon Peter, the rock (Matt., xvi, 18).

It was not His will that persecutions should cease altogether; they are too valuable a means for arousing the lukewarm, casting off the dead branches, exciting the faithful to heroic virtues, and making the glorious crown of martyrdom available to many. "We are persecuted, and we suffer it" (I Cor., iv, 12). "We suffer persecution, but are not forsaken" (II Cor., iv, 9). "If they have persecuted Me, they will also persecute you," said the Master (John, xv, 20), Who from His infancy suffered with the Church. "I am with you all days, even to the consummation of the World," He says (Matt., xxviii, 20), continuing His sacrifice and sufferings in His members. "Have confidence, I have overcome the world" (John, xvi, 33). And remember: "Blessed are they who suffer persecution for justice' [My] sake, for theirs is the kingdom of heaven" (Matt., v, 10).

The character-training and personality-forming values hidden in the lessons of the Epiphany, especially for spiritualizing and fortifying the young, are very evident.

CHAPTER XIII
More Divine Manifestations

THE LITURGICAL PERIOD after the Epiphany recalls several minor manifestations of Christ's divinity and of the scope of His future labors which may be profitably considered before we take up the two other great manifestations which, while commemorated on the Epiphany itself, actually took place at the beginning of Christ's public life.

Neither profane nor sacred history reports how long or where the Holy Family stayed in Egypt. The Evangelist merely states that after the death of Herod an Angel appeared to Joseph advising him to return to the land of Israel (Matt., ii, 19-20). At first Joseph intended to go back to Bethlehem, the tribal city of David, but on arriving in Judea he discovered that Herod had divided the country among his sons. One of them, who reigned over Judea and Samaria, had just killed three thousand citizens and the whole population was in an uproar (Josephus Flavius). Under these circumstances, Joseph decided to return with Jesus and Mary to Nazareth in Galilee, where Herod Antipas ruled.

From these historical facts it may be safely estimated that the sojourn of the Holy Family in Egypt lasted between two and two and one-half years. St. Luke, who records the youth of Jesus, does not mention the flight to Egypt, because it was not so important. It does, however, show the watchful providence of God and the fact that, when His own people endeavored to kill Jesus, the Gentiles gave Him a quiet shelter. This we find often repeated in the history of the Church. It has often occurred that, when Christ in His Church was persecuted in one country, other lands opened their gates to missioners who preached the Gospel with great success.

Christ's Hidden Life

During the thirty years of Christ's hidden life in Nazareth nothing is recorded except His official visit to the Temple in Jerusalem at the age of twelve years. This was the age when boys became full-fledged Israelites. The account of this visit is read on the Second Sunday after Epiphany and closes with the words: "And He [Jesus] went down with them [Mary and Joseph], and came to Nażareth; and was subject to them. . . . And Jesus advanced in wisdom and age, and grace with God and men" (Luke, ii, 42-52).

On this occasion Jesus publicly confessed Himself to be the Son of the Heavenly Father, and manifested Himself to be the Wisdom of the Father sent into the world "to give testimony of the truth." He sat among the doctors, hearing them and asking them questions, and "all that heard Him were astonished at His wisdom." Even as early in the Gospel as this we are left in no doubt about His divine origin and His divine mission: "Did you not know that I must be about My Father's business?"

This first official visit of Jesus to the Temple brings to our mind the earlier visit when He was carried thither by His mother, forty days after His birth. Mary went to the Temple to present her first-born to the Lord as prescribed by the Law, and to redeem Him by a sacrifice. The latter ceremony seems to be incongruous in so far as Christ is concerned. The Redeemer could not be redeemed from sacrificing Himself, because for this very purpose He had become Man. On His part as well as on the part of Mary, who needed no purification, it was a public manifestation of obedience to the ceremonial law that had not yet been abrogated for all Jews. The event is commemorated in the blessing of candles preceding the Mass of the Purification of the Blessed Virgin Mary celebrated on February 2.

St. Luke relates what took place (ii, 22-32). On this occasion the Lord whom Israel sought, "and the Angel of the Testament whom you desire," came to His temple (Mal., iii, 1). On this occasion also Simeon and Anna spoke about the nature and mission of the Child. Jesus is the Light of the world, "a light to the

MORE DIVINE MANIFESTATIONS

revelation of the Gentiles, and the glory of His people Israel." Commemorating this, the Church sings during the candle procession: "Adorn thy marriage-chamber, O Sion, and receive Christ the King. Give embrace to Mary who is the gate of heaven, for she bears the King in the glory of a new light." In consequence of what took place, Anna too "confessed to the Lord."

To this St. Luke adds: "The child grew and waxed strong, full of wisdom" (ii, 40). Because these words are repeated (ibid., 52), some heretics concluded that Jesus became gradually conscious of His divine nature and mission, but the fact that He revealed things gradually does not prove that He did not fully know them from the beginning. Besides His infused knowledge Christ also had acquired knowledge. He simply became in all things like man, sin excepted, as St. Paul writes: "It behoved Him in all things to be made like unto His brethren" (Heb., ii, 17).

Before turning to the mysteries that happened during His public life, a few words may be added concerning the part Mary played in the work of Redemption during the youth of Christ. Mary, instructed by the Angel Gabriel, knew that her Son was God and that she was the Mother of God; and although she was highly enlightened by grace, she was not all-knowing, and undoubtedly was gradually informed about the future and the divine plans. This prepared her for her rôle in the Redemption and in the Church. At the Circumcision, usually performed in the home, Joseph exercising his prerogative as foster-father called the Child, Jesus (Matt., i, 25), as the Angel had directed both Mary and Joseph to do (Matt., i, 21; Luke, i, 31). Both knew why: "For He shall save His people from their sins" (Matt., i, 21). How He would do this was still a mystery to them. The veil is lifted gradually at the Purification and at the visit to Jerusalem commemorated during this season.

During the two visits to the Temple Mary learned that Jesus was the Light of the world and the Teacher of mankind. This mission was clearly stated by Simeon enlightened from above, but at the same time it was foretold by him that not all would receive Him as such. For some He would be the occasion for damnation, instead of salvation. Mary learned about herself that the offering of her Son to God would be followed by pain and sorrow: "Thy own soul a sword shall pierce" (Luke, ii, 35). On the other hand, Mary could rejoice that by bringing forth and sacrificing her Son many would be saved. Here she appears as a type of the Church, who by daily sacrificing Christ leads mankind to salvation. The Liturgy expresses this relation by reciting in the Antiphon from the Feast of the Purification until Holy Thursday: "Salve radix, salve porta ex qua mundo Lux est orta." Christ submitted to the rite of Purification with Mary, that through her intercession the whole of mankind might present itself to Him with purified souls (Collect).

Twelve years later, during the Easter visit to Jerusalem, Mary was again enlightened by the loss and finding of her Son. She experienced what a void life would be without the graceful physical presence of her Divine Son, and that the time would come when He would no longer be on earth. Her words express the feelings of a mother's heart filled with anxiety about her child: "Son, why hast Thou done so to us? Behold Thy father and I have sought Thee sorrowing" (Luke, ii, 48). She also found out that the fulfillment of the will of the Father might, humanly speaking, not always please a mother: "Did you not know that I must be about My Father's business?" At the time, Mary did not fully understand what these words meant, but nevertheless she rejoiced over the finding of the beloved Son and kept all His words in her heart.

Jesus returned to Nazareth with Mary and Joseph, and continued to be subject to them until the time appointed by His Father for Him to appear in public. In His home, Jesus did not outwardly differ from other good sons. This may be gathered from the words found in the Gospel: "Is He not the carpenter's son? Is not His mother called Mary, and His brethren . . . and sisters [cousins], are they not all with us? Whence therefore hath He all these things?" (Matt., xiii, 55-56; cf. Mark, vi, 2-3). *We know who He was and whence His power and wisdom came.*

On this visit to the Temple, Mary shows again her close relation to the Church. She and Joseph have transferred their par-

MORE DIVINE MANIFESTATIONS 137

ental supernatural love to the Church. Mary, the Mother in the Holy Family, has become the Mother of the Church; and Joseph, her Protector, who shared in all joys and sorrows with Christ, now shares in all the vicissitudes of His Church. Mary lived and thought with the young Church, and transmitted the facts about Christ's youth to the Apostles and Evangelists, and through them to all following generations. In his Encyclical on the Mystical Body Pope Pius XII writes of Mary's care for the infant Church:

> "[Mary] through her powerful prayers, obtained the grace that the Spirit of Our Divine Redeemer, already given to the Church on the Cross, should be bestowed through miraculous gifts on the newly founded Hierarchy on Pentecost. Bearing with courage and confidence the tremendous burden of her sorrows and desolation, truly the Queen of Martyrs, she, more than all the faithful, 'filled up those things that are wanting of the sufferings of Christ . . . for His Body, which is the Church,' and she continued to show for the Mystical Body of Christ, born from the pierced Heart of the Saviour, the same mother's care and ardent love with which she clasped the infant Jesus to her warm and nourishing breast. May she then, most holy mother of all Christ's members, to whose Immaculate Heart We have trustingly consecrated all men . . . may she never cease to beg from Him that a continuous, copious flow of graces may pass from its glorious head into all the members of the Mystical Body."

Christ's hidden life is celebrated on the Feast of the Holy Family for the edification of the faithful, but this having already been considered, it is not necessary to enlarge upon it here.

Beginning of Christ's Public Life

After the Epiphany the Liturgy presents one manifestation after another without regard to time and place, but a certain uniformity and continuity of thought is preserved. The election of the Apostles is not mentioned on the Sundays before Lent, but among the feasts celebrated are the Chair of St. Peter and the Conversion of St. Paul, the two greatest among the Apostles upon whom as a foundation the Church was to rest. St. Peter was to be the rock, and St. Paul the Doctor of the Gentiles.

Hence, these feasts really have a liturgical significance in this part of the Liturgical Year. They belong to the parallelism between Christ and the Church or her members expressed and illustrated by the worship of the Church.

The Mass of the Octave of the Epiphany lays stress upon the words of the Baptist about Jesus, Who came to the Jordan to be baptized: "Behold the Lamb of God, behold Him Who taketh away the sins of the world" (John, i, 29). St. Matthew adds: "Jesus . . . came out of the water: and lo, the heavens were opened to Him: and He saw the Spirit of God descending as a dove, and coming upon Him. And behold a voice from heaven saying: This is My beloved Son, in Whom I am well pleased" (iii, 16-17). And the festal Gospel concludes with the words of St. John the Baptist: "I saw, and I gave testimony, that this is the Son of God" (John, i, 34).

This event clearly manifests that Christ, the Son of God, was the sacrificial Lamb of God selected to take away the sins of the world, Whose sacrifice would be pleasing to the Father. It also reveals that by Baptism and the Holy Ghost all men who believe in Christ will become beloved children of God (Luke, iii, 21-22). Moreover, the mission of Christ was authenticated by God Himself. The humiliation of Jesus by being baptized among sinners was immediately followed by a glorification, as always happened during His life (Marmion). Finally, Christ's baptism was the forerunner of the Baptism He was to institute, at which the whole Trinity would also be present, and through which we would be made beloved children of God, members of His Mystical Body, and partakers of His divine inheritance. All this, previously ratified, became effective after the Resurrection. None but the baptized would have a share in the Redemption or could enjoy membership in His Church.

In the early centuries the Gospels relating the temptation of Christ in the desert and the choosing of the Apostles were read in Rome on the following Wednesday and Friday, the regular days for the instruction of the catechumens. However, at the time of Pope St. Gregory the Great, some changes were made to suit the people, and some of the Epistles and Gospels used for

MORE DIVINE MANIFESTATIONS

instruction were transferred to other days in Lent, thus disturbing the chronological order somewhat.

The third great manifestation celebrated on the Epiphany, but commemorated on the Second Sunday thereafter, occurred during the marriage feast at Cana. On this occasion Christ wrought His first public miracle, "and manifested His glory [omnipotence], and His disciples believed in Him" (John, ii, 11). The Liturgy sees in the changing of water into good wine a picture of the transition from the Old to the New Dispensation, and a foreshadowing of the Holy Eucharist that also required the creative power. The marriage feast itself, at which Mary and the Apostles were present as guests, the Church considers to be a type of the perpetual union between Christ and His Church, which was cleansed in the water of Baptism and adorned by the Holy Ghost. To this Bridegroom demonstrating His divine glory and power, the Church, His Bride, sings: "Let all the earth worship Thee, let them praise Thy Name, O Most High. Rejoice in God, give glory to His name" (Introit).

Asked by His Mother, representing the Church, to provide wine, Christ answers implicitly by working the miracle: "Thou art always with Me, and all I have is thine" (Luke, xv, 31). For this reason, Mary unhesitatingly and confidently "saith to the waiters: Whatsoever He shall say to you, do ye" (John, ii, 5). This miracle was the first divine gift bestowed by Christ upon His royal Bride. "In all things you are made rich" in Christ Jesus (I Cor., i, 5), "having different gifts, according to the grace that is given us" (Epistle). Beholding this in spirit, the Psalmist exclaims: "With thy comeliness and thy beauty set out, proceed prosperously and reign" (Ps. xliv, 5). Hence, the Liturgy of this and the preceding and following Sundays reveals gradually the two natures of Christ and His relation to the Church and to ourselves individually.

On the Third Sunday after the Epiphany the Church sings in the Gradual: "The Lord shall build up Sion [His Church], He shall appear in His glory. The heathen shall fear Thy name, O Lord, and all the kings of the earth Thy glory [omnipotence]. The Lord reigneth; let the earth rejoice; let the multitude of isles be glad thereat" (Pss. ci and xcvi). The Gospel, describing the cures of a leper and the centurion's servant, concludes with Christ's declaration that the faith of the Gentile centurion was greater than that of Israel, and that faith was the cause of the cure of the servant. It is a picture of Christ laboring in His Church. He gives well-being to body and soul, because He is Master over sickness and health. But He requires faith, because without faith it is impossible to please God. There must be faith in His divinity and teaching, and membership in His all-embracing Church, as expressed in the Credo that follows the Gospel. The Offertory adds: "The right hand of the Lord hath done valiantly. The right hand of the Lord hath exalted me; I [the Church] shall not die, but live, and declare the works of the Lord" (Ps. cxvii, 16-17). This declaration is the universal task of the Church.

The following Sunday manifests that Christ is the Master over the elements: "A great tempest arose in the sea. . . . Then rising up, He commanded the winds and the sea, and there came a great calm" (Matt., viii, 24-26). His power was evident to the men that were with Him. The event is a picture of Christ protecting His Church and all her members who invoke His aid. Nothing happens against His will or without His permission. There is no danger that the Church will perish, because Christ guaranteed her existence unto the end, but individual members may suffer the shipwreck of their faith. Hence we pray: "O God, who knowest that, because of the frailty of our nature, we cannot be steadfast in the midst of such great perils grant us health of mind and body, that we may by Thy aid overcome what we suffer for our sins" (Collect). This prayer is necessary because, although the Church is divine in its Founder, Teacher, Bridegroom, and gifts of grace, the members are human beings still on the way to perfection.

The Gospel of the Fifth Sunday compares the Church "to a man that sowed good seed in his field, but . . . his enemy came and oversowed cockle . . ." (Matt., xiii, 24-30). The fault lies not with the Church if some of her children are wicked, but with men who, although receiving the necessary graces, do not resist

MORE DIVINE MANIFESTATIONS 141

the enemies who would separate them from God. To strengthen our wills to resist, we pray: "Watch over Thy household continually, O Lord, we beseech Thee in Thy mercy; that as it leans only upon the hope of Thy heavenly grace, so it may ever be shielded by Thy protection" (Collect). Hence, although there are reasons and causes for apostasy, there are no excuses. Christ manifests Himself as one having power over His and our adversaries, and assures us that He, and we united with Him, will conquer and triumph at the end when the weeds will be gathered and burned.

On the Sixth Sunday after the Epiphany the parables of the mustard seed and of the leaven are read (Matt., xiii, 31-35). By these parables Christ manifests Himself as one who would penetrate the body and soul of man. He Who came as a tiny Infant would grow in stature by drawing the whole of mankind under His power. "The Lord is King," begins the Introit. He is the leaven permeating all and saving all who wish to be saved. It was His strength that made the Church grow in the face of constant persecution and opposition. The end is not yet in sight, but Christ the omniscient God, Who told the parables, knew the future.

Summary

The manifestations of Christ as unfolded by the Liturgy of the weeks following Epiphany give us a clearer picture of Christ's own nature and that of His extension, the Church. There was no doubt about His human nature among those who saw Him and spoke with Him. Regarding His office and person, He revealed successively that He was to perform the business of His Father, Whose beloved Son He was, as Light of the world, as Teacher, example, and Saviour of mankind. He proved by His miracles and knowledge of the future that He was almighty and all-knowing, and that the hearts and thoughts of men were an open book to Him. He showed Himself to be the Creator in His control of the elements by orders that were immediately obeyed. Concerning His Church He made known that He himself was its Royal Bridegroom and Head, that He would endow His Bride, the

Church, with all the power needed for the salvation of men. This Church was to be built upon Himself as the corner-stone and upon the Apostles as a foundation. Mary was to be the Mother of the Church, even as she was His Mother. The gate for entering the Church is Baptism. Finally, Christ manifested Himself as the Prophet Who knew all about the future fate of the Church.

That Christ lives in the Church, that He is the Head and vital Principle of the supernatural life of His Church, and that the Church is the extension of the Incarnation are facts that the Liturgy, the Fathers of the Church, and the modern Popes will not allow us to forget. Pope Pius XII in his Encyclical on the Mystical Body gives us clear and profound doctrine on this great subject. For example, he writes:

> "The whole body of the Church no less than the individual members, should bear resemblance to Christ. Such was His will. And we see this realized. . . . From Him shines into the body of the Church whatever light illumines supernaturally the mind of those who believe; from Him comes every grace to make them holy, as He is holy. . . . For us today, who still linger on in this earthly exile, He is the author of faith, as, in our heavenly home, He will be its finisher. . . . He so sustains the Church, and in a certain sense so lives in the Church, that it is, as it were, another Christ. The Doctor of the Gentiles, in his letter to the Corinthians, affirms this when without further qualification he called the Church 'Christ.' Indeed, if we are to believe Gregory of Nyssa, the Church is often called 'Christ' by the Apostle; and you are conversant . . . with that phrase of Augustine: 'Christ preaches Christ.' "

Apologetical Notes

The fact that all these things are more or less known, does not mean that all Christians realize their importance and shape their views and lives accordingly. It seems that our young people educated in non-Catholic institutions have increased their knowledge but have at the same time wrecked or partially lost their supernatural faith. Having become imbued with the philosophies of such men as Descartes, Hegel, Kant, Fichte, and Schopenhauer, taught at all but Catholic seats of learning, they have

MORE DIVINE MANIFESTATIONS 143

arrived at the conclusion that truth is but subjective, relative, and therefore liable to change. This is the apex of private interpretation or, as they call it, the scientific view of religion which really does not fall under the domain of science.

All the modern views of religion are founded on man rather than on God, and thus give rise to the belief that there is no certitude in faith and morals. Many of our young men and women may not actually apostatize, but they acquire hazy notions which, unless counteracted, may lead to agnosticism and pragmatism without their realizing it. Some non-Catholics, becoming disturbed about their position regarding faith, eagerly turn to sects such as Quakerism, Methodism, Theosophy, and Christian Science, all of which are not founded on the entire Christian truth, but represent an individual following of a distorted mysticism. What impression would the aforenamed synthesis presented by the Liturgy make upon the different classes of people here mentioned? The standard skeptical response is: "We cannot know that." But they *can* arrive at religious certitude, as we shall see later.

When Jesus had miraculously changed water into wine, "His disciples believed in Him" (John, ii, 11). They were not easily satisfied in this matter. Even after His Resurrection, Christ complained about some disciples: "O foolish, and slow of heart to believe in all things which the prophets have spoken" (Luke, xxiv, 25). After Christ had established His mission by miracles, and had fulfilled the prophecies about Himself, they still hesitated for fear of deception. Our modern youth, being more "progressive" than the Apostles, accept everything from any well-advertised Tom, Dick, and Harry without a sign of authentication, and doubt the truths which Christ has revealed and confirmed by miracles.

Can man arrive at certitude in matters of faith to which the mind may adhere without fear of error? Yes, provided the objective is known and valid motives for belief are apprehended. The virtue of faith is a free gift of God, but at the same time it demands the cooperative effort of man. It consists in the freely willed acceptance by man's mind, aided by divine grace, of a doctrine, not because of an understanding of its content nor because of any human authority, but because of the authority of God or His accredited representative, the Church, which testifies to its truth. Christ is the only teacher of religion Who established His authority and veracity by miracles and prophecies (especially by His Resurrection, to which we shall return later). Other accepted teachers wrought miracles too, but they were performed in His Name, as the Gospels and the Acts explicitly state.

Confining ourselves to the miracles of Christ mentioned in this chapter, we find: (1) They are historically certain, because they form parts of the Gospel, the historical facts of which are proven beyond doubt. The miracles could not be rejected without rejecting the whole history of Christ. (2) The miracles were all performed to confirm Christ's divine mission, and were, as such, accepted by the people who witnessed them. This is especially mentioned after Christ changed water into wine: "His disciples believed in Him." This also happened on other occasions. (3) To the miracles should be added the prophecies of Christ. He not only fulfilled the prophecies concerning Himself, but added new prophecies about Himself, His disciples, and His Church, and prophesied about the Jews and the destruction of Jerusalem. These prophecies prove His divine mission, authority, and credibility, because so many of them have already been fulfilled.[1]

These and other motives for accepting the Faith should be stressed in religious instructions from the first grade through high school and even into adult life. Little good will be accomplished by merely mentioning miracles that occurred, unless their significance in religion is explained. After an analytical exposition, a synthesis should follow. The neglect of this means that parts of the truth are made known, but a picture of the whole is never seen.

The Church, preaching only the doctrines of Christ well established by His miracles and unbroken Tradition (of which Tradition the Liturgy forms an important part), needs no further

---

[1] More material in Tanquerey, 'Synopsis Theologiæ Dogmaticæ," vol. I, chap. ii.

miracles. *Lex orandi, lex credendi*.[1] If the Church or any other agency would teach new doctrines not founded upon Scripture and Tradition, as guarded and explained by the Vicar of Christ, protected against error by the Holy Ghost, we could unhesitatingly ask for a miracle before accepting them. Catholics are the most critical people as far as religious truths are concerned, and they are convinced that two opposing statements cannot both be true. Unfortunately, especially among students and educated Christians, we find some who readily accept, without any proofs from professors or writers, teachings at variance with the doctrines of the Church. This is foolish and stupid. Why do they not ask for a miracle in confirmation of the "new" teachings not in harmony with those of the Church?

Perhaps convincing proofs could be furnished by science? No, because religion is supernatural and beyond the realm of science. Religion can guide science, and science can help in explaining religious truths by furnishing at times examples taken from nature; but science cannot create new supernatural truths nor destroy old ones. Real scientists unhesitatingly declare that, as scientists, they know nothing about religion, and that true religion does not interfere with true science. This is true, because, although they have different immediate objectives, religion and science both have the same Author. Fake scientists, and this term embraces the majority of our "modern" professors and textbook writers, say, "We know nothing about religion," and this is one truth we may accept at its face value!

But is it not stupid to accept statements contradicting Revelation from teachers without a miracle to prove them? Especially from teachers and writers who ridicule, despise, and antagonize a religion about which they know nothing? It can only be imagined what their reaction and perplexity would be if they were asked for miracles to prove their intellectual concoctions. They would truthfully answer that they know nothing about miracles, and would falsely add that such things cannot happen. The very fact that miracles still happen does not induce modern

---

[1] The rule of prayer is the rule of faith.

scientists to retract their dogmatic slogan: "Miracles are impossible."

This is another sign of gross ignorance, if not wickedness, because the very existence of miracles proves their possibility. On the other hand, there is nothing to prove their impossibility. We, however, believe in miracles because with God everything is possible, except what is a contradiction in itself. This does not limit God's power, since that exception regards a limitation found in creatures themselves. Only the atheists, who deny the existence of God, and the pantheists, who deny a God distinct from the world, act logically by denying miracles, because if there exists no divine Factor, there can be no supra-natural acts. It is different with the rationalists, positivists, and others, who maintain that God would not interfere with the natural law; or if He did, we could not distinguish miracles from other extraordinary happenings, because no one knows the extent and operation of the laws of nature in all their details.

However, these reasons do not remove the possibility of miracles, because the latter do not destroy the natural laws, although miracles require their suspension or exception from the ordinary laws. Nor do miracles imply a change in God's wisdom or plans, for they were determined from all eternity as signs of His mercy, goodness, prudence, etc., not interfering with nor disturbing His universal plan of providing for the whole of creation. It may not always be easy to distinguish a miracle from other strange facts, and for this reason the Church is very slow in accepting miracles. This is wise, for in these matters she is the teacher of mankind, and these things cannot be in conflict with true science, because God is the Author of both religion and science. No one may entertain any doubt about the miracles of Christ and others related in Holy Scripture; but with regard to other events not declared miracles by the Church, individuals have sufficient freedom to accept or reject them.

Since the treatment of miracles so far has been mainly philosophical, we may conclude with the teaching of the Vatican Council in regard to miracles (Session III, Chapters 3 and 4). The Vatican Fathers declare: (1) that miracles are external and divine facts, signs, and arguments of Revelation; (2) that they are most certain signs of divine Revelation by which God's omnipotence and infinite wisdom can be fully demonstrated and they are, at the same time, accommodated to the intelligence of all. The same Council declares the following to be articles of faith: (1) that miracles can happen, and sometimes can be recognized with certainty, and that by them the origin of the Christian religion can be proven; (2) that divine Revelation can become credible by external signs (miracles and prophecies), and therefore men must not be moved to faith by their internal, personal experience alone or by private inspiration.

Christ wrought miracles to show His divine authority as Teacher, and we like His disciples believe in Him.

CHAPTER XIV

Liturgical Preparation for Penance

THE LENTEN LITURGY also has a variety of objectives. The first is to produce an increase in the number as well as in the holiness of the faithful. The preparation for the Baptism of the catechumens and the preparation of the faithful for Easter run parallel. For both, Baptism is the *terminus a quo,* and a glorious resurrection with Christ is the *terminus ad quem.* Hence, we clearly recognize in the Lenten Liturgy the efforts of the Church: (1) to prepare for Baptism, which creates a new life; (2) to impress the greatness and importance of Baptism upon all; (3) to increase the grace of Baptism or to restore it, if lost.

The first part of the Easter Cycle is the Pre-Lenten Season, beginning on Septuagesima Sunday and ending on Shrove Tuesday. This is followed by Lent (including Passion-Tide), Easter, and the following Sundays and feasts, and ends on the Saturday after Pentecost. The importance of this period for making converts, seeking to regain the lost sheep, and deepening the faith in all, is obvious. Grace accompanies penance, and the penance done by some will redound to the benefit of all mankind, but especially to the members of the Church. The acceptance of this grace must bear fruit in spiritualization: "Hodie, si vocem Domini audieritis, nolite obdurare corda vestra"[1] (Invitatorium). It is a special time for sowing the good seed, and God will grant the fruit.

Some general remarks about this most beautiful and moving cycle in the whole Liturgy may form an introduction to the consideration of its several parts.

Since the liturgical ceremonies and prayers of this season started to develop soon after the Christians in Rome emerged

---
[1] "Today if you hear the voice of the Lord, harden not your hearts."

from the catacombs, they are truly venerable. Very little substantial change has been made in the words of the prayers, although some of the ceremonies of a public nature have gradually been eliminated. In the Liturgy, then, we find a clear expression of the belief, piety, and worship of the early Roman Christians. The rite and discipline of primitive Christianity are adapted to conditions existing in Rome, the new terrestrial Jerusalem.

Every Sunday and week-day during Lent and Easter week were celebrated with more or less solemnity in the Station churches as indicated in the Roman Missal. For the information of the people, these churches were announced on the previous day or Sunday, as was also the church in which the faithful were to collect and form the procession. On the way to the Station church the Litany was sung, and when the procession arrived at the place of sacrifice, the Mass began with an Antiphon (Introit) which was directly followed by the Oration now called the Collect. The Kyrie was omitted during this season whenever the processions were held. The Liturgy of Holy Saturday furnishes an example. The Gloria is omitted in Lent.

Very often the Pope himself took part in the solemn celebrations on these days, and frequently the Mass was celebrated with a great concourse of people. All those who expected the baptism of water or penance during the Easter Season made it a point to be present as frequently as possible. It was a good and laudable practice, which is equally commendable and salutary today. More will be said about this when we come to speak of certain special days.

The Pre-Lenten Period

The period from Septuagesima to Quadragesima Sunday was the time of preparation for the Holy Season of Lent, especially as regards the catechumens who were still surrounded by the shadow of death. The Liturgy was intended to strengthen them in their resolutions and to draw God's grace upon them. It still has its significance at the present time in which so many baptisms are delayed for months and years.

The Liturgy of this period received its present form from Pope

St. Gregory, who had special reasons for introducing some changes in it. In his days the Eastern Christians, many of whom had gathered in Rome, considered the Saturdays as quasi-holydays without fast, and therefore began their fast three weeks earlier than the Romans. The idea of a semi-penitential period appealed to the latter. Another more important reason was the great desolation prevailing at that time in Rome, brought about by discord and pestilence.

A year before Gregory I was forced against his will to assume the supreme pontificate, a great inundation had visited Italy. People, farms, and buildings containing provisions were destroyed over a large area. Pestilence followed the disaster, corpses littered the streets of the cities, and there was a lack of healthy men to bury them. Rome had become a city of the dead, without business and other essential activities. Such were the conditions that confronted Gregory when he assumed the burden of the Papacy. During his pontificate (590-604), differences arose between him and the Lombards, the Franks, and the Empire which had its seat in Constantinople. All this increased the misery of the sick Pontiff.

With him, the populace of Rome turned to its great Patrons, Sts. Peter, Paul, and Lawrence. Processions were held to their resting places or basilicas, but in reversed order of importance so that the climax might be reached in the Lateran Church of Our Saviour on Quadragesima Sunday. The Masses following these public rogation processions express rather the physical misery of the time, but may equally well be applied to the devastation prevalent in the souls of many Christians brought about by a flood of worldliness and sin.

Septuagesima Sunday

On Septuagesima Sunday the picture of the all-powerful God is presented to the faithful steeped in spiritual and temporal misery. The Introit of the Mass forms an excellent introduction to our co-suffering with Christ, as exemplified by St. Lawrence in whose house the Church Militant gathers and whose intercession it implores: "The sorrows of death compassed me. The sorrows of hell compassed me about. In my distress I called upon the Lord. . . . He is my rock, and my fortress, and my deliverer." Here we find clearly presented the situation as it was—and as it is at present. We too are surrounded by physical and spiritual death caused (1) by war and its accompanying evils, and (2) by hell as manifested in the crimes, hatred, injustice, and widespread godlessness which have plunged so many into despair. But the Church is not without hope! The Christian knows that the Lord hears his voice, and we may rest assured that we who are justly afflicted for our sins, will nevertheless be mercifully delivered, to the glory of God's name (Oration). But this delivery from bondage, misery, and sin will not take place without our co-operation.

In the Epistle (I Cor., ix, 24-27) St. Paul describes how athletes prepare and run for a prize. Our prize is heaven. Hence, the Apostle advises us: "So run that you may obtain. And every one that striveth for the mastery, refraineth himself from all things: and they [the athletes] indeed that they may receive a corruptible crown, but we an incorruptible one. I therefore . . . chastise my body, and bring it into subjection." This requires exertion or penance, but God will help: "Thou, Lord, dost not forsake them that seek Thee. For the needy shall not always be forgotten; the expectation of the poor shall not perish forever" (Gradual). "There is forgiveness with Thee, O Lord" (Tract), for all who prepare themselves for the baptism of water or of penance.

The Gospel, as well as the Epistle, was chosen with a view to the catechumens, who on this Sunday were selected for probation during Lent. They were to receive more intensive instruction on the following Wednesdays, Fridays, and Saturdays. Hence, these days have a special significance during this season. The Lessons at Matins describe the creation and fall of man, which made Baptism necessary for all who wish to obtain a share in the Redemption by Christ. The admonition to preserve or regain baptismal grace is reiterated during these pre-Lenten days. All are invited to enter the vineyard of the Church and to labor in the garden of their soul.

Sexagesima Sunday

Sexagesima emphasizes the fact that Christian living is a battle against our interior and exterior enemies. The Liturgy of this Sunday is celebrated in the Church of St. Paul, who himself fought the good fight and received the crown. The Introit again expresses disconsolateness over existing conditions in even stronger words: "Arise, why sleepest Thou, O Lord? Arise and cast us not off to the end; . . . Our belly hath cleaved to the earth." To this the Collect adds: "O God, who seest we trust not in anything that we do, mercifully grant that, through the intercession of the Doctor of the Gentiles [in whose church we are assembled], we may be defended against all adversities."

In the Epistle St. Paul relates his own troubles and how he overcame them: Brethren, "you gladly suffer the foolish; whereas yourselves are wise" (II Cor. xi, 19). You suffer now; well, I suffered bondage, prison, stripes above measure. I was stoned; thrice I suffered shipwreck; I was in peril from robbers and persecutors. Hunger and thirst, fasting, cold and nakedness, were my lot, and in addition to these external things were my daily concern for the churches and my spiritual worry. Wherefore, "thrice I besought the Lord, that it might depart from me. And He said to me: My grace is sufficient for thee" (II Cor. xii, 8-9). It will enable us too to attain the things which God has prepared for those who love Him.

The Gradual and Tract add: "Let the Gentiles know that Thou alone art the Most High. Thou hast moved the earth, and hast troubled it. Heal the breeches thereof, for it has been moved." A very timely prayer, indeed!

The Gospel contains a valuable lesson for the catechumens as well as for the faithful. St. Paul scattered the seed, the Word of God, over a larger territory than any other Apostle. Yet, in many cases the fruits of holiness were not so evident. Our Lord Himself gives the reason for this phenomenon which might scandalize the catechumens. As Cardinal Schuster writes: "Shallowness of mind, excessive love of worldly things, and the hardness of a heart voluntarily closed to the promptings of grace often render profitless the labor of the sower."[1] Evidently the fault lies not with the sower nor with the seed, but with the soil in which it is planted, when the anticipated harvest is not reaped. Every individual must prepare "a very good heart," and then fruit will be brought forth in abundance—but in patience.

Since, to accomplish this, strength from above is needed, the Offertory prays: "Perfect thou my goings in Thy paths, that my footsteps be not moved: incline Thy ear, and hear my words; show forth Thy wonderful mercies, Thou who savest them that trust in Thee." To this the Secret adds: "May the sacrifice offered to Thee, O Lord, ever quicken and strengthen us. . . ."

The Communion addresses an admonition and consolation to the faithful hard-pressed by calamities and sin: "Then will I go unto the altar of God, unto God who gladdens my youth." And the final request is: "God grant that all who have partaken in the Liturgy and received Christ, may serve Him worthily by a life well pleasing to Him" (Postcommunion).

Quinquagesima Sunday

The Liturgy of Quinquagesima Sunday continues the recollection of the physical and spiritual misery surrounding the Church. On this Sunday Mother Church is assembled in the Basilica of St. Peter, the rock and the visible head of that Church against which the gates of hell shall not prevail. He is also the special Patron and Protector of Rome. These facts give added emphasis to the words of the Introit: "Be Thou unto me a God, a protector and a place of refuge. . . . For Thou art my strength and my refuge. . . . In Thee have I hoped; . . . deliver me in Thy justice." Knowing that our tribulations are caused by our sins and faults, the Church prays: "O Lord, graciously hear our prayers, and loosening the bonds of our sins, guard us from all adversities."

---
[1] "The Sacramentary," vol. II, p. 35.

On the preceding two Sundays St. Paul stressed faith and hope or confidence; today he takes up charity, which is the greatest of the divine virtues infused into our soul by Baptism. St. Paul, who had himself entered the third heaven, reveals to us the greatness and necessity of charity. By charity he understands the love of God and the love of neighbor based on regulated self-love. The perfect charity is sanctifying grace, which is inconsistent with grievous offenses against God. "God is charity: and he that abideth in charity abideth in God, and God in him" (I John, iv, 16). To this St. John adds: "If any man say, I love God, and hateth his brother, he is a liar. . . . For he that loveth . . . God loveth also his brother" (ibid., 20-21).

On these thoughts the Epistle enlarges (I Cor., xiii, 1-13). Unless we possess this charity and act accordingly, all other virtues and moral qualities are in vain. Even the virtue of charity, as portrayed by the Apostle, will not admit us to heaven without the garment of sanctifying grace, which is the basis of all merit. This grace is to be regained during Lent; all obstacles to its acquisition or development are to be removed by self-denial, penance, and mortification. We simply must die with Christ, in Whose death we were baptized and obtained supernatural life. If charity already dwells within us, it must be preserved and increased by the same means so that it may last forever.

But those who wish to follow Christ must suffer with Him. There is no easy way to come to a glorious resurrection; otherwise, the Saviour, Who loved His own until the end, would have announced it to us adults. However, this should discourage no one: "Nothing is wanting to you in any grace" (I Cor., i, 7). Hence, the Gradual adds: "Thou art the God that doest wonders. Thou hast declared Thy strength among us, [and] with Thy arm redeemed Thy people." Therefore, "serve the Lord with gladness. It is He that hath made us, and not we ourselves" (Tract). Knowing the frailty of our nature, God will come to the rescue of all who implore His aid.

This being the last Sunday before Lent, the Liturgy begins to unfold the mysteries of the following weeks.

The Master tells us in the Gospel: "Behold, we go up to

PREPARATION FOR PENANCE 155

Jerusalem, and all things shall be accomplished. . . ." (Luke, xviii, 31). The Son of Man will suffer and die, but "the third day He will rise again." But the disciples (although recently they had said: "Come let us go and die with Him") "understood none of these things." All left Him during the Passion, and none but the Beloved Disciple was found under the Cross, which He suffered willingly, and after three days He rose gloriously from the dead. They had no reason to doubt His power to accomplish what He foretold, because the cure of the blind man on the way to Jerusalem proved what He could do. This miracle of giving sight to the blind man, should have opened the Apostles' eyes, even as the light of faith would soon penetrate to the catechumens still surrounded by the darkness of sin and unbelief. As Christ suffered willingly for us, we should also follow Him in mortification and self-denial, making reparation for our own sins, and thus being united to Christ by grace share also in His merits.

The Secret expresses our desires: "May this victim, O Lord, we beseech Thee, cleanse away our sins, and sanctify the bodies and minds of Thy servants for the celebration of this sacrifice"— which is the renewal of Thy Passion and death. Our strength is Christ Himself in Holy Communion: "So they did eat and were filled, . . . and they were not defrauded of that which they craved." (Communion). Hence, the Postcommunion implores that "we who have tasted of the celestial Food may be fortified by it against all that is hurtful. . . ."

Ash Wednesday

In the fourth century Ash Wednesday inaugurated the canonical penances that public sinners had to perform before they received absolution on Thursday in Holy Week. These penitents were covered with sackcloth sprinkled with ashes, and as late as the seventh century they had to withdraw to some specified monastery. In the ninth century the imposition of ashes was still a separate ceremony, but in the eleventh century, when public penances were no longer imposed, all the faithful (including the clergy who before that time were excluded) received the blessed ashes. In Rome the ceremony was held very appropriately in the Church of St. Anastasia, the Basilica of the Resurrection. The resurrection with Christ in grace is the objective to be reached during the penitential season.

The present Roman ceremony dates from the twelfth century, and has been but little changed. From that time forward, Ash Wednesday (instead of the following Monday) became the first day of Lent. The prayers recited during the blessing of the ashes (obtained by burning the palms of the previous year) were taken over from the Frankish ritual and express the following thoughts: "Almighty God, spare those who are penitent . . . and conscious of their sins accuse themselves, deploring their sins before Thy clemency. Grant . . . that whoever may be sprinkled with these holy ashes for the remission of their sins, may receive health of body and safety of soul." The ashes, having been sprinkled with holy water and incensed, are signed upon the foreheads of the people whilst the priest recites: "Remember, man, that thou art dust, and unto dust thou shalt return."

During the distribution of the ashes which takes some time, the singers chant some responsories taken from Matins. These prayers express the sentiments that should be present in the penitents: "Let us change our garments for ashes and sackcloth: let us fast and lament before the Lord. . . . Between the porch and the altar the priests, the Lord's ministers, shall weep and shall say: Spare, O Lord, spare Thy people. . . . Let us amend for the better in those things in which we have sinned through ignorance; lest suddenly overtaken by the day of death, we seek space for penance and are not able to find it. . . . Hear, O Lord, and have mercy: for we have sinned against Thee." How many forget these sentiments during Lent and continue in their worldly ways! The closing prayer is indeed necessary: "Almighty and eternal God, who didst grant . . . Thy pardon to the Ninivites doing penance . . . grant us so to imitate their penance, that we may follow them in obtaining forgiveness."

In Rome, after the ceremony had been completed, a procession was formed and passed through a cemetery where the absolution over the tombs was given. Thence, the procession continued to the Church of St. Sabina, the residence of the Popes during the thirteenth century, and there the Divine Liturgy was celebrated. At present, the blessing and distribution of the ashes take place immediately before the Mass.

The Mass, which was formerly intended to inaugurate the penance of the public penitents, now serves this purpose for all Christians. The Introit is very appropriate and thought-provoking. "Thou hast mercy upon all, O Lord, and hatest none of the things which Thou hast made, overlooking the sins of men for the sake of repentance, and sparing them. . . ." The Collect pertinently asks: "Grant to Thy faithful, O Lord, that they may begin the venerable solemnities of fasting with suitable piety, and perform them with tranquil devotion." Fasting certainly is a venerable practice, having been observed and consecrated by Christ Himself and adopted by the Church from her very beginning.

In the Epistle the Prophet Joel announces the will of God: "Be converted to Me with all your heart, in fasting, and in weeping [sorrow for sins], and in mourning [prayer]. . . . Rend your hearts and not your garments, and turn to the Lord your God; for He is gracious and merciful, patient, . . . and will return and forgive, and leave a blessing behind Him. . . ." The Gradual and Tract are cries for help, mercy, and pardon.

In the Gospel Our Lord Himself explains to us the method of fasting. We should not fast in sadness, complaining like hypocrites seeking their own glory: "When thou fastest, anoint thy head and wash thy face; that thou appear not to men to fast, . . . and thy Father who seeth in secret will repay thee. . . ." Treasures in heaven will be the reward.

The Preface praises God for the benefits He bestows upon those who fast with the proper disposition. We sing: "It is meet and just . . . to give thanks to Thee, Our Lord. . . . Who by bodily fasting dost restrain vices, uplift the mind, bestow virtue and rewards. . . ." The Postcommunion asks: "May the Sacraments we have received, O Lord, afford us support, that our fasts may be pleasing to Thee, and be a healing remedy to us!" On all week-days of Lent a special final prayer is added. It is preceded by the words of the deacon or priest, "Bow your heads to God," and always ask for aid, mercy, and divine favors.

Beginning with Ash Wednesday all daily Masses *de tempore* have their own Gospels and other proper parts. These were all explained to instruct the catechumens and the faithful, but not all can be considered in detail.

Summary

During the Pre-Lenten Period the Church makes great efforts to dispose the people well for a fruitful fast and for the work that must be done in Lent if grace is to come to all souls. All Christians, as well as the catechumens, are to appear on Easter endowed with the New Life brought to man by the Redemption. Although these thoughts are unceasingly dwelt upon by the Liturgy, they are still but little understood by many Christians. All desire to be freed from temporal and spiritual evils, but not all see and adopt the means necessary to obtain the fulfillment of their aspirations.

The three days before Lent are often spent in a manner not conducive to prepare souls for penance. Carnival (*carni vale*, a valedictory to meat which was formerly not eaten until Easter) often goes beyond the bounds of propriety and morality. To make atonement for this, the Church recommends Eucharistic Triduums. Already before the Middle Ages these days brought sorrow to the Church, and the sobering ceremonies of Ash Wednesday were as necessary then as they are today.

Apologetical Notes

In liturgical groups or religious study clubs, the material presented above may suggest the question: "Why does God tolerate evil?" The fact that the Pre-Lenten Liturgy was introduced at a time of great distress might indeed provoke this question. Confining ourselves at present to temporal and physical evils, it may be said that God not merely tolerates them (as He can merely

PREPARATION FOR PENANCE

tolerate sin), but that He wills and sends them for various reasons. This holds true of all wars, and is not confined to any war in particular. However, it must be understood that God does not will the sins of those who are directly or indirectly responsible for the starting of a war. In view of the free will of man (which God, having once given, does not take away), He does not force anyone to do good and permits evils (sin only). He alone can do this, because He alone can use sin to bring about good results at the end. War in itself is not an absolute evil, like sin. It is an evil only if man draws no lesson from it to promote his eternal welfare.

We read in Holy Scripture that the Lord said to Solomon: "If I shut up heaven, and there fall no rain, or if I give orders, and command the locusts to devour the land [crops], or if I send pestilence [war and death] among My people: and My people . . . being converted, shall make supplication to Me, . . . and do penance . . . : then will I hear from heaven, and will forgive their sins, and will heal their land" (II Par., vii, 13-14). These words apply to Christians as well as to the Jews. Therefore, the Church continues to pray in the Litany of All Saints that we may be delivered from all the evils mentioned therein. The best delivery from these plagues would be if God should withhold them, but this would not serve His purpose nor satisfy His love. His desire and purpose is to draw all unto Him.

Among the greatest calamities God sends to mankind are wars, with their natural consequences of death, pestilence, hunger, hatred, poverty, destruction, etc. These afflictions touch the masses, and come upon the sinners and also upon the saints living among them, but for different reasons. These chastisements are aimed at the conversion of sinners, and incite the good to atonement, prayer, and intercession. Hence, all who suffer should benefit by tribulations.

Some complain that scourges come unexpectedly and at a time when everything seems to be in order according to the worldly standards of today. Such a complaint is not justified, because God plainly foretold them and no one can honestly say that they are not deserved. In times like ours in which so much injustice is found in the courts, in commerce and industry, in the home, in social and political life, the pillars of society are crumbling. Faith is waning in lands where the majority are already condemned because they do not believe in Christ as the Son of God. When there is but little private and public morality, when the quest for pleasure and well-being gets out of bounds, when penance is dissolved by dispensation, God has to assert His rights in a way that is felt and understood. When families bring up their children without religion to such a serious extent, and are torn asunder by divorce, desecrated by vice, and no longer sanctified by common Sunday worship, God must and does act.

Preaching that connives at worldly standards and passes over crimes and real evils which may embarrass certain classes, is no longer effective in bringing order into Christian living. Even if preachers should talk and threaten like the prophets of old, a firm belief on the part of the audience is absent. When such situations exist, God will reinforce the courageous preachers by visiting His people with afflictions and great tribulations. There is nothing new under the sun. *Experientia docet!*

In an old tome the writer found a sermon by an unknown preacher whose words are quite to the point at present. He said:

> "The sword of war shall come upon you, because the child is no longer safe in the streets, the home and in its mother's womb. The bridal state is no longer holy; youth is without chastity, and the home is desecrated by vices. Mourning garments shall take the place of robes of joy. Because you sinned in these things, God will cover you as He hid the shame of Adam and Eve.
>
> "Tears shall become your drink and hunger your food, because feasting and drunkenness become your occupation.
>
> "The things of the world enslaved all your energy, but 'thou shalt not have strange gods before Me.' Hearken, Christian soul, and walk in the way of the only true and loving God."

Just because the world does not listen to such undeniable truths and does not act accordingly, tribulations are our lot.

The great penitential season has the objective of bringing souls into union with God or making this union stronger and more perfect. The just also have to bear their crosses—not so much as a punishment for sins, but for the promotion of virtue and its reward. It is not the just who complain about God's ways. The good accept with resignation whatever God deigns to send them. Sinners, who do not realize what it means to love God sincerely, may consider the afflictions of the innocent rather cruel, but true lovers are willing to bring sacrifices for the Beloved. Love is nourished by sacrifices. Many virtues could not be practised without mortifications and self-denial. Fallen mankind needs restraint, whether self-imposed or demanded by God. Christianity cannot show its real strength to pagans except by heroic examples. These also encourage the faint and the weak. In this manner the just help to carry the burden of the sinners, and the just approach nearer to God and draw the others after them.

CHAPTER XV

The Days of Salvation

THE SEASON OF LENT may well be compared with an annual public retreat for all Catholics. The daily instructions are found in the Gospels, Epistles, and Lessons of the Liturgy. There are also special sermons and devotions. Simplicity of food and a more serious penitential and spiritual atmosphere add to the resemblance. Except the restrictions on food, everything affects the young as well as the old. In truly Catholic homes even the children are drawn into the prevailing spirit by the restrictions on music, parties, candies, etc.

Christ Himself is the divine Retreat-Master Who speaks to us by word and example. He enlightens our minds, moves our wills, and supports them by sufficient graces to follow His instructions. The pious observance of Lent in the spirit of the Liturgy will necessarily have a wholesome effect upon the humble Christian soul. Nor will the frequently heard words of Christ, and of the Apostles and prophets announcing the will of God, fail to impress sinners and make them long for forgiveness and open their hearts to grace. The clergy will find new motives for attempting progress in perfection, if they read attentively the words of the Fathers and Doctors of the Church quoted in Matins. The performance of the Lenten Liturgy, if conscientiously and intelligently carried out, ought to move stones!

Hence, the Lenten observance should bring about a reawakening of spiritual life in the whole Church. Everything is directed towards this end. In the larger cities, especially of Europe, following the example of Rome, sermons on the Gospels of the week are preached daily, at least in different churches on different days. There is an increase in attendance at week-day Masses even here and in the reception of Communion. Special devotions

THE DAYS OF SALVATION 163

are held, and a special Oration is said over the people at Mass to obtain a superabundance of God's grace. In some churches mission sermons have been substituted for the powerful Lenten orations. Liturgically speaking, popular missions disturb the Liturgy somewhat, and would fit in better with the harvest season of the Ecclesiastical Year—the last few months before Advent. However, since missions also aim at a reawakening of faith, they may help to achieve the purpose of Lent.

The Church does not exaggerate when she announces the holy season of penance in the words of St. Paul: "Behold, now is the acceptable time; behold, now is the day of salvation" (II Cor., vi, 3). Nothing is lacking to those of good will.

The First Week of Lent

When the beginning of Lent was established on Ash Wednesday, the Liturgy of the First Sunday was not changed. It still is called *initium jejunii*[1] in the Secret, most probably because it really was the first day in Lent on which all Christians were bound to attend the Holy Sacrifice. On this Sunday the Romans assembled in the Church of St. John Lateran (the Basilica of the Saviour, the cathedral of Rome, the mother church of all Christian churches), from whose apse the large mosaic of the Saviour looks down upon the congregation. This congregation was understood to represent the worshippers dispersed all over the earth.

Whilst the clergy entered the sanctuary with subdued solemnity, the choir and the people, including the catechumens, reminded the Saviour pictured before their eyes of His promise announced by the Psalmist: "He shall call upon Me, and I will hear, . . . deliver, . . . and glorify him. . . . He that dwelleth in the aid of the Most High shall abide under the protection of the God of heaven" (Introit). This was confidence-inspiring, and after repeating the cry for mercy the priest prays: "O God, . . . grant to Thy household, that what they strive to obtain from

---
[1] The beginning of fasting.

Thee by abstinence [the purification of their souls] they may secure by good works" (Collect).

St. Paul explains in the Epistle the real meaning of abstinence. Although the Church regulates food as to quality and quantity, it is easily understood that this alone will not bring about the great spiritual renewal that is desired. Those who cannot or need not fast must also attain the benefits of abstinence proclaimed by the Church and the Fathers. Other acts of abstinence and self-denial have already been regulated by the Commandments, which should be still more conscientiously observed during this holy season. The self-denial practised during Lent carries with it the additional merit of obedience, even if a legitimate dispensation from fasting has been obtained.

According to St. Paul, abstinence or penance also includes that we give no offense to anyone, that we practise much patience in tribulations, in necessities, in distresses, in persecutions, in labors, in fastings, in chastity, in long-suffering, in meekness, and in charity, "as sorrowful, yet always rejoicing" (Epistle). Adding to this "much praying," we clearly see that the practices of abstaining from strong drink, dances, dissipations, and other enjoyments that distract from the spirit of penance (practices that in case of necessity may be made substitutes for devotions and special family prayers), have an apostolic origin and are of much greater importance than many Christians today care to believe. But this modern aversion to self-denial does not excuse the preacher from making known the mind of the Church, guided and enlivened by the Holy Ghost.

The Gradual and the long Tract are decidedly encouraging. They are calls of the Beloved Master to repentant souls: "A thousand shall fall at thy side, and ten thousand at thy right hand: but it [evil] shall not come nigh thee. . . . For He hath given His Angels charge over thee, to keep thee in all thy ways" (Ps. xc, 7, 11).

Christ Himself illustrates these truths in the succeeding Gospel. After He had consecrated our Lent by His own forty days' fast, He permitted Himself to be tempted to lust of the flesh, lust of the eyes, and pride of life. In His victory He became a

THE DAYS OF SALVATION 165

model and encouragement to us in resisting all that may tempt us in the world (I John, ii, 16). All we need to do is to cooperate with the grace that is never withheld: "God shall cover thee with His wings. . . . His truth shall be thy shield" (Offertory). We pledge our cooperation whilst offering the Sacrifice at the beginning of Lent, and ask "that, while we restrain our carnal feasting, we may likewise abstain from all hurtful pleasure" (Secret).

The Postcommunion sums up all in the words: "O Lord, purifying us from our old life [of sinfulness] lead us on to fellowship in Thy saving mysteries [by sanctifying grace]."

On Monday of this week the Epistle refers to the great gift of Baptism, and the Gospel to the duties imposed by the reception of this Sacrament. The thought predominant in the Liturgy on Tuesday is: "Seek ye the Lord while He may be found; call upon Him while He is near" (Lesson), as the blind and lame who found Him in the Temple found also faith and health (Gospel). On Wednesday the Liturgy reminded the catechumens of the fact that the Israelites, the chosen and elect, being sinners did not do penance like the Ninivites, and many of them perished. Christ is greater than Solomon, listen to Him. There is mention of Moses, the great lawgiver who received the Ten Commandments from God. Then follows the account of Elias, and the miraculous food that was a type of the Holy Eucharist. On Thursday the Liturgy stresses the injunction to "do penance," and on Friday the living water symbolizing the Word of God is promised as giving everlasting life, if accepted.

The Ember Days in Lent

Before we continue, we may consider the Lenten Ember Days that occur in this week. These days seem to be out of place since they contribute nothing to the observance of Lent. In early times there were only three Ember Weeks during the year, but soon Ember Days were introduced also in the week following Quinquagesima Sunday. Later, when Lent began on Ash Wednesday, these days were transferred to their present position so as not to interfere with the ceremonies which inaugurate the penitential season. Hence the anachronism; but since the end of the fifth century they have served the purpose of final preparation of the candidates for the priesthood and the administration of Holy Orders.

Relative to the ordinandi, the following may be noted. On Wednesday the first scrutiny of the candidates took place in St. Mary Major, where the clerics were placed under the protection of the Mother of the Eternal High Priest. Probably the tonsure was conferred on this occasion. The next scrutiny took place on Friday in the Basilica of the Holy Apostles to insure also their protection and intercession. In this church the great mosaics of the famous deacons, Felicissimus and Agapitus, are especially venerated.

On Ember Saturday the ordinations took place after the Lessons, beginning with the lowest grade. For this occasion the Roman Church gathered around the tomb of St. Peter, the Prince of the Apostles, through whom the spiritual powers flow. The ordinations, however, did not take place on the altar above his tomb, but in one of the chapels, since the main altar is reserved for the consecration of the Pope, the Bishop of Rome. The text of the Mass does not contain any special references to the ordinations.

On the eve of the Sabbath Christ cured the sick man by means of the waters of Bethsaida. We have here a type of Baptism as well as of the tears of Penance, both preparing man for life eternal. The Liturgy of the Saturday endeavors to arouse an ardent desire for the glory of the resurrection from sin and death, and shows what this will mean for us. The night of sin and mortification will pass, and the light of day will shine. The Lessons announce to us how a contract was made between God and His people. The Israelites promised to keep God's laws and the faith in the one true God, and He in turn would bless them in all things. He asked His people to choose between blessing or curse; they would receive what they deserved according to their behavior. The third Lesson tells about the restoration of the ancient Temple, and refers to the miracle when fire came from heaven to enkindle the sacrifice sprinkled with water—a beauti-

THE DAYS OF SALVATION

ful type of the consecration of the temple of the Holy Ghost in our souls by Baptism, or its rededication by Penance. The fourth Lesson inculcates the fear of God, the beginning of wisdom; we must trust in Him. Finally, the Epistle reaches the climax by enjoining: "Pray without ceasing." This is necessary for the leading of a truly Christian life. The Gospel of the Transfiguration was well chosen to picture the change that had taken place in the newly ordained, who celebrated the Liturgy together with the consecrating bishop.

The Ember Saturday ceremonies which formerly began in the evening extended to the early hours of Sunday. On this account there was no other Sunday Mass (*Dominica vacat*). Later on, when in Rome and elsewhere the Liturgy was anticipated on Saturday morning, a Proper of the Mass was composed of parts used on preceding days. The Epistle alone forms an exception. St. Paul speaks to the Thessalonians about the precepts the Lord had given. The Sunday thus presented an occasion to instruct the catechumens about the Commandments and laws of the Church. This instruction would be further impressed by the Gospel, which introduces the lawgivers of both the Old and New Testaments.

The first week of Lent has been considered in some detail, day after day, in order to indicate the richness of thought and of ecclesiastical traditions found in the Liturgy. Much more can be found in the Breviary, Pontifical, Ritual, and St. Augustine's book "De catechizandis rudibus," of which a fine annotated translation has appeared in English.[1] For study clubs, or liturgical or doctrinal circles, such authentic works are recommended as additional sources.

It is not the intention of this writer to enlarge upon all the Sundays and ferials of Lent. This has been done by the authors of the books mentioned in the footnotes. The objective of these chapters is to give a picture of how the Liturgy molds Christian life, if applied to the faithful. For this purpose a selected condensation is sufficient. A more detailed description might become tedious and rather confusing.

---

[1] The Bruce Publishing Company, Milwaukee, Wis.

On all the days of *Quadragesima*[1] the main theme of the Liturgy is the deliverance from sin by Penance for Christians and by Baptism for the catechumens after having received a solid preparation. The explanation of the daily Epistles and Gospels tries to bring about this deliverance. Hence, the preparation of the catechumens serves equally well for those who need a good and fruitful Easter Confession. A change to a better Christian life is thereby assured for all.

In the Oration over the people on the preceding Friday, the aspiration was expressed that the Sacrifice "may preserve the faithful in mind and body." On this Cardinal Schuster makes the appropriate remark: "An exaggerated spiritualism which separates that which God has joined together [body and soul], is as inimical to true piety as sensual materialism."[2] But this danger is not great at present.

From the Third Sunday of Lent to Passion-Tide

The Liturgy for the Third Sunday is pronouncedly catechumenal, as far as the instructional parts are concerned. On this day those who were placed under the protection of St. Lawrence assembled again in his basilica where the Exorcism preparatory to Baptism took place. Entering the church, the congregation sang: "My eyes are ever towards the Lord; for He shall pluck my feet" from the bondage of Satan (Introit). In the Epistle St. Paul warns the catechumens as well as the baptized not to return to the slavery of Satan but to be followers of God, shunning fornication, uncleanness, covetousness, and other vices. "Walk then as children of the light; for the fruit of light is in all goodness" (Ephes., v, 8-9). Avoid all things that separate you from God and destroy love or sanctifying grace; otherwise you have not "any inheritance in the kingdom of Christ." A truly Christian life needs God's help and light, hence the cry: "Arise, O Lord, let not man prevail. To Thee have I lifted up my eyes" (Gradual and Tract).

---
[1] Lent.
[2] "The Sacramentary," vol. II, p. 92.

THE DAYS OF SALVATION

At that time Jesus, noticing the commotion of the people brought about by the driving out of a devil, said to them: "Every kingdom divided against itself shall be brought to desolation. . . . He that is not with Me is against Me" (Gospel). The doctrines expressed about the necessity of union with Christ and His Church were not more important in the early days of schisms and persecution than they are today. Without Christ or His Church there is no salvation.

After reciting the Creed, the faithful give the definite response: "The justices of the Lord are right . . . for Thy servant keepeth them" (Offertory). "O Lord, cleanse away our sins, and hallow the bodies and minds of Thy servants . . ." (Secret). The Christians have found a resting place for their souls. "Blessed are they that dwell in Thy house" (Communion). The catechumens and public sinners will soon enter the Church. The Postcommunion also refers to them: "Mercifully deliver . . . from all guilt and danger those whom Thou dost admit to fellowship in so great a mystery." It should always be kept in mind that the Roman Christians for many centuries knew the liturgical (Latin) language.

On the following Wednesday began the scrutiny of the catechumens who were to be baptized on the eve of Easter. Hence the instructional lessons of the ferial Mass. The second scrutiny took place on the following day, on which the instructions were continued, and the Gospel of Christ and the Samaritan woman was explained.

Lætare Sunday received its name from the opening word of the Introit, expressing joy over the consolation that will come to the Church in the near future. In the early days of the Roman Church the Byzantines celebrated at this time a feast in honor of the Holy Cross, and this was incorporated in the Roman Liturgy. The Station church was the Holy Cross in Jerusalem, a Roman replica of the old church in Jerusalem. A large particle of the True Cross is venerated there. During the Middle Ages the Pope went to this church in a solemn procession, holding a golden rose, which was afterwards sent to a prince or high Roman official. For these reasons some joy is expressed in the vestments and decoration of the altars. In the earliest times the very rigorous fast began on the following day.

The Introit for this Sunday is indeed appropriate: "Rejoice, O Jerusalem, and come together all you that love her; rejoice with joy you that have been in sorrow: that you may exult. . . ." The Church, the *Sancta Jerusalem*, celebrates the Liturgy in Christ's sanctuary, and the Collect asking for consolation in every affliction expects this as a fruit of the Sacrifice.

Equally appropriate is the Epistle of St. Paul, which explains the bondage wherefrom Israel was delivered through the Cross. "Brethren, we are not children of the bondage, but of the free; by the freedom wherewith Christ hath made us free." The Gradual and Tract exhort all to rejoice.

The fast being suspended on Sundays (but not the abstinence in those days), the Gospel relates the feeding of the multitude. This event had also catechetical value for instructing the catechumens about the Holy Eucharist. On account of the ancient secret discipline, this mystery was reserved for the last weeks before Baptism. A praise to the Lord for all He did for us, is expressed in the Offertory.

The Communion refers again to Jerusalem, but the Postcommunion seems to have in mind the Eucharistic instruction: "Grant . . . that we may treat with increased homage, and receive with faithful minds, the holy mysteries with which we are continually fed. . . ."

On the following Saturday the *aperitio aurium* of the elected catechumens took place. It was a long rite, a condensation of which is still found in the baptismal rite for adults. The whole Proper of the Mass is inspired by Baptism. During the Liturgy the Apostles' Creed and the Our Father were once more explained and rehearsed. It took place in the Station Church of St. Paul, the great catechumen and convert. On Friday the Sacrament of Penance was explained, and on Saturday the inner light or grace was the topic. The liturgical texts of these days fit the occasions.

Passion-Tide

Passing over minor details, although some of them are very interesting, we arrive at the last part of Lent preceding the Triduum before Easter. After having fought the battle against sin during Lent, the Church turns to Him Who died for the remission of sins. The center of the Liturgy is the Cross, emphasized by being veiled. The Christian must learn and more or less experience the mystery of the Cross, of his own as well as that of Christ: "In cruce salus."[1] The tribulations of life must contribute to our own glorious resurrection. In other words, the Christian goes in company of the Church with Christ to die with Him in a mystical manner.

The Station church is that of St. Peter, the sanctuary of the first Vicar of Christ, who was crucified (like his Master) on a spot where Pope Symmachus later built a church called *Sancta Hierusalem*. The text of the Mass formula is dedicated to the bloody sacrifice on Mount Calvary. At its beginning Christ appeals to His Father: "Judge Me, O God, and decide My cause against an ungodly nation: . . . let them lead Me and bring Me unto Thy holy hill . . ." (Introit). Inspired by these thoughts, the Collect prays: "Graciously regard Thy household that bodily they may be ruled by Thy bounty, and spiritually be guarded by Thy keeping." In other words, may God, moved by Christ's sacrifice, take care of the physical as well as the spiritual welfare of man, because both soul and body are destined for a glorious reunion after the resurrection of the body!

In the Epistle St. Paul pictures Christ as the High-Priest who enters to sacrifice, not as the sinful high-priests of the Jews (who cleansed themselves and the people by the blood of animals), but as the Innocent and Just One, Who by His own blood purified and redeemed mankind once and forever. It was no easy task, and the Church makes the Redeemer cry: "Deliver Me, O Lord, from Mine enemies. Teach Me to do Thy will." The will of the Father Christ accepted in the Garden of Olives: "Thou shalt lift Me up above those that rise against Me" (Gradual).

---
[1] "In the Cross there is salvation."

"Many a time have they afflicted Me, . . . yet they have not prevailed against Me" (Tract).

The Gospel furnishes an example of the afflictions heaped upon Christ by the Jews: "They took up stones to cast at Him: but Jesus hid Himself and went out of the temple." He separated Himself from the Synagogue and turned towards the Church of the New Dispensation. He will conquer at the end: "I will confess to Thee, O Lord, . . . I shall live . . . ; enliven Me according to Thy words" (Offertory). The Church confesses her faith in the Creed, and since the Mystical Body as a whole benefits by the Passion and death of the Head, so may each individual obtain freedom from the bonds of sin and the gifts of God's mercy (Secret).

Our hope is the Cross on which Christ conquered Satan and brought salvation and life to those who were dead in sin. "It is truly meet and just we should render unceasing thanks and praise to Him on earth and in heaven" (Preface).

The Holy Mass is a commemoration of the Passion, and to this the Communion refers: "This is My body. . . . This is My blood." May the sacrifice of both be not in vain: "Defend [O God] with continual support those whom Thou hast refreshed with Thy mysteries" (Postcommunion).

However, a superabundance of grace obtained by frequent or even daily Mass and Communion is of no avail unless the recipient cooperates. On this matter Cardinal Schuster remarks:

> "One of the greatest evils of the time is the want of spiritual vigor, which makes even preachers hesitate sometimes to declare to this frivolous generation how wide a gulf lies between the doctrine of Christ and the aims of the worldly minded. Even the faithful demand mitigations of the rules of the Church and compromises which often end by obscuring the Gospel teaching. . . . It would appear that it is no longer Christianity which is to convert the world, but the world which is fashioning Christianity after its own heart. Yet, Our Lord and His martyrs for our sake did not hesitate to declare the Gospel [of the Cross] in all its fullness, though they knew that for so doing they would incur the penalty of death."[1]

---

[1] "The Sacramentary," vol. II, p. 148.

THE DAYS OF SALVATION 173

During the following week the Passion of Christ and His Mystical Body are constantly emphasized, whilst the catechetical instructions on the Sacraments continue. On Friday the Sorrowful Mother also is remembered. Since she, the Mother of the Redeemer and all Christians, is also a type of the Church and Baptism, Mary could not well be passed over in silence. She remained with Christ in faith and presence until the end. In this regard Pope Pius XII states:

> "Free from all sin, original and personal, always most intimately united with her Son, as another Eve, she [Mary] offered Him on Golgatha to the Eternal Father for all the children of Adam, sinstained by his fall, and her mother's rights and mother's love were included in the holocaust. Thus she, who corporally was the mother of our head, through the added title of pain and glory, became spiritually the mother of all His members." [1]

Palm Sunday

Palm Sunday is the only one of the first four days of Holy Week that brings any great change in the Liturgy.

What was foretold by the prophets about the Messiah is now recalled as historical facts. A beginning is made on Palm Sunday with the dramatization of Christ's solemn entry into Jerusalem, as represented by the blessing of palms and the solemn procession. This rite came to us from liturgical exercises that were not followed by a Mass. Such rites or ceremonies were quite frequent among the Jews of the diaspora, who could not offer sacrifices outside the Temple, and whom the early Christians imitated in certain of their rites. Another outstanding type of this kind of ceremony is found in the Liturgy of Good Friday.

The great world drama of the crucifixion of the God-Man begins with His solemn entry into Jerusalem, when He was hailed with the words: "Hosanna to the Son of David. Blessed is He that cometh in the name of the Lord. O King of Israel: Hosanna in the highest." These words are now repeated by the Christians as representing the Gentiles. The Romans considered the

---
[1] "Mystici Corporis," June 29, 1943.

Church of St. Sylvester (where the blessing of palms and the reading of the Collect took place) as the Garden of Olives, and from there the procession moved to the Lateran. Seated in the square before the latter church, the Pope distributed the palms to the clergy, who in turn handed them to the people. Thereafter, the procession preceded by the clergy and the Pope entered the basilica, which had remained closed until the deacon carrying the processional cross gave the sign to open the doors. Apart from the outdoor ceremonies, all was much as it is today.

The blessing of the palms as performed at present is very solemn. After the singing of the Antiphon quoted above, the following Oration asks that God may grant us His "ineffable grace: and since through the death of Thy Son Thou hast given us hope of what we believe, make us through His resurrection arrive whither we are journeying."

The Lesson, taken from Exodus, refers to seventy palms under which the Jews rested in the desert, and relates how they murmured against Moses and Aaron. The Gradual reminds us of the conspiracy of the chief priests and Pharisees, who wanted to remove Christ from their midst. "But one of them . . . prophesied saying: It is expedient for you that one man should die for the people, and that the whole nation perish not." The Gospel relates the historical event now being dramatized, and, after an Oration modelled after the Secret of a Mass, a Preface and four Orations follow. These hallowing prayers are very beautiful, explaining the symbolism of the exercises in progress and of the mysteries they recall. They deserve a thoughtful reading.

The blessing of the palms having been concluded, the deacon calls out: "Let us go forth in peace." To this the people respond: "In the name of the Lord. Amen." The procession that now follows commemorates and reproduces the historical entry of Our Lord into Jerusalem. It was in some respects like the ordinary Station processions but, instead of the usual Litany, pertinent passages from the Gospel were sung and the clergy preceded, instead of followed, the people. The knocking at the door of the Lateran Basilica was the sign to open it in order that all might enter who bore the blessed palms in their hands and sang appro-

THE DAYS OF SALVATION 175

priate hymns and responses. This rite, too, deserves a thoughtful private reading in order to fathom and experience its significance and beauty. It expresses in different words and forms the victory of Christ over death.

The text of the Mass already refers to Easter, because He Who died for our sins rose to life for our justification. In fact, all Holy Week beginning with this Sunday was formerly called *hebdomeda paschalis*, because during this week Christ, our Paschal Lamb, was immolated.

In view of His approaching Crucifixion, the Saviour begins His sacrifice with the cry: "O Lord, remove not Thy help to a distance from Me; look towards My defense." (Introit). The Collect asks that we may imitate the patience of Christ, and have a share in His Resurrection. In the Epistle St. Paul describes the humility and obedience of Jesus, Who carried out the will of His Father, Who in turn "hath exalted Him, and given Him a name . . . [at which] every knee should bend, of those that are in heaven, on earth, and under the earth." The Gradual expresses the confidence of Christ in His Father: "Thou hast held Me by My right hand, and guided Me according to Thy will, and received Me to glory." The Tract reiterates the assertion that, notwithstanding the temporary victory of enemies over the Saviour, He will triumph and be glorified at the end.

The Passion of Our Lord according to St. Matthew takes the place of the Sunday Gospel, which had been previously read during the blessing of palms. In view of His Passion, the Saviour exclaims: "I looked for some one to take pity on Me, and there was none." The disciples had fled, and the women, like so many Christians after them, stood afar off. All the consolation He received was: "They gave Me also gall for my food, and in My thirst they gave Me vinegar to drink" (Offertory). The Secret asks for the grace of devotion and a happy eternity as a fruit of the sacrifice.

In the Communion Christ, speaking for Himself and His Mystical Body, asserts: "Father, if this chalice may not pass away, but I must drink it, Thy will be done." The Postcommunion asks for the disposition and strength to imitate Him. We simply must carry out the will of God, as Christ did; otherwise, our desire to share in His glory cannot be realized.

During the following three days the Church continues to consider the Passion. It is again read on Tuesday (Gospel of St. Mark) and Wednesday (Gospel of St. Luke) and the prayer over the people on Wednesday constitutes the Oration of the Divine Office until Holy Saturday at None inclusively.

Reflection

One cannot read the ancient but ever fresh liturgical forms and texts without admiring the understanding participation of the old Roman Christians. Much of this life with the Church still prevails, but it is beginning to wane and is practically unknown in English-speaking countries. This is unfortunate. If priest and people would drink from the clear fountain of the Liturgy more often, much of the prevailing religious ignorance, shallowness, and superficiality in word and thought would disappear, and with them much unbecoming behavior. Christians would once more realize the great difference that should exist between them and the pagans. The Liturgy, if studied, will point out to Christians the life-stream of the Mystical Body in which they are incorporated, and which should pulsate in the veins of everyone who is baptized. "Incorporetur ut vivificetur" [1] (St. Augustine). Hence the great care which the Church bestows upon the preparation of the catechumens and the reclamation of sinners during this holy season.

---

[1] "Let one be incorporated in order to be vivified."

CHAPTER XVI

Life through Death

"OUR EASTER LAMB is slain but will live again." Such is the constantly recurring theme of the solemn Triduum preceding the Feast of the Resurrection. It is applied to Christ's Mystical Body, to souls individually and collectively. Step by step the drama of the Passion is unfolded until it reaches a glorious climax: "Sepulchrum ejus erit gloriosum."[1] This applies also to the catechumens, who, buried in the waters of Baptism, rise to a new life in Christ. The antitheses occurring in the Liturgy of these three days are more frequent and consequential than at any other period of the Liturgical Year, but they are rarely explained to the faithful unless they are made the topics of a course of Lenten sermons. On the days themselves there is but little time for lengthy sermons, except perhaps during a Three Hours' service on Good Friday.

Yet, the Resurrection of Christ with its antecedent events is the foundation of our holy Faith, just as Baptism is our inauguration into the Christian life and final salvation. Active faith and charity are the essentials that will secure for us a glorious resurrection. On the Paschal Days Christ provides us with the means to live up to what they demand. He infuses faith by Baptism, strengthens it in Confirmation, and then furnishes an uncontrovertible basis for that faith by His Resurrection. This faith He nourishes by the Holy Eucharist. Charity also is infused by Baptism, and strengthened by Confirmation. It is restored by Penance. To preserve this charity, Christ likewise gave a new commandment, that we love one another as He loved us.

These are the Paschal mysteries, the transition from the Old to

---
[1] "His sepulchre will be glorious."

the New Dispensation, inaugurated and validated by the death of the Testator, but prepared beforehand. All these considerations establish within us a firm hope and confidence that we shall reach our own glorious resurrection: "In all things you are made rich in Him . . . , so that nothing is wanting to you in any grace" (I Cor., i, 4, 7). But, as we are reminded on entering the Passion with Christ, good will on our part is necessary: "Peace to men of good will" (Gloria on Maundy Thursday).

Maundy Thursday

Maundy Thursday commemorates the Last Supper, which immediately preceded the beginning of the Passion. Before withdrawing His physical presence by dying on the Cross, Christ gave Himself sacramentally in the Holy Eucharist to be with us until the end of time. This was His testament, to become effective after His Resurrection (Mark, xiv, 25).

The three Masses which were formerly celebrated in the Lateran (for many centuries the official residence of the Popes) are now condensed into one. The first Mass, celebrated in connection with the reconciliation of public penitents, was discontinued when public penances were no longer imposed, and the third Mass (during which the holy oils were blessed) was eliminated centuries ago and the blessings performed at this Mass were added to the second. Consequently, the former second Mass commemorating the institution of the Holy Eucharist is the only Mass celebrated today. The Liturgy of Maundy Thursday, although greatly simplified, is nevertheless still rich in thoughts and ceremonies. We shall consider it as it is celebrated in Rome and in cathedral churches, although we cannot enter into minor details.

Matins and Lauds having been anticipated on the evening of the previous day and the Hours having been recited, the Mass begins. The same order is observed as on the two following days.

The Introit announces solemnly: "But it behoves us to glory in the cross of our Lord Jesus Christ, in Whom are our salvation, life, and resurrection. . . ." Christians should no longer fear and despise the Cross, which is veiled in white during the Mass. Before the Redemption it was a sign of ignominy, but in the New Dispensation it has become the instrument to bring about our glorification. The Gloria is sung, not only to give a festive note to the celebration, but also because of the references it makes to the Lamb Who takes away our sins and to the peace that will come to men of good will. Christ delivered Himself for us and we must show our good will by delivering ourselves to Him in co-suffering; otherwise we shall not share the peace of His Resurrection. After the Gloria, the bells are no longer sounded until the Resurrection is announced.

In the Collect we find an allusion to the former absolution of public penitents and its effect. Judas, not asking for mercy, received the punishment for sin, whereas the thief crucified with Jesus, acknowledging and deploring his sins, received the kingdom of heaven as a reward. This introduces a serious note into the Mass.

In the Epistle (I Cor., xi, 20-32) St. Paul clearly shows that the first Christians were not all perfect nor all spiritual-minded. Baptism had cleansed them from sin and its guilt, but not from the consequences of sin—a darkened intellect and a weakened will. Abuses crept in among them. In those days the faithful gathered for three purposes in any suitable hall: to receive religious instructions, to attend the *agape* or charity meal, and to celebrate the Liturgy. As a rule, the *agape* preceded the other functions. For this charity dinner, held in the evening, the wealthier Christians brought food to be placed before the poor, who usually came after the completion of their work. The poor could not always arrive at the time appointed, and, instead of waiting for them, the donors themselves consumed the food and drink and not much was left for the needy. Since love and charity had brought them together, the Apostle criticized this lack of charity and wrote: "My brethren, when you come to eat, wait for one another" (verse 33): otherwise you scandalize the needy. This, and the excessive eating and drinking on the part of some, was not a proper preparation for the Mass to follow after midnight—for the divine banquet of love at which Christ gave Himself as the food for our souls.

St. Paul describes the institution of the Holy Eucharist by Christ as he had received it from the Lord. The power to change bread and wine into the Body and Blood of Christ was given to the Apostles and their successors at the Last Supper. From the transubstantiation and the subsequent Real Presence, he draws the evident conclusion that it is a sacrilege to receive Holy Communion in the state of mortal sin. This Epistle, also read on the Feast of Corpus Christi, is admirably chosen. It reminds us not only of the washing of the feet performed after the charity meal, but also of the fact that an unworthy communicant acts like Judas (who delivered Christ into the hands of His enemies), by forcing Christ into a sinful soul and body. Judas was not an Apostle in the full sense of the word, although he was one of the twelve chosen for this office; he did not receive the divine mission given to the Apostles on Easter Sunday.

The Gradual furnishes the first part of the final Antiphon recited at all the Hours: "Christus factus est obediens. . . ." The reference is to the willingness to accept the Passion and death which Christ expressed in the Garden of Olives.

The Gospel, which is also used in the antiphons during the washing of the feet with explanatory additions from Christ's last prayer, commemorates the betrayal of Judas and the love of the Saviour. He commands that all should imitate the fraternal love shown by His example. More will be said on this point when we consider the *Mandatum*. Here we emphasize merely the purity of conscience and the charitable disposition required for receiving Holy Communion worthily.

The Offertory of this last Mass celebrated before the Resurrection is self-explanatory. "The right hand of the Lord hath wrought strength [in the Garden], the right hand of the Lord hath exalted Me [on the Cross]. I shall not die [forever], but live [again], and declare the works of the Lord." These words are very consoling in view of what is to follow.

The Secret—as also the *Communicantes, Hanc igitur*, and *Qui pridie*—emphasizes by insertions that on this very day the Holy Eucharist was instituted.

Towards the end of the Canon, before the *Per quem hæc omnia*, the *Oleum infirmorum* was blessed with the formula found in the Pontifical. Formerly the faithful brought small vials with oil to the altar railing to be blessed and taken home. Between the Communion of the celebrating Pope or bishop and that of the clergy, the Holy Chrism and the *Oleum catechumenorum* were blessed with the beautiful ritual also found in the Pontifical. It is too long and too rich in thought to be considered here. After the Liturgy was completed, the priests who had received their Easter Communion at this Mass, took a supply of the holy oils along for use in their parish churches. This practice is followed in the cathedrals of today. On this day, therefore, all that was needed for the sick and the administration of Baptism and Confirmation was provided.

The Communion prayer refers to the love of Christ shown by the washing of the feet of His Apostles. The Postcommunion refers to the Easter Communion received by the clergy and faithful.

Since the next Mass would not be celebrated until the morning of the day of the Resurrection, a second Host is consecrated for consumption after the ceremonies on Good Friday. This Host is carried in solemn procession to a decorated side-altar for the adoration of the faithful until the next morning.

On this Thursday and the following day Vespers begin significantly with the Antiphon, "I will take the chalice of salvation," which is recited immediately after the Mass. Thereafter, the stripping of the altars takes place, leaving them without beauty and coverings and thus symbolizing Christ, the Man of Sorrows: "Diviserunt vestimenta mea" (Antiphon).

At a convenient time before Matins, a meal was given by the Pope or bishop to some poor men, after which the *Mandatum*, or washing of feet, took place. The rite is simple but very beautiful and significant. It deserves a reading in full, but the main and always recurring thoughts are: "I have given you a new commandment: that you love one another, as I have loved you, says the Lord. In this all shall know that you are My disciples, if you have love for one another. . . . Let these three, faith, hope, and charity remain in you: but the greatest of these is charity. . . . Where charity and love are, there is God. The love of Christ has gathered us together. . . . Let us fear and love the living God, and let us love one another with a sincere heart. . . . When therefore we are assembled, . . . let Christ our God dwell among us." After the *Pater noster* has been recited, the concluding prayer asks: "O Lord, we beseech Thee, . . . that as here the outward stains are washed away by us and from us, so inward sins of us all may be blotted out by Thee." Once this supplication has been granted, charity or sanctifying grace will permeate and elevate all. This prayer is certainly a glorious prelude to the blessing of baptismal water soon to take place.

Before proceeding further, we may point out a number of the antitheses presented in the Liturgy of Maundy Thursday. (1) At the very time when the Jewish leaders were planning to remove Jesus from among the people, Our Lord instituted a means by which He would remain with His own until the end of time. (2) Surrounded by the hatred of the Synagogue, Jesus gave a new law and an unparalleled example of His love. (3) Although oppressed at the thought of the approaching Passion and death, He gladly acquiesced in the will of the Father—for the sake of those who were the cause of all His suffering. (4) Showing Himself as the Omnipotent by casting to the ground the soldiers who came to arrest Him, He immediately thereafter gave Himself seemingly helpless into their hands. (5) A sign of friendship, a kiss, inaugurated the Passion and death, which were the greatest expressions of His love for friends and enemies.

Today's Liturgy includes only a few small parts of Christ's farewell address and high-priestly prayer, which is the most sublime and inspiring passage in all the Scriptures (John, xiv-xvii). Forgetting His own worries, Jesus addresses His Apostles: "Let not your heart be troubled," because He will be with them. A new commandment is given as the most important of all: fraternal love. Whatever we shall ask God in His name, He will do for us. He will send the Holy Ghost to comfort and teach us.

LIFE THROUGH DEATH 183

He will manifest Himself in those that love Him by keeping His commandments. He is the vine and we are the branches; separated from Him, we cannot have life nor bring forth fruit. He tells His disciples that, although they are in the world, they should not live according to the world. Finally, He predicts His Resurrection and Ascension—His victory over the enemies who would continue to persecute His disciples. But in Him and through Him His followers shall conquer with Him. Sublime words and thoughts, but unfortunately too often forgotten.

Good Friday

On Good Friday Christ, our innocent Paschal Lamb, was slain, and dying He brought life to all who believe in Him and follow Him. In harmony with the words of Christ, "It cannot be that a prophet perish, out of Jerusalem" (Luke, xiii, 33), the ceremonies on this day were performed in the Basilica of the Holy Cross in Jerusalem. Accompanied by the assembled faithful, the Pope walked barefoot from the Lateran to this Station church, swinging a censer before a relic of the True Cross carried in the procession. This Friday and Saturday were originally aliturgical (without distinctly liturgical worship), and continued so in the early centuries of Christianity. On this particular day, Good Friday, the Eternal High-Priest had offered Himself as a bloody sacrifice once for all. On the aliturgical days on which no Mass was offered, only the Psalter was recited at the usual hours and a synaxis took place in the evening. The synaxis was a religious service consisting in the reading and explaining of passages of Holy Scripture and the recitation of prayers or a litany. So it remained for many centuries.

The ceremonies of Good Friday, somewhat improperly called the *Mass* of the Presanctified, consist in the very ancient synaxis, the Adoration of the Cross, and the Communion service.

The first part of the ceremonies furnishes the finest example of an ancient synaxis retained in the Missal of today. It was already in use in the second century. There is no Introit nor Kyrie, but the celebrant and deacons prostrate themselves before the altar to make a private preparation. This was always done until Pope Celestine introduced the singing of verses and recitation of antiphons.

The Liturgy starts with the reading of a passage from Osee (chapter vi), referring to death and resurrection: "In their affliction [caused by the death of Christ] they will rise early to me. Come, let us return to the Lord; . . . He will strike and He will cure us. He will revive us after two days; on the third day He will raise us up, and we shall live in His sight." Very appropriate thoughts, applicable to Christ as well as to the catechumens! The Lesson is followed by a Tract from Habacuc, iii: ". . . In the midst of two animals [thieves] Thou shalt be made known; when the years shall draw nigh, Thou shalt be known; when the time shall come [Easter], Thou shalt be manifested. . . ." The Oration that follows is the same as that recited on Maundy Thursday, and recalls the difference between the fate of Judas and that of the repentant thief dying with Jesus. The Lesson was explained either before or after this prayer.

The second Lesson from the Old Testament is taken from Exodus, xii. It instructs the Israelites regarding the preparation and consumption of the paschal lamb: "It shall be a lamb without blemish, a male of one year. . . . They shall eat the flesh that night roasted at the fire, and unleavened bread, with wild lettuce. . . . There shall not remain anything of it until morning. . . . Thus you shall eat it: you shall gird your reins, and you shall have shoes on your feet, holding staves in your hands, for it is the Phase (that is, the Passage) of the Lord."

The Tract, taken from the Messianic Psalm cxxxix, refers to the treatment of Christ by His enemies, and contains the petitions: "O Lord, . . . overshadow my head in the day of battle. . . . Do not Thou forsake me." These verses anticipated what happened when Christ was dying on the Cross. The texts so far considered, except the Oration, may well have been taken over from the Synagogue, and hence their very early introduction into the Liturgy of the Church.

Logically, the description of the Passion and death of the true Easter Lamb introducing the New Dispensation follows immedi-

LIFE THROUGH DEATH 185

ately. For this day a portion of the Gospel according to St. John (chapter xviii) was selected. It is shorter than the three other accounts of the Passion, but it mentions incidents not related by the Synoptics. Among these are the commendation of Mary to John and of John to Our Lady, and the opening of the Sacred Heart by a lance. The catechesis following the narrative was concluded by the prayer service at which the catechumens were present.

Prayers in the form of litanies were undoubtedly taken over from the Synagogue at a very early date. St. Justin Martyr already mentions them, but the formula of the present prayers seems to have been prepared by order of Pope Leo the Great, as the special petitions and the wording indicate. It may be mentioned that the classes enumerated in the third petition as confessors, virgins, and widows signified at that time monks, consecrated virgins, and widows who had dedicated themselves to works of mercy, to the instruction of women, and to what is now called Catholic Action. The fourth petition and prayer for the Roman Emperor has been eliminated, although it is found in some of the older Missals still in use. The Eastern Rites still have such litanies in every Liturgy.

Our modern litanies were undoubtedly suggested by the ancient ones, and developed and became popular in the course of time. But there is no reason why the great Litany of Good Friday should not be used in the vernacular at public and private devotions. Its very text would bring us fifteen centuries nearer to the time of Christ. In fact, the whole first part of the Good Friday Liturgy might well be used at the beginning of the Three Hours' service in the vernacular, and the second part might similarly be used as a fitting conclusion. In between there would be plenty of time to speak and meditate on the Passion and to sing appropriate hymns. This procedure certainly would be no innovation in a liturgical sense. Rome does not start anything in the way of popular devotions, but approves of them after they have proved beneficial for the spiritual life of the faithful. The public recitation of the great Litany and other prayers would be greatly facilitated by the fact that many people already have the text in the widely distributed Holy Week books. It would certainly be worth a trial, and no fear of sentimentality need be entertained.

As in other ancient synaxes, the offering of gifts and their consumption should follow here as they did in the beginning. However, in the course of time the Adoration of the Cross, a separate ceremony, was inserted here, and fits in very well. First brought from Jerusalem to Constantinople and extended then to Rome, this ceremony was inserted in the Liturgy of Good Friday by Pope Sergius I, who himself came from the East. In the ninth century the ceremony had already spread widely, and was greatly amplified by the insertion of hymns and antiphons. The use of Greek invocations during the Reproaches may also commemorate its introduction by way of Byzantium.

Originally, the ceremonies were performed with a particle of the True Cross, but because such particles were not readily available everywhere, a crucifix of wood or metal was substituted and the unveiling arranged accordingly. The Veneration of the Cross, as performed barefoot by the clergy, is a reminder of the earliest procession held on this day in Rome.

The text found in the Missal needs no special explanation. In case the Veneration of the Cross is used at the close of a Three Hours' devotion, a particle of the Cross enshrined in a small ostensorium could be placed between two burning candles on an altar in which the Blessed Sacrament is not preserved, and finally be presented to the faithful to kiss. During this ceremony parts of the Reproaches might be sung. Either before or after the Veneration of the Cross, the blessing with the particle could be bestowed according to the approved rite. The relic could remain exposed between burning candles until the time of Matins.

The third part of the ancient ceremonies begins with the bringing of the offerings to the altar. But on this day not the usual offerings of food to be consumed at an *agape* are brought, but the greatest gift, Christ Himself as given to us on the day before, is brought to the altar in a solemn although somewhat mournful procession. It is a memorial of the death of Christ, as

LIFE THROUGH DEATH 187

the Hymn to the Cross, "Vexilla Regis," clearly indicates. On this day the Host is consumed by the celebrant alone.

The Sacred Host having been placed on the altar and incensed, the ceremonies move swiftly to the end. Wine and water are poured into the chalice, the altar is incensed as usual, the hands are washed, the *Orate Fratres* said, and the *Pater noster* and *Libera nos* recited in a clear voice. The Host is then divided and consumed, and the ceremonies close with the *Quod ore sumpsimus*. Having left the altar, the clergy recite the Vespers in choir or privately, and the altar is stripped of its cloths.

Holy Saturday

The Liturgy of the Vigil of Easter celebrated on Holy Saturday consists of three distinct but connected elements. The first part concludes with the *Exultet,* and the second with the baptism and confirmation of the catechumens; the third part is the Mass, to which the Litany of All Saints forms the transition and introduction.

The historic development of this Liturgy is very interesting. Here it should be remembered that on this Saturday, like on many others, there were originally no liturgical functions until the evening. It was the most quiet day of the Ecclesiastical Year. This calm was inspired by the resting of Christ in the tomb before the creation of a new spiritual world, as God had rested on the Sabbath Day after having created the old world which was changed with the Resurrection. But after sun-down the ceremonies multiplied.

The blessing of fire and light is of very ancient origin. Ever since God spoke the words, "Let there be light," and made the rainbow appear in confirmation of the promise given to Noe not to destroy mankind again, the pre-Judaic people used fire and light at their sacrifices. Ever since God appeared to Moses in a burning thornbush and established the manner of worship in the tabernacle, fire was brought and the seven-branch candlestick lit for the evening sacrifice. From this practice, fire and light entered into the Church, not only because Christ had said "I am the light of the world" and "I have come to bring fire upon the earth," but also on account of the purifying character of fire and of the darkness-dispelling symbolism.

When the Church took over the ancient rite, she gave it a Christian interpretation and substituted wax for animals. So the ceremony received a place in the Evening Liturgy of Holy Saturday. The *Eucharistia lucernaris*, as this part was called, has been mentioned by the earliest Christian writers. The name may have been inspired by the words of St. John, "Lucerna ejus est agnus" (Apoc., xxi, 23), meaning that the Lamb is the Lamp of the City of God and His Church. The ceremony, although celebrated in many places, was not made a part of the celebration of the Easter Vigil until the fifth century; in time, it was widely solemnized.

The rite as celebrated today begins with the blessing of fire. Originally the fire was blessed in the tomb of the Saviour in Jerusalem, and carried thence into the church. Now the fire is blessed outside the church or in the portico. The blessing of incense and light follows immediately, because these were used at the evening services of Jews as well as Christians. Arriving in the church, a triple candle carried by the deacon is lit, and the words *Lumen Christi* are sung. This is repeated three times, each succeeding intonation being made on a higher note. After the procession has arrived in the sanctuary, the offering of light and wax takes place in the form of a beautiful Preface, which will well repay a studious reading.

The large Easter candle around which the ceremonies are performed is blessed by the deacon. Formerly the candle bringing the light into the Lateran Church was broken into small pieces after the light service, and these pieces, distributed as "Agnus Dei," were highly prized by women as a protection from the dangers of childbirth. At present the blessing of these "Agnus Dei" is reserved to the Pope. Leo XIII composed a beautiful ode on the meaning and significance of the "Agnus Dei," as expressed in the formula for blessing them. Besides the aid in childbirth suggested by the symbolism of the tomb compared with the womb, the ode enumerates the following: "It shields from lightning and every harm; . . . it breaks the bonds of sin, and wars against the powers of darkness; . . . it gives grace to those who are worthy of it and quenches the fires of passions. Worn with devotion, it saves from perils of the sea, preserves from sudden death and from Satan's snares. He who holds it in honor shall triumph over his enemies, and a small portion of the 'Agnus Dei' shall have as much power as the whole. Lamb of God, have mercy on me. . . ."[1] This portion was quoted with permission, because neither the formula of blessing nor the ode is easily found in local libraries.

The second part of the rite on the Vigil of Easter consists in a final instruction of the catechumens, followed by the blessing of baptismal water and the administration of Baptism and Confirmation. It is a very long service even without the instructions following the Lessons and the baptismal rite for adults, which are now usually omitted. A study of the significance of the ceremonies, text, and what they express, will richly repay the student. The main points have been mentioned in an earlier chapter,[2] and some details regarding the Sacraments will follow later.

The third part of the Vigil Liturgy consists of the Mass. Formerly, owing to the length of the preceding evening services, the Mass could be celebrated during the early hours of Easter Sunday, but it is now anticipated on Saturday morning. The Litany of All Saints takes the place of the Introit and Kyrie in this Mass. The Mass proper begins with the Collect, as all early Station Masses did. Later on, the Psalm "Judica" was inserted. At this Mass the catechumens received their First Communion, and the short Vespers takes the place of the usual thanksgiving and conclusion (Postcommunion, etc.).

Since Easter has at present a Mass of its own, the Vigil Mass may well be referred to Christ as the archetype of catechumens and penitents rising from the death of sin; like Christ, both these have entered on a new life. As such, the symbolism pertains year after year to the Resurrection of Christ and His Mystical Body, the Church. Coming at the end of Lent, the Vigil not only commemorates an historical event, but is itself a recurring grace-giving mystery. The Collect, therefore, asks: "Preserve in the

---

[1] Schuster, "The Sacramentary," vol. II, p. 224.   [2] Chapter IV.

new children of Thy family [the baptized and converted] the spirit of adoption which Thou hast given [or renewed]: that being renewed in body and soul, they may give Thee a pure service." All is summed up in the prayer after the Communion, which asks "that those whom Thou hast replenished by the Paschal Sacraments may live in concord," with God, their neighbors, and themselves. The catechumens are expressly recalled in the *Hanc igitur* throughout the following week.

Reflection

In her Liturgy the Church, like her Divine Founder and Head, teaches through parables. She is the woman mixing leaven with the meal until mankind is leavened (Matt., xiii, 33). Having ground and prepared the *frumentum Christi* by penance, doctrine, and grace, she expects the whole mass to rise and to turn into good and palatable bread. But leaven, although it makes the meal sour, does not make it rise and expand unless a certain temperature is maintained. It is similar in the spiritual realm. Even though constantly instructed and replenished with grace, the Christian will not easily cooperate and live up to his baptism unless he cultivates some warmth or fervor. This temperature the Liturgy aims to supply. A fundamental knowledge of the significance of the Liturgy will bring about a favorable atmosphere. It will also supply the motives for dispelling the material frost, and, with the help of grace, will turn Christians into one bread, one body, and one Kingdom of God.

This is not pious sentimentality. Whence does the coolness and lack of fervor prevailing in many practising Catholics come? How can such a surprising worldliness and materialism exist alongside the frequent reception of the Sacraments and the daily celebration of Mass? One reason is because so many Catholics no longer live *with* the Church, and thereby fail to make the mysteries of religion their very own. "The declaration of Thy words giveth light: and giveth understanding to little ones" (Ps. cxviii, 130). This is equally true with regard to the lessons contained in the Liturgy and applied by the Church.

CHAPTER XVII

A New Life in Christ

EASTER IS THE CENTER of the liturgical cycle and also the principal mystery influencing Christian life. Advent, Christmas, and the Passion and death of Our Lord receive their full meaning only as a preparation for the Resurrection. All that follows—e.g., the Ascension, the Mission of the Holy Ghost, and the formation of the Mystical Body of Christ—rests upon the Resurrection as its foundation and corner-stone. St. Paul expresses this clearly and absolutely when he writes: "If Christ be not risen again, then is our preaching vain, and your faith is also vain" (I Cor., xv, 14). And again: "You are built upon . . . Jesus Christ Himself . . . the chief corner stone" (Eph., ii, 20). So it was promised and so it happened. "The stone which was rejected by . . . the builders . . . is become the head of the corner" (Acts, iv, 11), the cornerstone. This Church based on the Resurrection of Christ is speeding towards the glorious resurrection of His Mystical Body. Easter is, therefore, our mystery as well as the mystery of Christ, *our* Pasch. What happened in Him, also happens through Him in all Christians.

A regeneration of Christ was accomplished by the glorious Resurrection of His mortal body to a perpetual life in heaven. Our regeneration from a life in sin to a supernatural life took place in Baptism through the merits of Christ, but with our cooperation it must be made permanent, to endure beyond the period of our mortal existence. "Father, I will that where I am, they also whom Thou hast given Me may be with Me" (John, xvii, 24).

The Liturgy beginning with Easter follows this thought. First the Christian cycle of mysteries is completed, the Church is organized and consecrated, the means of grace given to her; thereafter all progresses towards the harvest, the "Day of the Lord." Some of these developments proceed simultaneously, but this is the general outline for the rest of the Liturgical Year.

Easter Sunday

Very appropriately and significantly does the Mother Church in Rome celebrate the Resurrection in the Basilica of St. Mary Major, where the Mother of God and His crib are venerated in a special manner. Christ, after rising gloriously from the sealed tomb, pays His first visit to her from whose womb He entered mortal life, leaving that womb inviolate. Mary is also a type of the Church in which the birth of Christ and all the following mysteries are daily renewed. Mary is truly the Mother of the whole Mystical Body, including Christ; as such her children visit her on Easter Sunday in her principal sanctuary, and the whole Christian world sings jubilantly: "Regina cœli lætare, quia quem meruisti portare, resurrexit sicut dixit. Ora pro nobis Deum"[1] (Breviary: Final Antiphon).

When we keep this in mind, and also the fact that Mary is a type of Baptism, we perceive that the Liturgy possessed an additional meaning for the catechumens. The clergy and faithful having arrived at the Station church, Christ greets His Mother and His brethren: "I am risen and am still with Thee." And turning to His Father, He continues: "Thou hast laid Thy hand [protectingly] upon Me." Well may Mary and the choir respond: "Such knowledge is too wonderful for me." It is a mystery, but: "O Lord, Thou hast searched me. . . . Thou knowest my sitting-down and my uprising. Glory be to Thee" (Introit). After imploring the divine mercy (Kyrie), the *Gloria in excelsis Deo*, sung with hearts filled with joy over the Resurrection, rises to the height of sublimity. The Collect sums up all that happened in our favor on this day. Eternal death has been overcome, the gate to everlasting life has been opened, and the means of entering heaven have been given us by Christ our Lord.

---

[1] "Queen of Heaven, rejoice, for He Whom thou didst merit to bear, has arisen as He said. Pray to God for us."

A NEW LIFE IN CHRIST

In the Epistle St. Paul admonishes all who have been so well prepared and are now in high spirits, to perpetuate their change from a sinful life to a life of justice and truth, because "Christ our Pasch is sacrificed." This sacrifice is renewed in each Mass. With all truth, therefore, the faithful may respond: "This is the day which the Lord hath made: let us rejoice and be glad in it. Christ our Pasch is immolated. O, give thanks unto the Lord ..." (Gradual).

The Sequence that follows and is recited daily during Easter week, begins with the words, "To the Paschal Victim," and is thus linked up with the Gradual. It is a devotional hymn in a dramatic form believed to be composed by Wipo in the eleventh century. Since the thirteenth century it is inserted after the Gradual, but not in its entirety and with some minor changes. The strophe which originally preceded the line, "Scimus Christum surrexisse," reads:

> "To Mary pure and true,
> Rather than to faithless Jew,
> Let credence full be given."[1]

The singing of the Sequence while the deacon was preparing for the singing of the Gospel added to the festive and joyful dispositions in the hearts of the faithful for receiving the good tidings. The Gospel relates but one event of the many that took place on Easter Day. The three pious women on their way to anoint the body of Jesus (a work of love that had been postponed owing to the interference of the Great Sabbath) were worrying about the removal of the great stone that sealed the tomb. But on reaching the sepulchre they found it open, and saw an Angel, who said: "Jesus of Nazareth, Who was crucified, ... is risen, He is not here. ... But go, tell His disciples and Peter that He goeth before you into Galilee; there you shall see Him, as He told you" (Mark, xvi, 6-7). Jesus had risen and His physical presence in the flesh on earth is in a glorified and supernatural condition. He will appear to His disciples repeatedly during the following forty days. Then He will not revisit the earth until He returns for the

---
[1] Schuster, "The Sacramentary," vol. II, p. 316.

Last Judgment. We express this belief in the Credo, which also is today a song of triumph.

The Offertory brings us the thought of judgment and God's Majesty: "The earth trembled and was still when God arose to judgment." The Secret asks that the Paschal mysteries now being renewed and commemorated may "avail us a remedy unto eternity."

The Paschal Preface recalls that Christ is "the true Lamb that took away the sins of the world. Who dying, destroyed our [eternal] death, and rising again [through His own power] restored us unto [spiritual] life . . ."—as it was in Adam (in whom we all have sinned) when he was created. During the whole Octave the *Communicantes* makes a more special mention of the Resurrection, and the *Hanc igitur* contains an intercession for the neophytes baptized on the Vigil.

The Sacrifice having been completed, the Communion extends the invitation: "Christ our Pasch is immolated; therefore, let us feast in the unleavened bread of sincerity and truth." The whole concludes with the Prayer: "Pour forth upon us, O Lord, the spirit of Thy love, that, by Thy mercy, Thou mayest make of one mind those whom Thou hast fed with the Paschal mysteries. . . ." This Oration is repeated during the whole Easter season whenever Holy Communion is distributed outside of the Mass. Its significance is deep and its meaning rich. Unless the faithful are of one mind with the Church, the union of the soul with Christ and His Mystical Body, a union of love, cannot be maintained. Without this union there is no salvation. A beautiful sermon might be built upon this prayer.

The Alleluia is repeated more frequently during Easter time as an expression of praise, joy, and thanksgiving, inspired by the greatness of the mysteries and gifts that are commemorated during this season. Christ and the Church, with all her actual and potential members, form but one unit, and are to be saved together by these very Paschal mysteries. The individual man, although he works for his own perfection, cannot attain this aim except as a member of a group. For this reason the Lord's Prayer and all general liturgical prayers are recited in the plural, but more about this later.

Easter Week

From the earliest days of the Roman Church Easter was celebrated for ten days, beginning with Maundy Thursday night. The last seven were dedicated to the Mystery of the Resurrection. In other words, Easter alone had an octave. All other great feast days, such as the Epiphany and Pentecost, lasted at first but three or four days. Later on, full octaves were added to these and other principal feasts. Hence, the Liturgy of Easter week is very ancient, and leads us to a better understanding of the liturgical life of the earliest Roman Christians. This furnishes us with an answer for the later would-be reformers who claimed they were returning to the original Christianity when they discarded the whole or greater part of the liturgical exercises.

All Propers of the Masses during the Octave refer to the neophytes, and indirectly to all the baptized. All these days have their own Station churches, and the Gospels follow the chronological order as far as possible. It is evident that Mother Church wished to lead her *agni novelli* from sanctuary to sanctuary in order to impress upon them indelibly the never-to-be-forgotten grace of having risen in Christ from the eternal death of sin through Baptism, and to make them realize the obligations arising from their being now children of God. The present honor and greatness of the newly baptized created responsibilities that were freely accepted. Their salvation, however, was only begun; it was not yet completed. The completion of their salvation requires the keeping of the baptismal vows. To achieve this, the Church extends her guidance, raises the fallen, and ever leads the erring back to her fold. On Easter she received the power to do so when Christ gave the Apostles power to forgive sins. Only a few words about each day can be added here.

On Monday the neophytes and faithful accompanying them assemble at the Church of St. Peter—the first of the Apostles to whom Christ appeared, the Apostle whom He had made His Vicar on earth. Jesus Himself welcomes the procession. Most appropriately, then, the Introit announces: "The Lord hath brought you into a land [the Church] flowing with milk and honey [the means of grace], that the law of the Lord may ever be in your mouth." The natural answer is: "Praise to the Lord, ... proclaim His works among the Gentiles." This response hints at the obligation of the baptized to contribute by word and example to the conversion of others. The Prince of the Apostles himself speaks through the Epistle (Acts, x, 37-48). His words could be expanded into a fine apologetic sermon that would not be out of place on Easter Sunday itself.

Tuesday leads us to the Basilica of St. Paul, where the Apostle of the Gentiles instructs us on the malice of sin and the mercy of God (Acts, xiii, 16, 26-33). The Gospel relates the appearance of Our Lord to His Apostles, convincing them all of His Resurrection and telling them "that penance and remission of sin should be preached in His Name unto all nations." His mercy should be offered to sinners, rather than His wrath threatened. The Communion reminds all that have risen with Christ: "Seek the things that are above, where Christ is . . . ; mind the things that are above." The Postcommunion asks that God's grace "may ever abide in our souls."

On Wednesday the Station church is the Basilica of St. Lawrence, one of the principal Patrons of Rome. He was among the Gentiles what St. Stephen was among the Jewish Christians in Jerusalem. The greeting extended to the neophytes was the same as that extended to the martyred deacon: "Come, ye blessed of My Father, receive the kingdom, which was prepared for you from the beginning of the world" (Introit). Today, as on the following days of the Octave, St. Peter—to whom Christ had given the command: "Feed My lambs, feed My sheep"—speaks again to us through the Epistle. He tells how the Jews had killed the Redeemer, but proclaims that God raised Him to life. The Gospel relates some further appearances of Christ, and the Offertory reminds us of the Easter Communion. The final prayer asks for a newness of life.

The Thursday Liturgy is celebrated in the Station Church of the Twelve Holy Apostles, where the relics of Sts. Philip and

A NEW LIFE IN CHRIST

James are preserved. The Introit again refers to the newly baptized: "They praised with one accord Thy victorious hand, O Lord; for wisdom opened the mouth of the dumb, and made eloquent the tongues of infants." The Epistle tells of the baptism of the eunuch of Queen Candace. The Gospel relates appearances of Christ to His Apostles and to Mary Magdalen, although the latter certainly took place on Sunday morning. The Liturgy considers the whole Octave as one Easter celebration. The Offertory, Communion, and Postcommunion all refer to entering the Church by Baptism.

On Friday the neophytes assembled at St. Mary's *ad Martyres*. In the early Church none but Mary, the Queen of Martyrs, and those who died a violent death for the Faith were venerated as heavenly patrons. There was a scriptural foundation for this practice, and this is still retained in the Canon of the Mass where none but martyrs are commemorated. To inflame the first Christians with the spirit of sacrifice, even unto death, was certainly necessary then as it is also today, when the pagans surrounding us may be less bloody but are more insidious. In this connection, the Introit introduces a fitting thought: "The Lord led them on in hope, and overwhelmed their enemies in the sea." The God who led Israel out of Egypt will also protect those who have been made His own in Baptism. The Collect adds to this: "O God, ... grant us, ... that we may worthily show forth in our deeds the faith which we profess." The Epistle enlarges upon this thought, and the Gospel is an abridgement of the constitution of the Church. Her rights, duties, and mission are stated. The Offertory and Secret refer to the neophytes, and the Communion asks for the remission of temporal faults.

The Saturday Station church is St. John Lateran, where the Baptism took place a week ago. Here the "Agnus Dei" were distributed while the *Agnus Dei* was sung during the Mass. The Introit again refers to the neophytes: "The Lord brought forth His people with joy, and His chosen with gladness." The Collect closes the Easter celebration. Henceforth, the *agni novelli* must strive manfully to reach their eternal destination. "O almighty God, grant ... that we who reverently have kept the Easter festival, may worthily come through its holy joys to those that are everlasting." In the Epistle St. Peter explains the dignity that came to the baptized when they were made children of God. The Gospel is taken from St. John, the Patron of the basilica, and recalls the visit of Sts. Peter and John to the empty sepulchre, on which occasion St. John granted the precedence to Peter. The Offertory exclaims: "God is the Lord, and He hath showed us light." The Communion proclaims: "All you that are baptized in Christ have put on Christ." Too many forget this, but all must lead a Christ-like life so that by their example and the help of God "the true faith may spread and prosper evermore" (Postcommunion).

The Sundays after Easter

The First Sunday after Easter, also called Low Sunday in contradistinction to the high Easter Sunday, is liturgically designated as *Dominica in albis* (White Sunday), because on this day the neophytes assisted at Mass for the last time in their baptismal robes. Hence, on entering the Station Church of St. Pancras, (the youthful martyr), erected at the end of the fifth century, the newly baptized were greeted with the words of St. Peter, the first supreme Pastor after Christ: "As new-born babes, desire reasonably milk without guile" (Introit). Some Protestant sects still call this Sunday by the words beginning the Mass, *Quasimodo geniti,* although they rejected the Mass itself centuries ago. More recently the Sunday has been also called the Octave of Easter, but this is not quite correct, as it is seen from the Collect: "Grant . . . that we who *have* observed the Paschal solemnities, may . . . ever keep them in our life and conversation."

In the Epistle St. John tells us that he who believes in Christ as the Son of God will overcome the world. He also explains the testimony given by the Blessed Trinity against the heretics of his time (Gnostics), that Christ was God before He was baptized in the Jordan. An Alleluia Verse takes the place of the Gradual until the Saturday after Pentecost.

The Gospel relates the institution of the Sacrament of Penance, the great Easter gift of the risen Saviour, and also His ap-

A NEW LIFE IN CHRIST

pearance to the doubting Thomas. Both events gave evidence of the infinite mercy of Christ towards all He had chosen to be His own. The power to forgive sins was given to the priesthood, but the right to exercise it (or jurisdiction, as it is called) was reserved to Peter and his successors. He received the "power of the keys," and he could communicate it to others and lay down conditions under which absolution could be granted or had to be withheld. The Gospel concludes with the remark that not everything Jesus did or said was written down, but what was written was laid down "that you may believe" (John, xx, 31).

The Offertory announces the fact that Christ is risen, and the Secret prays that the Mass being offered joyfully may bring everlasting happiness. The Communion asks us to be believing without seeing with mortal eyes, and the Postcommunion asks "that the most holy mysteries [of Baptism, Confirmation, Holy Eucharist, and Penance], which Thou, O Lord, has instituted to assure our redemption, may become a remedy for us now and hereafter."

During the forty days before His Ascension Christ instructed His Apostles about their future work in His kingdom, how the Church should be organized and divine worship be developed. This is clearly indicated in several passages in the Gospels and in the Acts of the Apostles (i, 3). Naturally, the Sundays after Easter are the most appropriate time to instruct the faithful about these matters.

On the following Saturday some dioceses and the Capuchin Franciscan Order celebrate the Feast of Mary, Mother of the Divine Shepherd, commemorating the relation between Christ and His Mother in the care of souls. The text of the Mass is very beautiful and may be found in some Missals among Masses celebrated *in aliquibus locis.*

The thoughts expressed in the Liturgy of the Second Sunday are that "the earth is full of the goodness of the Lord" (Introit), because Christ has "raised up a fallen world" and can bring all to "the fruition of eternal happiness" (Collect). Christ has given us an example that we must follow to reach this fruit. He was unjustly condemned to suffer and die for us that we might live justly; otherwise, all is in vain. For before you were baptized, "you were as sheep going astray, but you are now converted to the Shepherd and Bishop of your souls" (Epistle). The Gospel pictures Jesus as the Good Shepherd, Whom we have accepted in Baptism. He is truly good because He went so far as to seek out the lost sheep and gave His life for them. The hireling looks rather after his own welfare first, fleeing and hiding himself when the wolf attacks the flock. Christians acknowledge Christ as their Leader and Guide. "The disciples knew the Lord Jesus," and "I know My sheep" (Verse). The Offertory confirms our attachment to Jesus: "Thou art my God, early will I seek Thee, and lift up my hands in Thy Name" by celebrating Thy powerful mysteries. "Give us Thy benediction" (Secret). We conclude with the prayer that "possessing the grace of Thy quickening, we may ever glory in Thy gift" (Postcommunion).

On the following Wednesday the recently established Feast of the Patronage of St. Joseph is celebrated. The thoughts expressed in the Liturgy are that, as the Egyptian Joseph was an instrument for saving his family and his people, so Joseph of Nazareth was the protector and provider of Jesus in the Holy Family. This protection Joseph extended to the new family of God, mysteriously born in Mary, the Mother of the Mystical Body of Christ, the Church. The Mass, as well as the Office, is full of thoughts for preaching or meditation on St. Joseph. In the Breviary Lessons of the Second Nocturn for this feast St. Bernardine of Siena writes:

> "If you compare him [Joseph] with the whole Church of Christ, is he not the man, chosen and singular, through whom and under whom Christ was brought into the world fittingly and decently? If therefore the entire Church is a holy debtor to the Virgin Mother, because it was made worthy to receive Christ through her, so, certainly after her, the Church owes this man, singular gratitude and reverence. . . . Rightly therefore is he prefigured through that Patriarch Joseph, who kept wheat for the people. But our Joseph even excels the other, because he gave not only the bread of corporal life to the Egyptians, but with great care he provided for all the elect, the Bread of Heaven, that gives celestial life "

On the Third Sunday the Liturgy resumes the last thought expressed in the Gospel of the preceding Sunday: "There shall be one fold and one Shepherd," notwithstanding all difficulties that may arise. The power of God is great. Hence: "Sing joyfully to God. . . . Say ye unto God, how terrible are Thy works . . . ; in the greatness of Thy power Thine enemies shall lie before Thee" (Introit). But God expects cooperation on our part by prayer and good example. Therefore, we pray: "O God, Who showest the light of Thy truth to those who are astray, that they may return to the way of righteousness, grant to all who belong to the Christian faith to shun what is not, and to follow what is, in accord with this name" (of Christian). We must live in accord with our dignity and sublime profession (Collect).

St. Peter tells us in the Epistle what Christians must shun and what they must practise: "Refrain yourselves from carnal desires . . . , having your conversation good among the Gentiles: that by the good works they see in you, they may glorify God. Be ye subject to every human creature for God's sake: whether it be to the king . . . or governor, . . . for such is the will of God, that by well-doing you may put to silence the ignorance of foolish men. . . . Honor all men, love the brotherhood, fear God. . . ." It will not all be easy, but "it behoved Christ to suffer, and rise again . . . and enter into His glory" (Verse).

This truth, applicable also to the Mystical Body, is explained by Christ Himself in the Gospel. After announcing His Ascension after a little while, and His return after a little while for judgment, He explains what shall happen in between: "Amen, Amen, I say to you, that you shall weep and lament, but the world shall rejoice, . . . but your sorrow shall be turned into joy . . ." Persecutions and tribulations shall come but "I will see you again, and your heart shall rejoice, and your joy no man shall take from you."

In the Offertory we express our satisfaction with whatever God may please to send us: "I will praise the Lord in my life." Thereafter the Secret asks that the Mass now being offered may give us the grace to moderate earthly longings and to intensify heavenly desires. In the Holy Eucharist we do not behold Christ in His glory, but after a little while we shall see Him as He is in heaven (Communion). The Postcommunion asks that Holy Communion may "strengthen us with spiritual sustenance, and protect us with bodily safeguards," so that we shall surely reach our end.

On the Fourth Sunday the Liturgy returns to a thought expressed in the Epistle of the previous Sunday, and outlines what a truly Christian life demands: "O God, . . . grant unto Thy people to love what Thou dost command, and desire what Thou dost promise, that in a world of change our hearts may there be fixed where true joys abide" (Collect). Considering this prayer, **we may well exclaim:** "How far have many drifted away from living with the Church as expressed by the Liturgy!" The spirit of the world and the spirit of God which all the baptized have received, are contrary and cannot be mixed. Where one is, the other is absent. Faith inspires heavenly inspirations that are followed by an eternal reward. But faith must be accompanied by good works and remain firm (Epistle). The words of St. James are a classic to refute the errors of Protestantism. In the Church alone, "the right hand of the Lord has brought strength . . . and exalted me" (Verse).

In the Gospel Jesus declares that, unless He goes to the Father, the Paraclete will not come. But Jesus will send the Holy Ghost Who shall convince the world of sin, judgment, and justice. "He shall receive of Mine, and shall show it to you." Nothing that is good comes to us except through Christ. The Offertory adds: "Come and hear, all ye that fear God, and I will declare what He hath done for my soul." The Secret refers to the most important gift of faith, and asks "that, as we know Thy truth, so we may securely exemplify it by a worthy life." It is truly remarkable how the Church always prays for the most necessary things, for which many of her children would not dream to ask. The Sacrifice concludes with the petition: "Assist us, O Lord . . . , that by these mysteries . . . we may both be purified from vice and delivered from all dangers. . . ."

The Fifth Sunday after Easter recalls the Resurrection of Christ and His victory over Satan and death. The Introit, Offertory, and Communion express our thanks for these great blessings.

The Collect calls upon God, the origin of all good created and uncreated, that He may inspire us to "think what is right, and under His direction, perform it." In the Epistle St. James tells us that religion is not sentimentality but is an active force, a way of life; it is the practice of charity and the overcoming of sin by self-denial or penance.

Knowing that we cannot do anything good without Christ's grace, we must pray for it: "Amen, amen I say to you, if you ask the Father anything in My name, He will give it to you" (Gospel). This the Church does by concluding all her liturgical prayers with the words, "through Christ our Lord." The *Pater noster* alone does not need this conclusion, because it is Christ's own prayer, and for this reason the priest (representing Him in celebrating Mass) responds himself with "Amen." The first petition we address to the Father after the instruction is "that, by these services of pious devotion [the Mass], we may pass to heavenly glory, through Jesus Christ . . ." (Secret). The Postcommunion asks that the Lord may grant to us "to desire what is right, and to obtain what we desire." This is the true spirituality of the New Dispensation.

Rogation Days

During the weeks after Easter, on the three days preceding the Feast of the Ascension, called Minor Rogation Days, the Litany of All Saints is recited and the Rogation Mass celebrated. A few words about the origin and meaning of these may be added, since they may serve to encourage the faithful to attend Mass in greater numbers on these days.

The great procession on St. Mark's Day (April 25), the Major Rogation Day, is very ancient, and was substituted for a pagan festival held to obtain from the gods of Rome an abundant harvest. The Church changed the pagan concept to the Christian truth that the best protection against all misfortunes is a devout life accompanied by prayer. The saints were called upon to intercede for us, because they themselves had passed through life and as fruits of the Redemption had been harvested by God.

The Triduum before Ascension was taken into the Roman Rite from the Franks at a much later date, but the fast observed by the Franks on these days was dropped.

The Litany is very ancient, except for the addition of a few names in the thirteenth century. Originally it ended with the *Kyrie eleison,* which was followed immediately by the Collect of the following Mass. In the Middle Ages the Penitential Psalm and the ancient diaconal Litany still in use among the Greeks were added. Finally, the sacerdotal prayers were attached, and an Introit provided for the Rogation Mass, making both independent of each other for private use.

The Mass text is full of thoughts inspiring hope in the efficacy of prayer. After having laid practically all spiritual and temporal needs before God in the Litany, we confidently pray in the Collect: "Grant, we beseech Thee, O almighty God, that we who in our affliction confide in Thy mercy, may be ever shielded by Thy protection against all adversities." And we repeat at the end: "Mercifully hear our prayers with favor, . . . that while we receive Thy gifts in tribulation, we may in consolation increase in Thy love."

A thoughtful consideration of these liturgical rites makes one wonder why the Litany is not more frequently recited publicly in times of distress, and why this Mass is not said oftener as a Votive Mass to draw down God's mercy and comfort.

Reflection

The religious instruction of the neophytes and catechumens did not cease after the Easter celebrations, but continued on the Wednesdays and Fridays throughout the year. It may easily be imagined what an important part the Liturgy played in these instructions at a time when books, pictures, and statues were scarce or not available at all. In those days when Catechisms were unknown, the Liturgy provided dramatic teaching, applied understanding, and community exercises, and at the same time furnished the grace to make Christian life possible and truly fruitful.

In our days many aids are available for instruction, but all of them together do not really provide what the Liturgy presents. Without it, grace-giving exercises and life with the Church are often neglected. Our people no longer understand the liturgical language as the early Christians did, and in consequence have lost actual contact with the celebrating and administering priest. However, there are now an abundance of Missals available in the vernacular at a very low price, and all that is needed to reestablish the connection between celebrant and faithful is a series of fundamental instructions on the meaning of the Liturgy. For this purpose the present book has been written. Mere reading may appear somewhat tedious, but if used as a brief commentary on the Masses of the Sundays and holydays, it will open to our people a rich and but little known source of true spirituality. The interest of the faithful will not be found lacking.

CHAPTER XVIII

The Glorification of Christ

SOME MYSTERIES OF CHRIST of great importance in the life of the Mystical Body and its individual members cannot be passed over in silence, but at present we must confine ourselves with merely indicating truths that are of special significance for the spiritualization of Christians. Writing on this subject, Abbot Marmion states and demonstrates that Christ's mysteries are also our very own, and that each mystery celebrated in the Liturgy bestows its peculiar grace upon those who contemplate and live it.[1]

The Ascension

The Ascension of Christ, concluding His earthly career and beginning His glorious life as God-Man in heaven, was certainly a most important event as far as His Sacred Humanity was concerned. It was the bestowal of the eternal reward for His obedience to the will of His Father unto death. In Rome the ancient feast was formerly celebrated with great splendor. The ceremonies included a solemn procession held at noon and proceeding from St. Peter's where the Mass had been offered. It symbolized the going forth of Christ and His Apostles to Mount Olivet, His last "station" on earth.

Both the Office and the Mass are one continued jubilation over the triumph of Christ and a rejoicing with the Saviour in the glorious finale of His work and care for all mankind. We certainly have reasons to rejoice in the Ascension, because, as the Preface points out: "Christ . . . was taken up to heaven that He might bestow on us fellowship in His Godhead." Can any mortal fully realize what this means? Such a realization is impossible,

---

[1] "Christ and His Mysteries," pp. 393 sqq.

THE GLORIFICATION OF CHRIST 207

but we can definitely conclude that He went to heaven for our glorification as well as His own. Hence, it is the duty of the Mystical Body and every one of its members to be ready when He calls: "He shall come as you have seen Him going up into heaven" (Introit). We must never forget the things that are eternal (Collect). The Apostles returned with joy to Jerusalem after the Ascension, and remained there to prepare themselves for the coming of the Holy Ghost. Thereafter they were to preach and to extend the Kingdom of God "to the uttermost parts of the earth" (Epistle). The reason for their joy is expressed in the Verse: "God is ascended with jubilee. . . . He hath led captivity captive."

In the Gospel Jesus promises the Holy Ghost and the gift of miracles to His disciples. The Secret and Postcommunion ask that we may obtain invisible graces by celebrating the visible Ascension: "Now this is eternal life, that they may know Thee, the only true God, and Jesus Christ Whom Thou hast sent," and Who has returned to Thee (Gospel of Vigil).

During the following days the disciples remained in prayer awaiting the "Gift from above," and the Church imitates them by commemorating every ferial of the novena: "Grant us . . . ever to continue in thanksgiving . . ." (Sunday within Octave).

The Coming of the Holy Ghost

Since the time of Tertullian the Vigils of Easter and Pentecost have been set aside for the solemn administration of Baptism. Both mysteries were most intimately connected with the new life and sanctification produced by Baptism. The rites of both Vigils are similar, although the rite for blessing baptismal water on the Vigil of Pentecost has been shortened by eliminating six of the prophecies with the prayers following them. The remaining prayers refer to Baptism and are very beautiful. The Liturgy was celebrated in the Church of the Lateran, the cathedral of Rome. The Mass refers to the Holy Ghost, Who confirms our Baptism, although Baptism and Confirmation are two distinct Sacraments. Holy Orders are conferred during the Octave, the three Sacraments complementing one another for definite purposes. As the Vigil of Easter has already been commented on, and the commentary applies with the necessary changes also to this Vigil, we pass over to the Feast of Pentecost as it is celebrated among us today.

Pentecost commemorates for seven days the infusion of the divine life-giving Spirit, Who consecrated the Church founded by Christ as a living body. This Church, the new Mystical Body of Christ, was to extend over all the earth and was to embrace all mankind. The Descent of the Holy Ghost was the consecration of this Church built mystically upon the foundation of the Apostles and completed by all Christians as stones cemented together by a common faith and common love. Christ preached the faith, and the Holy Ghost poured out the love. This is beautifully described in the Liturgy for the "Dedication of Churches," especially in the hymns and antiphons. Pentecost celebrates, therefore, the baptism to a new mystical life and its confirmation in charity. Moreover, the Coming of the Holy Ghost is the final confirmation before the Last Judgment of all that Christ taught and did, including His Ascension into heaven. Henceforth, Christ sits at the right hand of the Father, and the Holy Ghost operates and sanctifies the Church. Hence His importance for us.

The Office of Pentecost (like that of Easter) has but three Lessons. They were read by a Canon, a Cardinal, and the Pope, who also intoned the *Te Deum*.

The Mass (celebrated after Tierce, in which the usual hymn is exchanged for the *Veni Creator*) begins with the words: "The Spirit of the Lord has filled the whole earth" (Introit). All the Orations ask for faith, love, and their fruits as the result of the outpouring of the Holy Ghost, through Christ, "Who poured out this day the promised Holy Spirit upon the children of adoption" (Preface). The Epistle describes the coming of the Holy Ghost upon the Apostles, their first preaching, and its wonderful effects. Even the Jews shared indirectly in the graces from above through the gift of tongues enabling them to understand the good tidings.

The Verse and Secret ask that the faith of Christ may fill the world, and that the fruits of the Redemption imparted by the Holy Ghost may change the face of the earth. The Sequence invokes and praises the sevenfold gifts of the Holy Spirit that are infused into our soul through Baptism, Confirmation, and the other Sacraments, and are intended to accompany man's life from the cradle to the grave and bring forth the most precious fruits. Every one of its verses may be used as the basis for a solid instruction. It is the Holy Ghost Who now sanctifies the Mystical Body, and it would be highly salutary if its members knew a little more about Him than the mere historical facts.

The Gospel relates the words in which Jesus promised the sending of the Paraclete from the Father and the Son as one source. It was a great consolation for the Apostles, and would remain such for the present and future generations if the faithful would but know what He is and what He does for them.[1]

The ancient Octave of Pentecost ends with the Mass of the following Saturday. The theme of the Mass on Monday is Baptism by water and the Holy Ghost. On Tuesday the Sacrament of Confirmation is commemorated. The Epistle gives the reason why the bishops are the ordinary ministers of this Sacrament, and the Secret distinguishes the Holy Eucharist as sacrifice and as food for the soul.

Ember Wednesday fittingly recalls that in the Church there are many races and tongues, and that all must be influenced by the Holy Ghost. To achieve this, an interior deepening of the faith and an exterior extension of the Church must be brought about. The fast seems to be out of place within the Octave of this high feast, but the fasts were already observed before Pentecost was extended from three to seven days. For a short time, the Ember Days were transferred to the following week, but they finally were put back to their original place, where as a preparation for ordinations they serve very well.

---

[1] Very useful in this connection and at the same time clear and practical is the book entitled "God the Holy Ghost," by James E. Carroll, C.S.Sp. (Kenedy, New York). Also recommended is "The Abiding Presence of the Holy Ghost," by Bede Jarrett, O.P. (Westminster, Md., 1943). Cf. also "Mystici Corporis," June 29, 1943.

The Mass on Thursday is the same as on the feast, with the exception of the Epistle and the Gospel. These refer to the miracles and progress accompanying the preaching of the Gospel. The Mass on Friday proclaims the Holy Ghost as Comforter, and illustrates the powers given to the Apostles to drive out devils and to cure diseases as related in the Gospel of the previous day. Both Gospels point to the administration of Penance and Extreme Unction.

On Ember Saturday the ordinations took place at the tomb of St. Peter. Hence, the five Lessons referring to the Holy Ghost, after which the Holy Orders were administered *gradatim*. The Orations are of a general nature, because the specific rite of conferring Holy Orders is taken from the Roman Pontifical. This rite is very beautiful, and supplies an abundance of thoughts which are not only useful for instructions on the priesthood, but also for sermons during the first Masses celebrated on the following Sunday. The Epistle of the Mass is a beautiful epitome of Christian life built upon faith, hope, and charity, and the feast concludes with the Postcommunion: "May Thy holy mysteries [celebrated on Pentecost], O Lord, with godly fervor quicken us, and make us to delight both in them and in their blessed fruit."

The Most Holy Trinity

The cycle of Christological mysteries culminates in the mystery of the Blessed Trinity, the source and the end of all that exists outside of the Godhead. It is the greatest and deepest mystery, not because we do not know much about it, but rather because we know so much about it (perhaps more than about any other mystery) and still cannot reach the end nor fully understand (much less comprehend) it, since this is the essence and life of Divinity itself. This, however, does not mean that what can be known and is known about the Blessed Trinity is not of interest and supreme importance to the faithful in general. After all, the Trinity is the cause and the end of the Redemption.

Unfortunately, this mystery is not only the deepest but also the darkest for the largest number of people. This is not always

THE GLORIFICATION OF CHRIST

their fault. Many were never told much about it, beyond what is contained in our traditional dogmatic formulas expressing our belief in the Blessed Trinity. This might suffice for salvation, but not for deep spiritualization nor for resisting the onslaughts made by so many unbelievers and modern scientists. Theology teaches that there must be one God with intelligence and will power, both simple and absolute, constituting the Word and the Holy Ghost, the substantial Love between the Father and the Son. The mystery has been revealed to us. It tells us that it is necessary that there are three divine Persons, and that more or less are simply impossible.

This immediately brands as wrong the belief of Unitarians and idolaters, and also those who deny the divinity of the Son or the Holy Ghost. The latter constitute by far the majority of the American people. Still, "this is eternal life, that they may know Thee, the only true God, and Jesus Christ, Whom Thou hast sent" (John, xvii, 3). From this it is at once evident that the current and frequently heard statements such as "We all believe in God," "the Fatherhood of God," "the brotherhood of man," are all nonsense unless they are founded on the true belief in the Most Holy Trinity. May these few practical thoughts suffice! [1]

The Liturgy of the Feast of the Most Holy Trinity contains several authentic formulas and dogmatic texts expressing our correct belief in the Blessed Trinity. In the Office we find scriptural passages, doxologies, and the so-called Athanasian Creed. The Mass has some fine antiphonal passages, the *Gloria in excelsis Deo,* the Nicene Creed, and the Gospel explaining and praising the Trinity. The main thought running through the Mass and the Office is praise to the Blessed Trinity and undivided Unity, because He has shown mercy to us. This is indeed the objective of all our worship. The whole New Dispensation is the creation of the one True God: "For of Him, and by Him, and in Him are all things" (Epistle). In the name of the Father and of the Son and of the Holy Ghost, salvation is to be preached and brought to all men until the consummation of the world (Gospel).

---

[1] Preachers may find abundant, practical, and interesting material in "The Doctrine of the Trinity," by the Abbé Felix Klein (Kenedy, New York, 1940).

It so happens that the Mass of the First Sunday after Pentecost is supplanted by the feast, but the Sunday Gospel read at the end of the festal Mass explains beautifully the charity and mercy of God that man should imitate. This should be the fruit of the mysteries of the New Dispensation of love. The Postcommunion is a fit conclusion to the feast as well as to the Sunday Mass: "May . . . the confession·of the holy and eternal Trinity, and its undivided Unity, profit us unto salvation of body and soul, and . . . grant that we who have been sated with such great mysteries may receive Thy saving gifts and never cease from Thy praise."

With this consideration of the Blessed Trinity we might conclude our exposition of the Liturgy of the Church as an outstanding means for spiritualizing individual souls. The whole work of Redemption, the founding of the Church, and her means of grace to sanctify man have passed in review. However, there are some outstanding liturgical celebrations that could not receive adequate attention in the chronological order in which they were commemorated, and, being supplementary, cannot well be passed over in silence.

Corpus Christi

The first Thursday following the Octave of Pentecost is dedicated to the glorification of the Holy Eucharist by the Solemnity of Corpus Christi. The institution of the Blessed Sacrament was commemorated on Maundy Thursday, but under the prevailing circumstances it was not timely to render outstanding honor to this exalted mystery. Hence, a celebration takes place on the first free Thursday after the chronological date. A new viewpoint is added—the Real Presence as a mystery of faith. The feast dates from the time of St. Thomas Aquinas, who composed this Liturgy, one of the most beautiful in the Roman Rite.

The Holy Eucharist in all its aspects is truly a mystery of faith to be believed and appreciated. Hence, the Liturgy is intended to be a confession of our faith, an expression of praise of its greatness, and a solemn act of thanksgiving for the love that Christ showed us by instituting it. These sentiments run through

THE GLORIFICATION OF CHRIST 213

the Office as well as through the Mass. The Holy Eucharist can only be accepted by faith. The three Divine Persons in God were manifested at the Baptism of Jesus by the voice of the Father, the appearance of the Holy Ghost in the form of a dove, and Jesus was proclaimed as the beloved Son. The Incarnation was manifested by the birth and life of Jesus and by the works He performed, which required a divine power. The Redemption was visibly indicated by the voluntary and bloody sacrifice on Mount Calvary, where He was physically present. The Humanity of Christ was present when He taught the people and worked miracles of grace, and all this gave to our belief in Him a tangible foundation. With the Holy Eucharist all is purely a matter of faith. It is true that Christ multiplied loaves of bread and foretold the transubstantiation, but this did not satisfy the mind of His hearers.

Not without reason and perfect justification were the words, *mysterium fidei*, inserted in the form of consecration. Not only the transubstantiation, but also the Real Presence and its multiplication, its effects as an unbloody sacrifice differing only in the manner of offering from the bloody Sacrifice of the Cross, the identity between the Priest and Victim, and all else that constitutes the Holy Eucharist, are objects of faith.

This wonderful memorial of the Passion which Christ bequeathed to us at the Last Supper is clearly portrayed in all its aspects in the Liturgy of the Feast of Corpus Christi. The lessons, antiphons, and hymns of the Office are full of sublime thoughts dogmatically and concisely expressed. Confining ourselves to the Proper of the Mass, we find that the Introit refers to the time of the institution of the Blessed Sacrament: "He fed them with the fat of wheat: and filled them with honey out of the rock." Truly a *Panis dulcedinis*, but at the same time it is a memorial of Christ's bitter Passion (Collect).

In the Epistle St. Paul describes what took place "the same night in which He was betrayed." Jesus answered the perfidy of the Jews by giving to mankind the greatest sign of His love: "Take ye and eat; this is My body. . . . This do for a commemoration of Me." After the first Pentecost, the Church began to

comply with this command of her Divine Founder. Throughou
the Christian centuries, "the eyes of all hope in Thee, Lord, an(
Thou givest them their meat in due season." To this Chris
responds: "My flesh is meat indeed, and My blood is drink in
deed; he that eateth My flesh and drinketh My blood, abidetl
in Me, and I in him" (Gradual).

Then follows the most beautiful dogmatic Sequence found iı
the Missal. It recounts the mysteries connected with the Hol
Eucharist. To explain it fully would require a good-sized book
but for our purpose a few indications of its contents will suffice
leaving the rest to private or group study.

The Sequence is an exhortation directed to Sion (the Churcl
and her members) to praise the Redeemer unceasingly. Thei
follow the reasons, taken from the mystery of the Holy Eucharisı
why our praise and gratitude should never end. Among thes
reasons are: Christ the Good Shepherd gave Himself as livin
and life-giving bread to nourish the spiritual life of His sheeɼ
He did so in the midst of His Apostles, when He substituted fo
the old paschal rite (which was but a shadow of things to come
Himself as a real sacrifice by consecrating bread and wine int
His own flesh and blood. About this consecration the Churc
maintains that the bread is changed into the substance of flesł
and the wine into the substance of blood, although the accient
appear to remain the same. This is beyond our comprehensio
and exceeds the experience of our senses, but faith, not boun
by the material, "leaps to things not understood."

Some of the mysteries that require our faith are the invisibl
facts that Christ is but one and indivisible, all communicanı
receive Him entire, whether one or thousands participate in th
divine banquet. Another mystery is that the same food may hav
a contrary effect in the receivers. It gives more life to the jus
but is poison to the sinner. Furthermore, Christ is not only livin
and entire in every Host, but also in every least part of It. It
the mysterious multiplication of the Real Presence that startlɛ
us. Finally, we have on our altars in an invisible manner th
Manna that mysteriously descended from heaven, and also th
Sacrificial Lamb that, having died for us .on the cross, ascende

living into heaven, substituting an eternal and universal unbloody Sacrifice for the temporal, local, and bloody sacrifices of the Old Dispensation.

The conclusion is a beautiful prayer that this gift of love may not have been given to us in vain, and that Christ as Viaticum may accompany us on our way to life everlasting. No wonder that we sing after the solemn procession and at every Benediction of the Blessed Sacrament: "Tantum ergo Sacramentum veneremur cernui."

The Gospel of the Mass recalls the occasion on which Christ promised the institution of the Holy Eucharist, and ends with the words: "He that eateth this bread shall live forever." The Offertory introduces the Eucharist as a Sacrifice by referring to the sacrifices in the Temple: "The priests [and the people] offer incense and loaves to God, and therefore they shall be holy to their God, and shall not defile His name." If this was required from the Jews, how much more may this be expected from Christians who offer together with the priest, not mere material gifts, but the Most High Son of God Himself! The Secret asks for unity and peace in the Church, "mystically figured under the offerings we make." For to the making of bread and wine many kernels of wheat and many grapes contribute.

The Communion points out that the Holy Eucharist must be received in the state of grace; otherwise, "you shall be guilty of the body and blood of the Lord." Having this in mind, the Postcommunion prays: "Grant us, . . . O Lord, to be filled with the everlasting fruition of Thy divinity, which is prefigured by our reception here of Thy precious body and blood." "He that eateth Me, the same also shall live by Me" (John, vi, 58).

The theophorical procession that forms a part of the Solemnity of Corpus Christi, should remind us of Christ's walking among His people on earth, doing good and receiving from them homage, love, and adoration.

Owing to the sublimity of this Mystery, it sometimes happens that intelligent adults preparing for unconditional Baptism experience difficulties with regard to the Holy Eucharist. They are not unwilling to accept it, but somehow consider it either too good to be true or seemingly impossible. In such cases, the writer has found that more explanations only increased the difficulties, but as soon as they were baptized and had received the supernatural virtue of faith, these persons became outstanding in their devotion to the Real Presence and zealous in the reception of Holy Communion, all former apprehensions having disappeared.

The Feast of the Sacred Heart

As the commemoration of the death of Christ follows the institution of the Holy Eucharist on Maundy Thursday, the glorification of the love of Christ, shown by His death on the Cross, follows on the Friday after the Solemnity of Corpus Christi. It is the resumption of the celebration of Good Friday from a different viewpoint. The feast considers, not so much what man inflicted upon the God-Man, but what Jesus bestowed upon man. He loved man to the end of His life and unto the end of His infinite love and mercy, as far as man is capable of receiving them.

Although the Sacred Heart had been honored for centuries in religious orders and some dioceses, the extension of the cult and the feast to the universal Latin Church and its high liturgical rank with a privileged Octave is quite recent. But the mystery it extols was unfolded by Christ Himself.

In some ways the feast supplements the Solemnity of Corpus Christi as a memorial of the Passion. It is the new testamental version of Good Friday as seen through the eyes of faith. This concept was stimulated by the writings of Sts. Bonaventure and Bernard, and received a new impetus from the private revelations made by Christ to St. Margaret Mary Alacoque. The adoration of the Sacred Heart has a solid dogmatic foundation, notwithstanding the emotional aspects prevailing in some books. United with the rest of the Sacred Humanity of Christ, the Sacred Heart is adored as a symbol of Christ's human and divine love for us. The Sacred Heart of the Crucified draws all unto Himself (John, xii, 32), until all things have been subjected to him (I Cor., xv, 28).

The Matins of the feast begin with the Invitation: "The Heart of Jesus wounded for love of us, come let us adore." [1] This love urged Him to assume a mortal body in order that the new Adam might restore what the old Adam had lost. He, the Son of God, came to reconcile us to the Father and to assume our guilt of sin and to atone for it. Having completed this work, His Heart was opened to pour abundant grace upon us all (Hymn). The Lessons of the Second Nocturn describe the origin, spread, and meaning of the devotion and end with the Consecration to the Sacred Heart. The Homily is by St. Bonaventure, who points out that the blood and water flowing from the Sacred Heart signify the sacramental graces originating in the fountain of the Saviour, and that the Heart was opened to be a refuge of peace for men. The Lessons of the Second Nocturn within the Octave are taken from the Encyclical, "Miserentissimus Redemptor," of Pope Pius XI, who raised the feast to its present high rank and also amended the Act of Consecration annually to be recited on the feast day.

Many beautiful thoughts are found in these documents, outlining the objectives of the cult. One of these objectives is that we should make atonement to Christ for those who do not respond to His love, who reject or do not know Him. The cult of the Sacred Heart is directed to the physical Heart of Jesus inseparably united with the rest of His Humanity, which is ever united with His Divinity, and as such, humanly speaking, the Sacred Heart is the symbol of Christ's human as well as divine love. They cannot be separated in practice.

The Introit, Gospel, and Preface of the Mass give us a picture of the content and significance of the Liturgy. "The thoughts of His Heart extend to all generations, to deliver their souls from death, and feed them in famine" (Introit). Here the Heart stands for the Saviour, Who wills the salvation of all men and gave Himself to man, dying on the cross and living in the tabernacle.

---

[1] Pope Pius XI granted the latest Mass and Office for this feast in 1929.

The atonement we offer for unrequited love is expressed in the Collect: "O God, who hast given to us the Sacred Heart of Thy Son, wounded by our sins, as an infinite treasure of love and mercy, mercifully grant that this expression of our devotion may also constitute an act of satisfaction. . . ." We ask God Himself to accomplish in the Sacrifice of the Mass what we ourselves cannot do sufficiently. How appropriate such a satisfaction is, St. Paul tells us in the Epistle: "To me was given the grace to preach among the Gentiles the unsearchable riches of Christ." And after we have been enlightened about the extent of His love for us, Christ Himself adds: "Learn of Me, because I am meek and humble of heart; and you shall find rest to your souls" (Gradual). This rest is the prize for a victorious active love, which is utterly different from sentimentalism and pious quietism.

The Gospel relates how the Heart of Jesus was opened by the soldier's lance, and "immediately there came out blood and water." It closes with the words addressed to the enemies of Christ: "They shall look upon Him Whom they have pierced." In the Offertory Christ speaks through the mouth of the prophet: "My Heart has expected reproach and misery, and I looked for one that would grieve together with Me, but there was none." This deplorable defection is to be remedied by the Mass now being offered that "it may be an expiation for our delinquencies" (Secret).

The special Preface implores that the Sacred Heart pierced by a lance may be for us a treasury of divine bounty, and that from it may flow torrents of mercy and grace; that our love may never grow cold; that the pious may find rest therein, and penitents a refuge.

The Communion repeats a sentence from the Gospel, and then the Postcommunion asks "that having tasted the sweetness of Thy most Sacred Heart, we may despise earthly things and love those that are eternal." May this petition become a reality!

An additional abundance of dogmatic thoughts on the feasts of Corpus Christi and the Sacred Heart are found in the liturgi-

THE GLORIFICATION OF CHRIST

cal Litanies of the Holy Name and the Sacred Heart, since both refer to the God-Man. Truly inspirational and practical matter is found in "Christ in His Mysteries"[1] and "Werde Licht" (vol. III).[2] Such reliable sources are undoubtedly the best, and protect us from trivialities and errors.

The Feast of the Immaculate Heart of Mary

To crown the consecration of the world to the Immaculate Heart of Mary (October, 1942), Pope Pius XII instituted the feast of her Immaculate Heart to be celebrated by the universal Church on the Octave of the Assumption, August 22, as a feast of the second class.

The motives for the institution of this feast are the truths regarding Mary's maternal love and power and the ever-deepening confidence of the faithful in her mediation with Christ, which inspired bishops and people to petition for the extension of this feast to the whole Church.

The Holy Father hopes that this feast and the accompanying increase of devotion to Mary's Immaculate Heart will accelerate the coming of a just peace for the world, liberate mankind from its present miseries, promote the freedom and prosperity of the Church, encourage the just in virtue, and hasten the conversion of sinners.

The significance and dogmatic content of this devotion are clearly expressed in the Decree, "Cultus Liturgicus," and in the Mass and Office of the Feast of the Immaculate Heart of Mary.[3]

---

[1] Columba Marmion, "Christ in His Mysteries," (Herder, St. Louis, 1924).
[2] Benedict Baur, "Werde Licht," 3 vols. (Herder, Freiburg im Breisgau, 1937-1938).
[3] *Acta Apostolicæ Sedis,* February 28, 1945 (Washington, June 20, 1945), pp. 44-52.

CHAPTER XIX

The Final Preparation of Mankind

AFTER HAVING COMPLETED the consideration, celebration, and dramatization of the historical mysteries of the Redemption, the Church turns to the execution of the command of her Divine Founder: "Teach ye all nations, baptizing them: . . . teaching them to observe all things whatever I have commanded you: and behold I am with you all days, even to the consummation of the world" (Matt., xxviii, 19-20). This command expressed the content, extension, and duration of the soul-saving labors of the Church. This work will continue and will not be completed until the day of judgment and final victory. Up to that day, the Church will teach that "this is eternal life: that they may know Thee, the only true God, and Jesus Christ, Whom Thou hast sent" (John, xvii, 3). She will announce: "This is my commandment, that you love one another, as I have loved you. . . . Do the things that I command you" (John, xv, 12, 14). The Church will provide the means of grace, and will guide and govern the faithful to their final destination.

This is a compendium of "teaching them to observe all things": faith and charity expressed by keeping the Commandments of God and of the Church, based upon them. Christ promised His unfailing aid through His own intercession and the operation of the Holy Ghost. Without God, we can do nothing.

The Sundays after Pentecost cover about one-half of the Ecclesiastical Year, and this period is dedicated to the missionary work. The thoughts expressed in the Liturgy of these Sundays are not systematically arranged, but follow generally the contents of the Epistles and Gospels. However, some historical references on the march of the Church can be noticed. There is a kind of *anabasis* (or ascent) until about the end of August. Thereafter, the

FINAL PREPARATION OF MANKIND 221

thoughts of the Liturgy are directed to Christ reigning "in splendoribus sanctorum." Certain feasts and ferials serve as milestones on the way of Christianity. These, being symbols of truth, arouse joy and confidence, and deserve special mention here as we hurry to the end of the Liturgical Year. The main thought of the Masses, usually found in the Gospel, will be pointed out briefly. The Epistles are principally of a moral nature, but sometimes illustrate and explain the Gospels.

On all the Sundays after Pentecost the Liturgy seems to emphasize continually a devout participation in the Holy Sacrifice. It is the memorial of the death of Christ, in which all are baptized and have risen to a new life of grace. On practically all week-days the heroic examples of ancient and modern saints are kept before the eyes of the faithful for imitation. On week-days men are mostly away from their Christian homes, and liable to be influenced by the world surrounding them. They are exposed to the many dangers expressed in the Epistles. Many of the faithful fortify themselves against temptations by attending daily Mass, but on Sundays all must hasten to the house of the Father, participate in the Mass, and drink from the fountains of living water, dispensing instruction and grace. This idea of the Sabbath in the New Dispensation, as a rest on the bosom of Christ, runs through the whole Liturgy of this season, and it might become tedious if we pointed this out in every instance. An abundance of texts occurring in the Office as well as in the Mass will corroborate this. Hence, we turn to the historical progress indicated in the Liturgy.

The Sundays after Pentecost (I-IV)[1]

The Apostles having received the mission to teach all nations, the nations are told in turn that the blind cannot lead the blind; therefore, they must follow the teaching of the messengers of the Master who have been endowed with wisdom and charity from above (I). The Church has been founded, the banquet is ready, and all are invited to come; those who refuse, cannot be saved (II).

---
[1] The roman numerals indicate the respective Sundays.

Not even the sinners are excluded because it was especially for the sick souls that the Divine Physician came (III). So, the Apostles went forth to cast out their nets in the name of Christ and caught a multitude of fishes (IV).

Sts. Peter and Paul

The development of the Liturgy kept step with the progress of the Church. Very early it became the custom to hold vigils and celebrate Mass at the tombs of the martyrs in the catacombs. Naturally, the Apostles Peter and Paul received outstanding honors in the Church at Rome, together with the secondary Patron of the city, St. Lawrence the Deacon. The two Apostles—one the Patriarch of the West and the other the Doctor of the Gentiles who labored principally among the Greeks—may symbolize the forms of the Liturgy. Hence, Peter the Rock and Paul the Vessel of Election stand for the unity of Christ's Kingdom on earth. They are never completely separated in our worship.

The spread of the Church over large and populous districts made a closer organization of the ecclesiastical hierarchy necessary. This became very urgent after the death of the Apostles when several schisms and heresies threatened the Mystical Body of Christ. All the faithful believed in Peter as the Vicar of Christ, but not all could get directly in touch with him or his successors. A gradation in the ranks of the clergy had to be defined, from local pastors up to the Supreme Pontiff endowed with infallibility and final authority. These institutions became objectives of liturgical celebrations, and entered the deposit of faith.

Originally two celebrations were held on June 29: one in St Peter's Basilica and one in St. Paul's outside the Walls. At both of these the Pope assisted. In the course of time, most probably on account of the great distance between these basilicas, the second celebration was transferred to the next day under the name of Commemoration of St. Paul, with the same Octave for both. On the feast itself St. Peter predominates, but the Oration refer to both. On the following day St. Paul holds the first place

FINAL PREPARATION OF MANKIND 223

and St. Peter is commemorated. The whole world joins Rome in celebrating the feast, although it is no longer a holyday of obligation in a number of countries.

The Mass begins with an historical reference to the imprisonment of St. Peter. "Now I know in very deed that the Lord has sent His Angel, and has delivered me out of the hand of Herod, and from all the expectations of the people of the Jews" (Introit). It was a great manifestation of the aid God was to extend to the Prince of the Apostles, and through him to the Church at large. Hence, we pray in the Collect: "O God, who hast consecrated this day by the mysteries of Thine Apostles Peter and Paul, grant that Thy Church may in all things follow the precepts of them from whom it first received the faith." There is nothing more important than that. It goes right back to Baptism: "I do believe" and "Keep the Commandments," including those of the Church.

The Epistle describes the event to which the Introit refers. The leading thoughts of the celebration are found in the Gradual: "Thou shalt make them princes over all the earth; they shall remember thy name, O Lord. . . . Thou art Peter: and upon this rock I will build my Church." In the Gospel Christ receives Peter's testimony: "Thou art Christ, the Son of the living God." And Christ makes Peter the rock and foundation of the Church, with full powers to bind and to loose. *"I believe . . . in the one, holy, catholic and apostolic Church."*

In the Secret we confidently ask that the prayers of the Apostles may accompany the offerings consecrated to God's Name and by these same offerings we beg to be purified and defended. The Communion is again Christ's promise; "Thou art Peter; and upon this rock I will build my Church."

In the Mass of the Commemoration of St. Paul the Epistle recalls how Saul persecuted the infant Church, and how he was converted into Paul and made a preacher to the Gentiles. Christ Himself instructed him in the desert for three years. Thereafter Paul presented himself to Peter, the head of the Church, who commissioned him to preach.

In the Gospel Jesus speaks about the future of the Apostles and their successors. He foretold: "They will deliver you up in councils, and they will scourge you in their synagogues. And you shall be brought before governors, and before kings. . . . You shall be hated by all men, . . . but he that shall persevere to the end shall be saved." All these things happened, and are repeated in the history of the Church.

The Offertory reminds us of the governing power and the dignity of the Apostles and their successors: "To me thy friends, O God, are made exceedingly honorable: their principality is exceedingly strengthened." The Communion guarantees that all "you who have left all things, and have followed Me, shall receive a hundredfold, and shall possess life everlasting." All who have followed the Apostles in this, will share in their reward. The Postcommunion asks that this may come true through the intercession of St. Paul. The teacher and preacher will find an abundance of practical material for fostering loyalty to Christ and His Church in the Offices of these two feasts.

In our days it cannot be clearly understood what an impression such celebrations made upon the faithful. For more than ten centuries the Liturgy with its instructions and ceremonies was practically the only means for bringing the knowledge and realization of the Faith and its mysteries to the majority of the people. Books were scarce, and the number of those who could read was comparatively insignificant. In those days the Faith was spread and kept alive by the Liturgy, by living with the Church and celebrating with her the sacred mysteries. This also supplied the necessary grace. The Liturgy is the "People's Catechism."

When the liturgical life was neglected, the door was opened for schisms and heresies, but the influence of the Liturgy lost none of its importance during the centuries. It is still invaluable for Christian living. The Feast of the Princes of the Apostles vividly recalls the foundation of the Church upon Peter the Rock, and that where Peter or his successor is, there is the Church that Christ founded and nowhere else. It also recalls the fact that in this Church there is a divinely established hierarchy that speaks with unerring authority. This one Church is a living organism kept healthy and in truth by the Holy Ghost through the infallible Vicar of Christ. There cannot be a federation of

FINAL PREPARATION OF MANKIND 225

Churches of Christ, since those founded by men not in union with St. Peter are evidently not of Christ. Catholics must not only know this, but must also realize and live this. Much loose talk would be left unspoken if the faithful were really imbued with this fact. The fact must be kept clearly in mind, while charity requires that we rather lovingly guide our erring brethren to the truth without needlessly offending them, but without compromising the truth.

The Sundays after Pentecost (V-VII)[1]

On the following Sundays the Church continues the moral instruction of her children, stressing what is most important for growth in perfection. Preserve charity; be not angry with your brother nor hate him; but if offended, be speedily reconciled (V). Christ has compassion with your physical and spiritual weaknesses; confide in Him (VI). A good tree brings forth good fruits; your good works will be rewarded by your Father with the glories of heaven (VII). This glory follows the keeping of the Commandments (Feast of the Transfiguration, August 6).

Assumption of the Blessed Virgin Mary

About this time the Church presents to the faithful the first and the most precious fruit of the Redemption, Mary who was assumed into heaven with body and soul and crowned as the Queen of Heaven. She is the only human being who did not have to await the final resurrection of her body in order to enter into the full possession of the complete eternal reward. Dwelling gloriously in heaven, she is for us a source of inspiration and joy.

Therefore, the Liturgy invites all Mary's children: "Let us all rejoice in the Lord, celebrating a festal day in honor of the Blessed Virgin, in whose assumption the Angels rejoice and give praise to the Son of God." And Mary answers our jubilation with the assurance: "My heart hath uttered a good word; I speak my works to the King" (Introit). Her good will is the salvation

---

[1] The roman numerals indicate the respective Sundays.

of all, and her work is to assist us in reaching heaven by obtaining for us the help of God. Since our own deeds "are unable to please Thee, O God, may we be saved by the intercession of the Mother of Thy Son" (Collect).

Through Mary as a type of Baptism and as the Mother of Christ's Mystical Body, each one of us was "established in Sion [the Church] and . . . took root in an honorable people, and in the portion of my God, His inheritance; and my abode is [to be] in the full assembly of Saints" (Lesson). May this come to pass, "because of truth, and meekness and righteousness . . . Hearken, O daughter [Christian soul], and see and incline thine ear, for the King hath greatly desired thy beauty" (Gradual). This Mary did and confessed in her words: "Behold the handmaid of the Lord"; and by doing so, "Mary has chosen the best part, which shall not be taken away from her" (Gospel). The perfect observance of God's will leads infallibly to the eternal possession of God. But since this is not so easy, we ask: "May the prayer of the Mother of God assist Thy people, O Lord, and though we know she has passed hence after the manner of all flesh, now that she is with Thee in the glory of heaven may we feel the benefit of her intercession . . . and be delivered from all impending evils" (Secret and Postcommunion).

The Sundays after Pentecost (VIII-XXIII) [1]

On the following Sundays (VIII-XXIII) the Church continues her efforts in the doctrinal parts of the Liturgy to sanctify, strengthen, and comfort her children.

The Liturgy of this period has two noticeable objectives in mind: it desires to prepare as many souls as possible for the coming harvest symbolized by the Ember Days in September, and to fortify the faithful against the Antichrist. There is no chronological order nor definite plan in the instructional part of the Mass texts, but the most important truths and laws regulating private and public life are presented in the Gospels and Epistles. Behind the life of the individual, the Church beholds the life of

---

[1] The roman numerals indicate the respective Sundays.

the Church and of the whole of mankind, which is after all but the sum total of the lives of individuals woven into one great pattern. Hence, in addition to caring for her individual members, the Church endeavors through them to prepare all mankind for the last great catastrophe prophesied and described on the Last Sunday of the Ecclesiastical Year.

The perversion of man preliminary to the final onslaught may already be under way. Therefore, the Church intensifies her instructions and prayers to counteract all evil influences militating against Christ and His Mystical Body. She has especially in mind the things that will lead to the battle of the Antichrist as foretold by Christ (Matt., xxiv, 4-13). Jesus, revealing the events preceding the end of the world, said: "Many will come in My name saying: I am the Christ." The several hundred so-called Christian sects in our land can no longer be ignored, because "they will seduce many." There will be tribulations for the members of the Church, and she will be molested and persecuted by *all* nations.

At present, all governments having any real power belong to one or more of these three varieties: Atheistic Communism, State Absolutism, and Masonic Liberalism. This may not yet be so evident in domestic policy, but it is clearly seen in international diplomacy. In this field, it is not nations but individuals that decide the destiny of peoples. Forthright Catholics are often barred from these circles, and if sporadically admitted they have at times little chance to protect the Church and bring about decisions that are just and charitable. Moreover, all three varieties of ideologies mentioned are expressly condemned by the Church, and those who favor them know and remember this and await an expedient moment. How much harm will come is a matter of degree and of how much God will tolerate. But "because iniquity hath abounded, the charity of many shall grow cold."

This is already evident all over the world, and has been stressed in papal pronouncements. For example, the present Holy Father laments persecution of bishops and faithful in his Encyclical on the Mystical Body:

"We are deeply pained when we hear that not a few of Our brother bishops are being attacked and persecuted, not only in their own person, but—which is more cruel and heart-rending for them—in the faithful committed to their care, in those who share their apostolic labor, even in the virgins consecrated to God; and all this just because they are a pattern of the flock from the heart and conserve, with justifiable energy and loyalty, the sacred 'deposit of faith' confided to them; just because they insist on the sacred laws that have been engraved by God on the souls of men and, after the example of the Supreme Shepherd, defend their flock against ravenous wolves. Such an offense We consider as committed against Our own Person. . . . We cannot but plead with all to love Holy Mother Church with a devoted and active love. Let us pray every day to the Eternal Father for her safety, and for her happy and large increase. . . . And while the skies are heavy with storm clouds and untold dangers menace all human society and the Church herself, let us commit ourselves and all that we have to the Father of mercies with the prayer: 'Look down, we beseech Thee, O Lord, on this Thy family, for which Our Lord Jesus Christ did not hesitate to be betrayed into the hands of evil men and to undergo the torture of the cross.' "

Besides spiritual trials there will be physical evils like wars and their consequences: death, pestilence, and famine. About these we need not be unduly alarmed, because they are in the hands of God Who alone can regulate them and use them for a good purpose. The principal concern of the Church is that her individual members remain in faith and charity to the end. For this the Church must and does labor, and in this labor the Liturgy is an outstanding means. But all the things enumerated above are only "the beginning of sorrows." The end is not yet in view. All these things have happened before, and may be repeated many times until the Antichrist is finally conquered.

Christ the King

The final victory of Christ over all His enemies is celebrated by the Liturgy on the ancient Feast of All Saints, which is introduced by the Invitation: "The Lord, the King of Kings, let us adore; because He Himself is the crown of all the Saints." In 1925 the Feast of Christ the King was introduced into the Liturgy with the same objective of adoring Christ as King of Kings, but from the special viewpoint that Christ is *now and forever* the King and Ruler of mankind. Several reasons for introducing this feast (to be celebrated on the Last Sunday of October which immediately precedes the Feast of All Saints) may be found in the conditions prevailing at the end of the first World War and the political situation that caused it.

The false doctrine of the supremacy of the State, independent and therefore above morals, and similar doctrines had uprooted Christian morality in the hearts of many. For years this false theory of expediency had been and still is taught in many secular universities in Europe and in all publicly supported colleges in the United States. Among liberal youth, this false doctrine is already taken as a truism. The State, being supreme in its own right, is considered not to be responsible to anyone, including God. A logical conclusion is that the most powerful State or combination of States could control and rule all others. Since God's rights are denied and practically removed from public and political life, it seems a logical conclusion that religion is a private matter and of no concern to the State as long as it does not interfere with the conduct of public life. It is true that Jesus standing before Pilate said: "My kingdom is not of this world." However, this was in answer to a question about a political kingship. In an absolute sense, Christ's answer was: "I am a king." Good and evil come from within a man, and there Christ should reign. This truth is of the greatest importance at present.

More beautiful and practical truths are expressed in the Liturgy, especially in the Preface, and in the Encyclical introducing and explaining the feast. At the end of the Encyclical on the Kingship of Christ, Pius XI writes:

> "If (as We have shown) to Christ the Lord is given all power in heaven and on earth, if mortal men bought by His most precious blood are subject to His sway by a certain new title (Redeemer), if, finally, this power embraces all human nature, it is clear that nothing is exempt from such an empire. He must, therefore, reign in the mind of man, and man with perfect submission must assent firmly and constantly to revealed truth. . . . He must reign in the will, which should obey divine laws and precepts. He must reign

in the soul, and . . . in the body and its members. . . . If all these things be thoroughly explained and proposed for the consideration of the faithful, they will be more easily led to the most perfect things."

Study clubs especially should be interested in the meaning, significance, and dogmatic content of this feast.

The Feast of All Saints

The Feast of All Saints, celebrated shortly before the end of the Liturgical Cycle (November 1), forms a fitting conclusion, because heavenly beatitude with Christ is the final end of the creation and Redemption of man. It places before our eyes how the promise made to us in Baptism is being fulfilled in the multitudes that have arrived at their destiny with God. It also solves problems hard to understand in mortal life, and proves that everything will be squared in eternity. "Why dost Thou not vindicate our blood?" asked the first martyrs for Christ. They received the divine response: "Wait a while until the number of your brethren has been completed" (Office of the Holy Innocents). Heavenly glory is the reward and the vindication of all who suffered a bloody or unbloody martyrdom for Christ, and to one of these two classes belong all who were baptized in the death of Christ and tried to live up to their baptismal obligations.

After St. John pictures the multitudes he saw in heaven (Epistle), the Gradual of the Mass adds: "They that seek the Lord shall not be deprived of any good." The sum of all good things is heaven. In heaven we shall be with God. The conditions for obtaining this exceedingly great reward are announced by Christ Himself in the Beatitudes (Gospel). They are the norms for our judgment, and will decide whether we are to enter heaven or be eternally rejected.

At the particular judgment the question is not how much and how grievously one has sinned. This is settled in every valid confession. One dying in mortal sin has already condemned himself. A multitude of forgiven sins and a lack of penance may

FINAL PREPARATION OF MANKIND   231

indeed influence the intensity of purgatory, but they do not exclude a soul from the eternal possession and enjoyment of God. The question at the particular judgment is how much you have done or neglected. The measure of eternal glory is determined by that. It is true that these deeds or omissions are covered by the Great Commandment, but how few in examining their conscience bother about the works of charity and mercy and try to purify their intentions! It is also true that matters of this kind overlooked or forgotten are pardoned by penance; but if this penance was not sufficient during life, the shortage has to be made up in purgatory.

The Feast of All Saints should urge the faithful to do penance during life, by showing that the prize expected is worth striving for. "Almighty, eternal God, . . . we beseech Thee, . . . bestow upon us . . . the fullness of Thy mercy we long for . . ." (Collect).

All Souls' Day

On All Souls' Day the Church Militant asks this same mercy for the Church Suffering. The Mass, celebrated in black vestments reminding us of the night in which no one can work for his soul, begins and ends with imploring: "Eternal rest grant to them, O Lord; and let perpetual light shine upon them." In other words: "Let all those still detained in purgatory come to the enjoyment of God's presence."

Shortly before the end of the Liturgical Cycle, the Church desires to do special good to those of her elect children who have not as yet entered their final glory, and also to remind her living children of the things to come. All Souls' Day should bring consolation to all.

Our merciful Mother the Church, most anxious to come to the rescue of her saved but not yet beatified children, permits the celebration of three Masses with the altar privilege on this day (since 1915) and grants a *toties quoties* indulgence applicable only to the faithful departed, under the usual conditions. The conditions for all indulgences of this type are the reception of the Sacraments, a visit to the church, and the recitation there at each visit of six Our Fathers, Hail Marys, and Glorias. Confessors have the faculty to substitute other good works for those who are sick or invalids. These great privileges were granted during the first World War, wherein so many perished, and are of an even greater significance in World War II, with its heavy toll of deaths through battle, bombings, famine, and pest. It would be rash to assume that all those who die suddenly in consequence of a war waged in a good cause, go straight to heaven.

Secondary but nevertheless important objectives of this Commemoration are to direct the minds of Christians to the end of their earthly life and to urge them to prepare for that solemn moment. The Liturgy strives to bring about a wholesome fear of God and His infinite justice (Epistle, *Dies iræ*, Gospel), but also inspires hope in God's infinite mercy (Orations, Offertory, Communion, and final Absolution). A note of consolation and Christian fortitude is added by pointing out that death does not destroy life but changes mortality into immortality (Preface).

Here a short explanation may be inserted about the words "*this* day" and "enter not into judgment," occurring in the Requiem Mass and burial rite. They sometimes puzzle the faithful who read or hear them recited for souls departed from this world for a considerable time. It must be remembered that, in offering our suffrages, we place ourselves sometimes in the condition of the deceased, and this may give a different meaning to our expressions. At the moment of physical death, the flow of time ceases and a perpetual present takes its place. Eternity has no succession and no change. This may be difficult for us to understand, since we have no experience to aid us, and because we are still *in via* during which acts and time succeed each other. But our last day on earth has no successor. That day is and remains the *last* day forever. At the moment of judgment God, being all-knowing, applies to a soul all that will be done for it until the end of the world. Hence, our intercession, if needed, never comes too late. This thought ought to help also to enlighten people who insist too much on the celebration of Masses on days when it is very difficult or impossible to grant the request.

FINAL PREPARATION OF MANKIND

Some writers compare the time between All Saints and the end of the Liturgical Year with the period between the conquest of the Antichrist and the Last Judgment. This is to be a time of peace and tranquillity for the Church to make the final efforts to save all men. It is like the quiet and peace of an old age matured in the Faith and resigned to comply with God's will. These are beautiful thoughts, but the Liturgy does not substantiate them.

CHAPTER XX

The Church Triumphant in the Liturgy

ALTHOUGH CATHOLICS DO NOT worship the saints, veneration of them has been intimately connected with divine worship in the Church since the beginning of Christianity. This veneration is not only reasonable but also necessary. Man is made up of body and soul. In practice the spiritual element cannot be severed entirely from the material and temporal. The Sacred Scriptures tell us how the Chosen People of old venerated their holy men even though God had commanded them not to have strange gods before Him. The Jews paid great tribute to their father Abraham and to the patriarchs and others on account of the noble service these had rendered the people of God. It was only the would-be reformers who cast aspersions on the veneration of saints and their relics. Against such reformers the Council of Trent reaffirmed the original Christian belief in the invocation, veneration, and intercession of the saints and in the veneration of their relics and images (Sess. XXV). Such practices on the part of the faithful ultimately redound to the greater glory of God. The sublime doctrine of the Mystical Body, taught by Christ and the Apostles, and brought to greater development in our day, gave the Church added reasons for the veneration of the saints and belief in their powerful intercession.

Mother Church has a hierarchy in the degrees in which she honors Christ's saints. Mary receives an eminent veneration because she is the Mother of God, the Co-Redemptress, and Mediatress of All Graces. St. Joseph receives prime veneration and all other saints receive ordinary veneration. Mother Church also classifies the liturgical celebration of feasts according to the importance of the mystery or according to the contribution a saint made to the welfare of the whole Mystical Body, aside from his personal holiness.

The degrees of solemnity among feast days are indicated in the Roman Calendar or Ordo. The ranks of feasts are, beginning with the lowest: simple, semidouble, double, double major, second class, and first class. According to these ranks the antiphons in the Divine Office are duplicated at each psalm or merely intoned at the beginning and recited in full at the end of each psalm (simple and semidouble). These ranks also indicate the number of orations and other prayers to be recited in the Divine Office and Mass.

The feasts of first and second class are again subdivided as primary and secondary. The primary first class feasts may have privileged octaves that are of the first, second, or third order. Thus Easter and Pentecost are doubles of the first class with octaves of the first order. Some feasts have merely a common octave such as the Assumption or a simple octave such as the Nativity of Our Lady. Other feasts are again subdivided into primary and secondary. Certain feasts have a Credo at Mass, other feasts have both a Gloria and a Credo.

Besides a general calendar or order observed by the entire Roman Rite, various countries, dioceses, cities, and religious orders have particular feasts in honor of some event or of their sainted patrons, founders, and other persons. In this way various calendars and orders of feasts originate. Thus a feast celebrated by the rest of the members of the Roman Rite may be postponed in a particular place or religious order owing to some special feast of a certain calendar. Bishops and religious superiors regulate the feasts for their respective subjects, with the approval of the Holy See. Hence some vernacular Missals used by the laity have certain feasts proper to various countries or religious orders.

The Blessed Virgin Mary

Mary has a unique place in the Liturgy and the Church honors her and prays to her in every Mass and Divine Office. Besides that, she has many special feasts. Mary has been honored by the

Church since the dying Christ gave her to be the Mother of those who believe in Him. St. John represented the Church at the foot of the Cross, when Christ told him; "Behold thy Mother." To Mary Christ said: "Behold thy son." The modern Popes have been particularly insistent on Mary's privileges, honor, power, and place in the economy of salvation.

Pope Pius IX defined the dogma of her Immaculate Conception. Pope Leo XIII pointed her out as the hope of mankind and especially urged the recitation of the Rosary. Popes Pius X and Benedict XV taught her great intercessory power and proclaimed her the Mother of all men through grace. Pope Benedict XV declared Mary the Queen of Peace.

Pope Pius XI was so devoted to the Mother of God that special treatises could be written on his Marian doctrine. He praised her and extolled her power as Co-Redemptress and Mediatress of All Graces on many occasions. To commemorate the fifteenth centenary of the Council of Ephesus (1931), he granted the Feast of Mary's Divine Maternity (October 11). The present Holy Father has called upon the world time and again to pray to the most holy and most powerful Mother of God for grace and world peace. He has dedicated the human race to her Immaculate Heart (October 1942, on the occasion of the twenty-fifth anniversary of the last apparition of Our Lady at Fatima) and in the Encyclical on the Mystical Body he gives her special praise and asks her to protect the Church.

Devotion to the Virgin Mother of God is as old as the Church. She it was who offered her Son for mankind. Her prayers hastened the coming of the Holy Spirit on Pentecost. She encouraged and consoled the infant Church in the days of persecution and early growth. Since her Assumption into heaven no grace is given to mankind except by her intercession and through her means. Little wonder, therefore, that Mother Church honors the Queen of Heaven and Earth in so special a manner in the Liturgy and in many other ways. St. Anselm writes that when Mary prays all the saints pray and when she is silent no saint prays.

From early times Mary's name is mentioned in connection

with the divine mysteries and gradually feasts were instituted to honor her privileges and offices as well as the main events of her life. The feasts of her Conception, Birth, Annunciation, Visitation, Purification, and Assumption are ancient. Other feasts were added through the centuries. Modern Popes have given us new Marian feasts such as that of Our Lady of Lourdes, the Holy Family, the Divine Maternity; and, for certain places and religious orders, the feasts of Mary, Mediatress of All Graces, Mother of the Good Shepherd, and Queen of the Apostles. These newer feasts do not celebrate new doctrines but emphasize and explain the truths regarding Mary and her glorious position and offices in God's plan of salvation.

Throughout the year Mary is with Christ in His great feasts. Thus it was in His life. Mary is united with Christ in the eternal decree of salvation. She shares glory with Him. She is close to Him in prophecy, in life, in heaven, and in the Liturgy. In the course of the year's feasts her relations to the Mystical Body are stressed in prayerful contemplation. Thus the Liturgy again confirms the doctrine regarding the Mother of God and her power.

We live in a wonderful Marian age. Modern saints such as Gabriel of the Sorrowful Mother, Conrad of Parzham, Thérèse of the Child Jesus, Gemma Galgani, Don Bosco, and Mother Cabrini have all been noted for their extraordinary love and devotion to the Immaculate Virgin Mother of God. Modern Popes teach her glories and power with ever-mounting clarity and insistence. Mary herself has visited our earth at Lourdes and Fatima on various occasions in 1858 and 1917, confirming and encouraging devotion to her Immaculate Conception, her Rosary, and the use of her Scapular as Queen of Mt. Carmel. The faithful are responding to Mary, with increased devotion to her as Mother of Divine Grace in the Miraculous Medal devotions, in the May and October manifestations of love for her, and in other forms.

The great and venerable religious orders are drawing new treasures from the vast heritage of their ancient devotion to Mary. The Franciscans present her as the Immaculate Queen; the Capuchin-Franciscans, as the Immaculate Mother of the Good Shepherd; the Benedictines, as their Delight. The Dominicans spread the devotion of her Rosary; the Carmelites clothe the faithful with her scapular. The Augustinians honor her as the Mother of Good Counsel; the Passionists, as the Mother of Sorrows; the Redemptorists, as the Mother of Perpetual Help.

No matter how we multiply titles and feasts in honor of Mary, we cannot praise her or honor her sufficiently since she has a most exalted and mysterious dignity as Mother of God! She helped in our Redemption in a unique way and she distributes the fruits of that Redemption. Pope Pius X, in his Encyclical, "Ad diem illum" (February 2, 1904), teaches that Mary by her union of will with her Divine Son, merited to become the "Dispenser of all the gifts which Jesus procured for us by His death and precious Blood."

Two great saints of the Franciscan family, St. Bernardine and St. Conrad of Parzham, have contributed notably to the cult and spread of devotion to Mary, our Spiritual Mother and Mediatress of All Graces.

St. Bernardine's doctrine on the Blessed Virgin in her various privileges and offices is clear and advanced for his time. In fact, he teaches the present and future ages. He adduced new proof for her Immaculate Conception over four centuries before the doctrine was defined as a dogma. Pope Leo XIII, in his Encyclical, "Jucunda semper" (September 8, 1894), quotes St. Bernardine, to teach us that "every grace that comes to this world has a triple process: from God to Christ, from Christ to the Virgin, and from the Virgin to us" (Sermo vi in Annun. B.M.V.). St. Bernardine ranks with the famous Marian Doctors, Sts. Ephrem, Bernard, Anselm, Thomas Aquinas, Bonaventure, John of the Cross, Robert Bellarmine, and Alphonsus Liguori. To this list we must add several who are not yet Doctors of the Church, namely, Sts. Antonine, Lawrence of Brindisi, Germanus of Constantinople, John Eudes, Don Bosco, and Grignion de Montfort (whose canonization lacks merely the external solemnity of declaration).

St. Conrad of Parzham, the humble Capuchin-Franciscan lay

CHURCH TRIUMPHANT IN THE LITURGY 239

Brother of modern times, was neither a preacher nor a writer. Yet by his ardent love for the Mother of God he inspired thousands of pilgrims with greater devotion to her whilst he lived at her shrine at Altötting, Bavaria, for over forty years. He exhorted the people to trustful prayer to the Mother of God, who is all powerful with her Son and he distributed the Mt. Carmel scapular to the pilgrims. St. Conrad has been compared to the Marian Doctors of the Church, especially Sts. John of the Cross and Alphonsus Liguori.

In concluding this part on Marian feasts and devotion it is recommended that the various texts given in the Masses and Divine Offices of Our Lady's feasts be studied and contemplated. They will yield a rich fruit if thus prayerfully considered.

*

St. Joseph

St. Joseph had a place of honor in the East for long centuries. In the West a church was dedicated to him for the first time at Bologna in 1129. But the devotion to St. Joseph soon spread in Europe. Pope Benedict XIV ascribes this fact to the Fathers of Carmel who came to Europe in the twelfth century. Among the great saints who wrote about St. Joseph and his unique place among saints, the more important writers are Sts. Bernard, Thomas Aquinas, Vincent Ferrer, Bernardine of Siena, Gertrude, and Bridget of Sweden.

Towards the end of the fourteenth century the Franciscans and Dominicans introduced a feast in honor of St. Joseph. At first it was celebrated only by their orders but soon some dioceses adopted the feast. John Gerson wrote an Office of the Espousals of Joseph and Mary and defended the cult of St. Joseph at the Council of Constance (1414). Sts. Bernardine and Vincent Ferrer were ardent defenders of St. Joseph and his cult. The writings of St. Bernardine have served the Church in this regard for five centuries. We have already mentioned the fact that the Breviary Lesson for the Second Nocturn on the Feast of the Patronage of St. Joseph is taken from one of Bernardine's sermons. Other writings of this Saint have also been employed by the Holy See in defense of St. Joseph.

The devotion and zeal of the Carmelites, Franciscans, and Dominicans, together with the work of Gerson and Peter d'Ailly, spread the cult of St. Joseph so far and wide in Europe that Pope Sixtus IV (1471-84) introduced the Feast of St. Joseph on March 19 into the Roman Calendar. Pope Gregory XV made the feast a holy day of obligation in 1621. Pope Paul III granted the Feast of the Espousals of Joseph and Mary to the Franciscans in 1537. This feast had first been granted by Pope Leo X to the Franciscan Nuns of the Annunciation in 1517 (January 23). Pope Benedict XIII in 1725 granted this feast to all orders and dioceses requesting it.

True to their tradition, the Carmelites continued to cultivate St. Joseph's devotion with special zeal. St. Teresa of Avila is known to have had an extraordinary devotion to him. In her Autobiography she writes:

> "I took St. Joseph for my patron and advocate, and I recommend myself unceasingly to his protection. I do not remember ever having asked anything of him that I did not obtain. . . . Our Lord wished us to understand that, as He was obedient to His Foster-father here upon earth, so He can now refuse him no request in Heaven. . . . I have never met anyone who had devotion to him who did not advance rapidly in the path of virtue, because he mightily aids all who recommend themselves to his intercession" (chapter vi).

In 1621 the Discalced Carmelites chose St. Joseph as their Patron and in 1689 the Ven. Pope Innocent XI granted them the feast of the Saint's Patronage on the Third Sunday after Easter. This feast spread through the Spanish Kingdom and to other places. The nineteenth century saw an immense increase in devotion to St. Joseph especially among the poor and working classes. Pope Pius VII granted various privileges and a Votive Mass in honor of St. Joseph.

Sensing the ever-mounting devotion to this great Saint, Pope Pius IX extended the Feast of the Patronage of St. Joseph to the universal Church in 1847. At the end of the Vatican Council

CHURCH TRIUMPHANT IN THE LITURGY

on December 8, 1870, the same Pope declared St. Joseph the Patron of the Universal Church and raised his feast on March 19 to a double of the first class but without an octave. Pope Leo XIII ordered prayers in honor of St. Joseph and gave the Church the splendid examples of virtue exhibited by the Holy Family. Pope Benedict XV extended (1921) the Feast of the Holy Family (on the Sunday within the Octave of Epiphany) to the whole Church. Pope Pius X granted a litany in honor of St. Joseph in 1909.

The Capuchin-Franciscans have ever been most zealous preachers of devotion to St. Joseph. They exerted a remarkable influence in extending the feast of his Patronage to the whole Church. Proper to their order is the Scapular of St. Joseph enriched with many indulgences by modern Popes. Many are the churches and Provinces of the Capuchin-Franciscans, as well as of the Carmelites, Franciscans, and other religious, dedicated to St. Joseph. The Capuchin-Franciscan José Calasanctius Cardinal Vives y Tuto has compiled a "Summa Josephina" containing fine sermons and poems as well as various Acts of the Holy See in honor of St. Joseph.[1]

The Church hopes great things from this new increase in love for the Foster-Father of Christ. As Protector of the Universal Church in these difficult times, St. Joseph stands before the Church with new luster. Undoubtedly the greater liturgical cult of this hidden Saint will focus attention on him ever more as the decades roll on. There is hope that this cult will unfold new glories of St. Joseph for the consolation of the whole Church.

The Apostles

The Apostles venerated in the Liturgy are the men chosen by Christ to carry on His mission and to bring the fruits of Redemption to the world. These men, with the exception of Judas Iscariot, fulfilled their task, and their successors, the Popes and bishops, continue this work through the ages. Mathias was

---

[1] Typographia Instituti Pii IX, Romæ, 1907.

chosen by the Apostles, after prayer, to fill the place of Judas. After His Ascension into heaven, Christ chose Paul to be a special Apostle of the Gentiles. Barnabas was one of Paul's most important companions in this sublime work. Peter was Christ's Vicar on earth, yet Paul also had a very distinguished place among the Apostles.

The Apostles and the Evangelists had the highest mission of spreading the great news of salvation throughout the world. By word and work, by writing and example, the Apostles taught the world the path of peace and held before it the Cross and Resurrection of Our Lord Jesus Christ. The Apostles are the first channels of Christ's truth. Their veneration is almost as old as the Church herself. This cult increased in the course of time; but Peter and Paul have been honored since the day of their martyrdom.

Classes of Saints

All other saints are considered either as *Martyrs* or *Non-Martyrs*. The latter class is again subdivided into Popes, bishops, non-bishops, virgins, and widows. Twenty-eight saints are honored with the special title of Doctor of the Church, besides some other title such as martyr or bishop. Of these Doctors two were Popes, eighteen were bishops, seven were priests, and one, St. Ephrem, was a deacon. Their ranks will be increased as the centuries pass.

Martyrs in the liturgical sense are those who give up their lives for Christ. They profess their faith by suffering a violent death. They witness to the true Faith in an heroic way and hence their name, martyrs, which is a Greek word meaning witnesses. In the early days of the Church only Mary and the martyrs were venerated. It was easy to establish the cult of the martyrs since the fact of martyrdom was obvious and the people rightly considered these victims as heroes of the Cross. Since the Church underwent fierce persecutions in the early centuries and, at many times since then, there is a vast phalanx of martyrs honored in the Liturgy. The age of martyrs is ever with us and our days have

CHURCH TRIUMPHANT IN THE LITURGY 243

seen many thousands put to death for the Faith of Christ on all continents of the globe.

A saint may have an Office and Mass proper to himself, but generally the texts for both Office and Mass are taken from the Common of a certain class of saints. Thus we have a Common for Apostles, Evangelists, Popes, one Martyr, many Martyrs, Confessor Bishops, a Confessor who is not a Bishop, Abbots, many Confessors who are not Bishops, Virgins, and Non-Virgins.[1] Besides these Commons there are special texts for the feasts of the Angels; also a Common for the ordinary feasts of the Blessed Virgin and another for the Dedication of a Church. The newest Common is that for Sainted Popes, issued by Pope Pius XII on January 9, 1942, in virtue of the decree, "Sancta Mater Ecclesia." It has a complete Mass, "Si diligis me," but there are merely special prayers and a homily for the Office. The other parts of the Office are taken from the Common for Martyrs or Confessor Bishops respectively, depending on whether the Pope laid down his life for the Faith or not.

In regard to the cult of the *Angels* the Roman Rite took this over from the East. The Church distinguishes Archangels and Angels in her cult. She does not honor spirits of other choirs specifically. The Roman Rite pays tribute to the Archangels Michael, Gabriel, and Raphael on account of their relation to the Redeemer, the work of Redemption, or the help of the Church. Michael is considered the Protector of the Church as he was formerly the defender of the Chosen People. Uriel, who is mentioned in the Byzantine Liturgy, is not inserted in the Roman Rite; but the Feast of St. Michael (September 29) embraces all the angelic spirits. The Guardian Angels are honored by a special feast on October 2.

These feasts of the Angels testify to the fact that God "gives His angels charge over us." At least all baptized persons, as well as nations, dioceses, cities, and other communities of the Church and Christian States have a heavenly spirit to protect

---

[1] There is also a Common for Apostles and Evangelists in Paschal time, and a Common for Martyrs in that time.

them and to offset the evil influence, which the satanic hordes can still exert. The honor paid the angelic protectors is an act of thanksgiving for their services, an admonition to reverence their presence, and a reminder to have greater confidence and more frequent recourse to them in all our needs both spiritual and temporal. We have encouraging examples of such angelic help in the lives of God's servants, especially Sts. Don Bosco, Frances of Rome, and Gemma Galgani.

Some *Patriarchs* and *Prophets* of the Old Law are venerated in various Liturgies of the Catholic Church. Even the Roman Rite honors some of them in the Martyrology; and St. John the Baptist receives special honor in the whole Church. The Carmelites reverence Sts. Elias and Eliseus with special feasts. But the Catholic Church also has patriarchs, such as the archbishops who rule over a great see founded by an Apostle or raised to such dignity by the Popes. The Holy Father himself is the Patriarch of the West. Of course here we use the term patriarch in a different sense than in the Old Law. Thus, too, the Church has prophets because the Pentecostal gifts are always present in the Church in some form. Through her saints in the course of ages, the Church has the gifts of tongues, miracles, and prophecy. The Apostles foretell events in various parts of their letters. St. John especially is a prophet in the Apocalypse. However, there is no Common for either Patriarchs or Prophets. Saints who were of these classes come under the title of Martyr, Bishop, Confessor, or some other proper title.

Confessors, Virgins, or *Non-Virgins* are the respective titles of all saints who did not die as martyrs. They may have suffered otherwise but they are said to have confessed or witnessed Christ not by a violent death but by an heroic life of Christian virtue. Their number is exceedingly great, for St. John tells us in the Apocalypse: "And I heard the number of them that were signed, a hundred forty-four thousand were signed, of every tribe of the children of Israel. . . . After that I saw a great multitude, which no man could number, of all nations, and tribes, and peoples, and tongues, standing before the throne and in sight of the Lamb, clothed with white robes, and palms in their hands: And they cried with a loud voice, saying: Salvation to our God . . . and to the Lamb" (Apoc., vii, 4, 9, 10).

However, the number of canonized persons who are not martyrs is rather small. The reason is that for canonization much more is required by the Church than the mere fact that the person entered heaven. Otherwise infants and children who die in their innocence could be canonized. The Church demands heroic virtue of those whom she canonizes in order to set splendid examples of holiness before her children. There are comparatively few youthful confessors and virgins canonized for the very fact that heroic virtue, and the maturity of faith with its influence on others, ordinarily come much later in life. Moreover, the exacting process of canonization and beatification requires many testimonies and much probing—all of which are not normally carried out in a short time. Some processes last for centuries.

In modern times, however, we have seen some extraordinary cases quickly come to a happy end. Thus St. Conrad of Parzham's cause began in 1910. It was introduced into Rome in 1924. He was beatified in 1930 and canonized on May 20, 1934. This case is exceptional, for it was the speediest in modern centuries and the first one begun and completed under one and the same Pope. The Little Flower was canonized only twenty-eight years after her death—a record for modern times.

The process of beatification and canonization is the most exacting in the Church. Popular demand begins such a process under the auspices of the Bishop. If that process is satisfactory, Rome calls the case to herself and examines further. Some cases are dropped entirely, while many others await further testimony or miracles that can be proved beyond doubt to have been wrought at the intercession of the person in question.

We see that besides canonizing a person, the Church declares them in some class of saints. The main classes are Martyrs and Non-Martyrs. Some saints have special glory in heaven. They are the Martyrs, Doctors, and Virgins. A certain saint may have all three glories before God and yet only one or two will be recognized liturgically. Virginity is proper not only to women but also to men. In fact St. John in the Apocalypse ascribes it first of all to men. "They . . . who were not defiled with women . . . are virgins. These follow the Lamb wherever He goeth. . . . They are without spot" (Apoc. xiv, 4-5). Yet, liturgically the title of Virgin is used only for a woman.

It is consoling for the faithful to know that even though they may never be canonized, even though they will remain hidden on earth, in heaven they may have the special glories of one or more of these titles as martyrs, doctors, or virgins. Even the desire of martyrdom and heroically bearing the burden of life's duties give us a share in the martyrs' glory. To teach others to justice by word and example in the family, in the school, or at work and in social life, gives us a share in the glory of the doctors. And who will deny that the number of virgins of both sexes is very great in heaven? These considerations should be incentives to the faithful and the clergy to strive for higher things and to bear life's trials and temptations with patience and even with joy.

Saints are also classified in the Liturgy according to their influence on their own and subsequent times. The fact that some man or woman is an appealing example of holiness, or has some special relation to some mystery of faith, or has extraordinary power before God, will determine his or her place and rank in the Liturgy.

St. Francis of Assisi

Among the saints not closely connected with the life of Christ, very few enjoy such popularity and constantly increasing veneration as St. Francis of Assisi. He was not of noble birth nor the scion of a very wealthy and prominent family having a great influence in Church and State, but rather a son of the common people. His life is sufficiently known and will not be repeated here except in so far as it is necessary to understand his universal veneration and his position in the Liturgy. How could St. Francis, the simple confessor, arrive at this status, is the question to be answered at present.

Like his Divine Master, he had to be born in a stable presaging his future humility. Unlike his Master, he was not brought up in a perfectly holy family. The care of his saintly mother, although sowing the seed for future holiness, was not able to neutralize the worldly influence of his father. So Francis grew up as the son of Bernadone rather than the child of God. Although he lacked the true Christian mentality, he was according to the standards of the surrounding world, a good youth and a likable companion. He was in quest of pleasure as well as of conquest. However, the plans of God with regard to Francis were different. Christ wanted him to find his pleasure in other things and his conquests in fields that were not of this world. God made use of natural inclinations to reach a supernatural end. His grace led Francis to the first step absolutely required for every conversion, to self-reform. Without this step Francis could not reform others.

This step having been taken, Francis resolved to imitate his Divine Master as closely as possible. God revealed to Francis that the distinguishing feature of his life and that of his companions, who were attracted by his good example, should be absolute poverty as far as it was humanly possible. Thereafter, singular and significant events proceeded rapidly.

One of the first things St. Francis did was to compose a rule, in order to acquaint his brethren and followers more definitely with the requirements of a life in conformity with the teachings of the Gospel, such as he and his associates were to live. Although his rule was inspired by God, Francis desired, for good reasons, a special approval from God's Vicar on earth. He had already received the consent and encouragement of his Bishop in Assisi, but he realized that more was required to fulfill the task which God had predestined for him.

By his frequent meditations Francis saw that without progress in sanctity a successful spiritual labor for others is impossible. He realized that his own personal standing and the authority of a single bishop would not bear much weight in a Christianity that was in his time as secularized and worldly minded as it is today. He needed a help without which, humanly speaking, not much of a spiritual reform could be brought about. His thoughts were directed to the Pope.

In this he differed substantially from past and future "reformers" who inaugurated their reforms from without instead of from within the Church. Francis saw in the Pope more than an outstanding and powerful personality. He saw him in his full stature and was convinced of the ancient dictum "Where Peter is, there is the Church." For him, the visible head of the Church was a perceptible representation of the unity, infallibility, indestructibility, and authority of the Church. The physical Vicar of Christ was also the visible head of the Mystical Body and the symbol of Christ's enduring presence among us as the Shepherd of His Flock. Consequently, it was inconceivable for Francis to engage in any work without the Pope's approval.

Francis asked the papal confirmation of his rule of life and the apostolic mission for the labors of his order. The future revealed more clearly the significance of this fact. Francis and his order became destined not only to labor in and for the Universal Church, but also in union with and in obedience to the Church. His example was subsequently followed by other holy founders.

St. Francis is the founder of three orders. The first order is for men, and the second for women, living a community life with solemn vows and the obligation to follow the binding precepts of their rule. The third order, called the Order of Penance, he founded for all men and women living in the world, beginning with the Pope and ending with the humblest member of the laity. For each of these autonomous orders, Francis himself wrote the rule of life according to the Gospel. Hence, they are essentially the same, the variations being necessitated by the different states and modes of life. Only those communities who follow these rules are founded by St. Francis. The Third Order Regular and the multitude of Franciscan Congregations are later developments of the Third Order.

Another outstanding factor that greatly affected the religious life of the whole Church was the combination of the contemplative life with the active apostolate. It worked splendidly and so did the transplanting of the regular life into the secular world by means of the Third Order. It enlivened faith and reformed morals and so stabilized the tottering Church that Pope Innocent III had seen in a dream with Francis supporting it.

Whilst the work was spreading and the first fruits appeared, Francis received from God the assurance that his work would last until the end of time, and with it came the consolation that henceforth some heroic souls would always earnestly strive to lead a more perfect life according to the Gospel, in community as well as in the world. That the processes of canonization of Franciscans have been almost uninterrupted establishes this sufficiently.

Now all the facts enumerated so far, and several more, enrich the Liturgy of the Franciscans found in every part of the world. But one outstanding fact deserves special mention because it affects the Liturgy of the whole Church. Jesus desired visibly to manifest the zeal and love that burned in the heart of St. Francis and to give an evident approval to his life and labors (Proper Preface). Christ did this by appearing to him crucified, surrounded by wings of Seraphs, and impressed upon Francis' body the wounds which He Himself bore. In addition, the nails were visible on both sides of the hands and feet of the Saint. Thus marked, he could with St. Paul call upon Christ as a witness of his divine mission. "I bear the marks of the Lord Jesus in my body" (Gal., vi, 17).

The Church celebrates this event on September 17, and the Liturgy on that day expresses the theological content of this singular distinction. This stigmatization differed from all others that ever took place. Concerning it, St. Bonaventure, the Seraphic Doctor of the Church, writes that it was presaged by the Angel in the Apocalypse sent by God to mark the elect with a cross. Facts like these are significant for the entire Church; otherwise they would not have been made a part of the universal Liturgy.

Other facts which increase the veneration of the Saint, such as being chosen as special Patron of countries, dioceses, cities, pious organizations, and lately of Catholic Action, cannot be enlarged upon here. It must suffice to state that the veneration of St. Francis has never lapsed but has been kept on a high level throughout the Church for over seven centuries.

Some Other Significant Saints

The significance of St. Francis for the Church, which we have but feebly sketched, is not an isolated phenomenon. In every crisis of Christianity and for every class of persons God has called holy souls to assist the Church, and especially the Pope, by prayer and labor. With some saints this special help became apparent at once; with others it became known only after their death. Sometimes a saint's influence hastens his canonization. But if he was involved in public life and especially if he wrote much, the process of canonization takes longer, in order to investigate the life and writings.

Here we can refer only to a few of the saints who have had special influence in the Church. St. Dominic fought and conquered the Albigensian heresy of his day. St. Catherine of Siena helped to bring the Popes back to Rome from Avignon and has been declared principal Patroness of Italy, together with St. Francis of Assisi.[1] Sts. Ignatius Loyola, Peter Canisius, Robert Bellarmine, Pius V, and Lawrence of Brindisi were among the great leaders of the Catholic Counter-Reformation. St. Lawrence was also an apostle of the Jews in Europe. St. Charles Borromeo merits special honor as a great Bishop at the close of the Tridentine Council. He set an example of episcopal zeal and reform in Lombardy.

Young and old, rich and poor, active and hidden people find their models in the saints. The Church, therefore, is happy to place before us youthful examples of sanctity, such as St. Aloysius Gonzaga, Gabriel of the Sorrowful Mother, and the Little Flower. Some saints encourage missionary activity, such as Fidelis of Sigmaringen and Francis Xavier. Again, the Church is pleased to allow all the faithful to honor those whose devotion and work in life laid emphasis on some special truth or devotion, such as St. John Eudes and St. Margaret Mary Alocoque for devotion to the Sacred Heart, and St. Bernadette for devotion to the Immaculate Conception, although her feast is not yet celebrated by the whole Church. St. Conrad of Parzham and the

---
[1] By Pope Pius XII in April, 1939.

CHURCH TRIUMPHANT IN THE LITURGY 251

Little Flower are modern wonder-workers, while St. Don Bosco and the latest Doctors, Sts. John of the Cross, Peter Canisius, Robert Bellarmine, and Albert the Great, stress the office of teaching, preaching, and writing for young and old. Our own day glories in Sts. Gemma Galgani and Francesca Cabrini, whose canonization lacks only the external declaration. St. Gemma assisted the Pope by her prayers. St. Thérèse of Lisieux helped the Pope and the missions by her fidelity and love.

This hidden power of sanctity will continue in the Church till the end of time. Some of these saints will become known, but most of them will remain hidden. God alone knows who those saints are who are helping the Church and the Pope in the present crisis of Christianity. Their sufferings and prayers will bring happier times to the Church and the Holy Father.

It is in God's plan that certain saints receive a world-wide veneration within a comparatively short time and that some saints arrive at the honors of canonization only long after their death. In April, 1944, for example, the Pope canonized Margaret of Hungary who died in 1270. What God does is well done. All the elect, whether known on earth or not, do great good to the Church. Heaven will surprise us with many hidden saints on the last day. For further material the reader is referred to the Breviary, reference works, and biographies of the saints.

CHAPTER XXI

The Liturgy and Christian Life

THE PRINCIPAL OBJECTIVE of the Liturgy is the glory of God directly, while indirectly it seeks to enhance this glory by making men Christ-like. To God it renders praise, thanksgiving, and atonement; for men it provides a means of petition and a norm of life as members of Christ's Mystical Body. Baptism incorporated us into Christ; but unless our life is based upon His views, motivated by His principles, and guided by His attitudes, there is division and no union. These are undeniable truths: "If you be risen with Christ, seek the things that are above . . . : mind the things that are above, not the things that are on earth" (Col., iii, 1-2). All the baptized have risen with Christ, "for you are dead; and your life is hid with Christ in God" (ibid., 3). Christian life, to be worthy of the name, must conform to, be hidden in, or merged with the life of Christ, if we now constitute one body with and in Him.

At the present time there is nothing more urgent than the recovery of the necessary and only correct viewpoint and attitude announced by Christ, true God and true Man: "Seek ye . . . first the kingdom of God," (Matt., vi, 33). He did not qualify this statement, although He knew all the modifications, excuses, and objections that later ages would make. He simply added the assurance that God will take care of the rest.

In very fact, this assertion of Christ is not doubted by Christians; but it has been so modified by personal interpretations that its vital significance has become obscured, if it is remembered at all. The "everything else" has taken the place of the one thing necessary. In consequence of this, the number of those who are trying to live or cultivate a truly spiritual life is rapidly

THE LITURGY AND CHRISTIAN LIFE 253

diminishing, whilst the seekers after mere temporal improvement grow by leaps and bounds.

How can this evil tendency be stemmed and the balance restored?

Seemingly not by spiritual preaching and writings alone. These exhortations are heard and read by some, but the reader or hearer is often like "a man beholding his own countenance in a glass; for he beheld himself, and went his way, and presently forgot what manner of man he was" (James, i, 23-24). Moreover, truly spiritual and spiritualizing books are scarce; and when they occasionally appear, literary editors and reviewers no longer realize what they are about, and dismiss them with some generality. Hence, they have only a very limited sale, and cannot be sold at a popular price. And, in turn, their cost becomes a further handicap to the distribution of these books and the author's first purpose is frustrated. For material profit is the last thing that the author sought.

Nor are the usual Sunday talks apt to bring about a greater spirituality. In many listeners the soil is already too cold to make the seed sown bring forth good fruit. Besides, an effective spiritual sermon requires a highly spiritual preacher. Since recent preaching methods were not effective in maintaining the spirituality that once existed, they evidently cannot revive what has vanished.

The thoughts so far expressed are not mere personal opinions of the writer, but are also expressed and corroborated by high ecclesiastical authorities. One may find them in the Encyclical of Pope Pius XII addressed to the Church in the United States. The praises contained therein are often quoted and enlarged upon, but the urgent pleas for the removal of specified evils mentioned are left buried in the *Acta*. This is, alas, a psychological tendency. People, as a rule, do not like to be reminded of things that they ought to know and realize; consequently, even the soundest advice is often wasted.

In his "Manual of Catholic Action" Msgr. Luigi Civardi writes: "What we have to lament to-day . . . is not so much widespread ill-behavior, . . . as the loss or distortion of the moral sense."[1] Where there are spiritual and intellectual disorders, this is but a natural consequence. Archbishop Samuel Stritch put the matter concisely, when speaking to a gathering of prominent laymen he said: "If there is a single criticism that one would make of the greatest Catholic laity in the world, the Catholic laity of the United States, it would be that they have not a sufficient intellectual foundation for their religion. They have not a Catholic mentality."[2] Much less do they have a spiritual-mindedness, for this is more difficult to acquire and cultivate.

While the Archbishop was addressing himself strictly to the laity, his words may be safely extended to all who spend the greater part of the most impressionable period of their life as members of the laity. Seminaries and novitiates will not easily bring about a sudden and permanent change in fundamental attitudes. Such changes may come in later years as the result of some kind of shock.

During the earlier part of human life there is no true spirituality. There are few exceptions to this general rule. Young confessors and virgins were canonized for reasons of their love of God and their early victories over the world, Satan, and the flesh. Valiantly they kept the Commandments for the love of God (John, xiv, 15). The child saints, guided by the fear of God, were carried to heaven in the arms of Mother Church. With these, the early impressions received in the home were the most decisive factors.

The Liturgy and Spiritualizing the Masses

The Liturgy is a most desirable means of respiritualizing the masses. Although conditions are deplorable, there is no reason to doubt that an improvement can be brought about, for the Holy Ghost is still active in the Church. As used at present, the word Liturgy does not merely connote the collection of perceptive and directive rubrics necessary for the dignified celebration of the sacred mysteries; in its primary meaning and significance,

---

[1] Page 41. Quoted with the permission of the publishers, Sheed & Ward.
[2] *Catholic Herald* (Milwaukee), January 15, 1935.

THE LITURGY AND CHRISTIAN LIFE 255

it embraces divine worship as practised by the Mystical Body as a whole. This worship comprises the life, thoughts, desires, words, and actions of the "kingly" priesthood, as well as of the hierarchical.

To render this worship to God completely and adequately, in a manner highly profitable to man, it is necessary that we rise above mere physical needs and conveniences, because "if you live according to the flesh, you shall die; but if by the spirit you mortify the deeds of the flesh, you shall live. For whosoever are led by the Spirit of God, they are the sons of God" (Rom., viii, 13-14). These words of the Apostle of the Gentiles are not gainsaid by modern Christians; but they are conveniently put aside, which amounts to the same thing. It remains infallibly true that a material or purely natural life divorced from the supernatural cannot lead to eternal life with God.

How the Liturgy can and does help man's spiritual progress is clearly seen when we examine the pattern and methods as revealed by its texts and forms. Its doctrinal parts stress unceasingly the most important dogmas of Christianity, and relate them to other subsidiary truths. Corollaries are always connected with the basis upon which they rest. In all forms of worship, taken either separately or in a series, the Trinity of God and His perfections or attributes are recalled. The creation and fall of man are commemorated at least in their consequences. The Incarnation and Redemption are constantly kept before our eyes by emphasis on the benefits they brought to man. The activities of the Holy Ghost are reiterated in various ways in the Liturgy. He is the Vivifying Principle of the life of the Mystical Body; we are told of His work in the Church in applying the fruits of the Redemption through the means of grace; we learn of His intimate relation to Christian life. Pope Pius XII enlightens us on the Holy Spirit when he writes:

> "Just as at the first moment of the Incarnation, the Son of the Eternal Father adorned with the fullness of the Holy Spirit the human nature which was substantially united with Him, that it might be a fitting instrument of the Divinity in the sanguinary task of the Redemption, so, at the hour of His precious death, He

wished that His Church should be enriched with the abundant gifts of the Paraclete in order that, in dispensing the divine fruits of the Redeemer, it might be for the Incarnate Word a powerful instrument that would certainly never fail. . . . Christ is in us through His Spirit, Whom He gives to us, and through Whom He acts within us in such a way that all divine activity of the Holy Spirit within our souls must also be attributed to Christ. . . . This communication of the Spirit of Christ is the channel through which flow into all the members of the Church those gifts, powers, and extraordinary graces found superabundantly in the head as in their source, and they are perfected day by day in those members according to the office they may hold in the Mystical Body of Jesus Christ. Thus the Church becomes, as it were, the filling-out and complement of the Redeemer, while Christ in a sense attains through the Church a fulness in all things. Here We touch the reason why, to the mind of Augustine, the Mystical Head, which is Christ, and the Church, which on this earth, as another Christ, bears His Person, constitute one new man, in whom heaven and earth are yoked together in perpetuating the cross' work of salvation: By Christ, we mean the Head and the Body—the whole Christ." [1]

The keystone of all liturgical worship and also its central theme is that the Resurrection brought not only a new life of glory to Christ, but also a new life leading to glory for all who believe in Him and have been "baptized in His death."

Such is an outline of what God did for man, whom Christ elevated to a high estate. What man must do in return follows as a logical consequence. The child of God must preserve his dignity, and must make atonement for sin to his Heavenly Father. The divine adoption must be made secure and permanent by loving our God made known to us by faith, by the cultivation of various virtues, and especially by practising penance—which consists in denying our own will for the love of God. By doing all this, the child of God will infallibly come to rest in the bosom of the Father.

The Liturgy insists frequently on doing penance, but does not neglect to point out its double character. The essence of penance is a turning away from creatures to the Creator Himself; the

[1] "Mystici Corporis," June 29, 1943.

penitential exercises are all intended to make the flesh subservient to the spirit. Unfortunately, the noble, beautiful, and highly desirable aspects of penance are not grasped by a carnal man, although it is exactly the virtue of penance that makes the yoke of Christ sweet and the apparent burden of Christianity light.[1] The Liturgy teaches these corollaries, but never fails to point out at the same time the sources from which they spring, and so establishes their importance and obligatory nature. The Church in her Liturgy preaches sin and punishment, virtue and reward; she does not overlook them in teaching dogma, and makes them a part of our baptismal obligations.

As judged from the Liturgy, then, it is not of the greatest importance that every Christian shall know the exact meaning of various teachings, since faith supplies such deficiencies; nor need we know the accepted names and the varying gravity of all the sins about which moralists write for the enlightenment of confessors, but that all sins must be shunned as much as possible. Hence, liturgical doctrine is free from many things that might confuse the "little ones."

In the early Church the Fathers did not waste much time with minor details when speaking in public. They did not do so, because doctrines were not yet fully developed, but because of the entire lack of spirituality among the pagans and the neophytes. This does not mean that moral discussions and conferences are not valuable and even necessary for confessors and spiritual guides; it only indicates that the essence of Christianity and the solution of the problems of life are communicated to the faithful through the Liturgy in a manner that will profit them most. From the day of her foundation the Church was never without all the means necessary for the guidance and sanctification of souls. The simplest form of the Liturgy used by the Apostles contained all the elements needed to carry on the work begun and endowed by Christ.[2]

---

[1] The author has treated this more fully in the *Franciscan Herald and Forum* (Chicago), January to May, 1943.

[2] Cf. Gaspar Lefebvre, "Catholic Liturgy" (Sands, London, 1937).

FORMING A CHRISTIAN MENTALITY

Steady Progression of the Liturgy

If we examine the liturgical documents from the very first, we shall find a steady progression starting with the origin of physical and spiritual—of natural and supernatural—life, and leading step by step to immortality and glory. We find this historical progress, not only in the portrayal of the life and mysteries of Christ and in the development of His Church, but also in the application of these mysteries to the life of every individual. The four seasons of the year are used as a basis to guide the infancy, youth, manhood, and old age of the individual, as well as of mankind as a whole. This beautiful symbolism is not always clearly seen by the casual observer, because a strictly chronological order is not always observed. The various factors are not considered independently of each other; they often run parallel, each having its own significance, but the student cannot fail to grasp the progression.

In Advent, a season when nature and humanity grow colder, the foundation is laid for the coming of Christ to humanity and individual souls. Beginning with Septuagesima, the creation and regeneration of man is the principal topic. Easter introduces the new life, and its effects and postulates are explained together with the development of this life in the Kingdom of God in the world and in souls. Pentecost is followed by a portrayal of the battles of life and how they can be won. In the fall, the season of harvest when nature prepares for rest, the tranquillity of mature faith and its progression towards eternal stability in the Beatific Vision are kept in mind. Thus, the end intended is securely gained.

This pattern of the Liturgy, woven under the assistance and inspiration of the Holy Ghost, is divinely psychological. It is adapted to all conditions of life and their peculiar requirements. As far as Christian life is concerned, it begins with the forceful inculcation of the fear of God (Sundays in Advent), and slowly progresses to the love of God. It satisfies the heart at a time when the intellect is not yet capable of explicit faith, and emotion holds the place of conviction. Corresponding with these two

THE LITURGY AND CHRISTIAN LIFE 259

faculties of the soul, religion or worship is an affair partly of the mind and partly of the heart. Both should be combined, but in some situations one or the other may greatly predominate.

The Liturgy Appeals to Both Intellect and Emotions

The Liturgy, taking this into consideration, endeavors to develop both faculties. It is not possible to enumerate in detail all that the Liturgy (including the Holy Sacrifice, Sacraments, sacramentals, and prayers) presents to the intellect. This would require a work of theology in several of its branches. A treasury of thoughts for further development is contained in the Missal, Breviary, Pontifical, and Ritual. Nearly all prayers and blessings have a dogmatic content and a significance of their own. Often the Lessons in Matins give beautiful and exact explanation of the mysteries and feasts celebrated. Their very richness of thought, owing to divine inspiration, is the reason why they will never be completely evaluated, and why every treatise on the contents of the Liturgy will differ from others in some respects.

As far as the heart or emotion is concerned, it is true that this is not a spiritual power in itself, but with the aid of grace emotions often influence the will considerably. Dramatic presentations like solemn celebrations, processions, music, song, and decorations, fill the heart with joy. A dignified worship, enhanced by appropriate vestments and furnishings of the house of God, also attracts the senses, and draws the heart away from the cold materialism and formalism of the secularized world. Devotional acts and sacraments (e.g., genuflections, kissing of relics, holy water, etc.) help to bring about an other-worldly disposition, if understandingly performed.

The force of emotions is usually not neglected as a means of attracting people to certain kinds of devotions. They are continually announced and made known by other channels of publicity, and often these devotions themselves have an emotional appeal. All this, if done in a manner not incompatible with religion, is not blameworthy, so long as one of the main ends, the spiritualization and formation of the Christian character of the faithful, is not entirely neglected. These more or less private parish devotions should contain something for the mind and the will (as is found in all strictly liturgical functions); otherwise, character formation and guidance of the will are neglected. Perhaps, an example may make this point clearer.

In a certain parish, a devotion to the Holy Family every Wednesday evening was traditional for decades. All the members of the Congregation of the Holy Family and many others attended regularly. The devotion was very popular. The prayers were recited in the form of the ancient diaconal litanies. The meaning of the series of invocations and petitions furnished material for a short talk. Among the petitions were such as the following:

> "*Priest.* Grant to all who are married the full knowledge of their duties and a holy and pure love.
> "*Faithful.* Protect them against the storms of passion and keep them united. . . .
> "*P.* Grant them strength to carry their cross together in patience:
> "*F.* For they that have been divorced and marry again, commit adultery." [1]

Other devotions may emphasize similar truths of a timely nature in the form of prayers. The recitation of such prayers week after week by large congregations, or even smaller ones, becomes imperceptibly a spiritualizing and character-forming influence, and will contribute greatly to the maintenance of Christian public opinion. Some of the congregation may not like this form of reminder, but those that are sick must submit to operations. By preaching or by prayer, therefore, salutary lessons can be inculcated.

Returning to strictly liturgical worship, we find that, if it is integrated with life, it is a truly strong force for directing the mind to the things that are above, to eternal verities. The influence exercised by the Liturgy will thus become, not only occasional, but constant, so that thoughts about the happy hereafter and the conditions for its acquisition will come when decisions

---
[1] "Parish Devotions" (Sunday Visitor Press, Huntington, Ind.)

THE LITURGY AND CHRISTIAN LIFE 261

have to be made. Consequently, the Liturgy is not only a form of prayer but a worship of God by the whole man.

The Liturgy and the Perpetuation of Faith and Morals

To acquaint groups or individuals with the Liturgy, it is not necessary to explain to them its history, development, or content in detail. This may be done with profit in study clubs; but while highly interesting and profitable to some, it would not greatly profit the masses. What all people should know is the meaning of the more important elements, and what they should do to influence Christian life. Hence, the explanation of liturgical forms is not of so much importance as the utilization of the truths and the application and illustrations found in the Liturgy of the day or season. Bishop Schlarman undertook to do this, and has succeeded quite well in his volume on "Catechetical Aids."[1] In this connection, the fact that most people do not know Latin, may be disregarded. The reading or hearing of liturgical texts alone does not contribute much to the understanding of the Liturgy as a whole or to its application to daily life. Nowadays, the most important parts of the Liturgy are found in the vernacular in nearly all prayerbooks, sometimes with short annotations. The Sacraments are presented in various liturgical monographs,[2] but although these contain adaptations to life, they still need an integration if the faithful are to realize, and be impressed by, the transcendent beauty of the whole.

An acquaintance with the Liturgy cannot fail to be profitable to the faithful. An extensive use of liturgical thoughts in sermons and instructions ought to spiritualize the hearers. To turn to the Liturgy for aid to accomplish this, does not mean a turning away from the standard sources of Christianity, because the Liturgy is a compendium of all sources of the Faith—of the Scriptures, Tradition, and infallible pronouncements.

---
[1] B. Herder Book Co., St. Louis, Mo.
[2] Liturgical Press, Collegeville, Minn.

CHAPTER XXII

The Domestic Liturgy

As TOPIC FOR THE FINAL chapter we have selected one feature of Christian life that is related to the Liturgy—a feature which, although perhaps not so well known to the younger members of the clergy, should be interesting and enlightening for all. The Psalmist says: "From the morning watch even until night, let Israel hope in the Lord" (Ps. cxxix, 6). The hope of Israel was based upon personal worship and service, in addition to the liturgical sacrifices, and so it should be with us today. This personal worship and service can be rendered by turning frequently and more or less regularly or habitually from creatures to the Creator. For this personal worship the Liturgy furnishes the plan as well as the occasions and incentives.

Not only individuals, but also the family and the sanctuary of the home, should be strongly influenced by the Liturgy. The Christian home is a place where not only the domestic virtues (enumerated by Leo XIII in the Lessons of the Feast of the Holy Family) must flourish, but where God is also remembered and worshipped in different ways. It must be a seminary of the Faith, where the word of God must be implanted as seed and cultivated to bring forth fruit and increase from generation to generation. The home is truly the sanctuary wherein the worship of faith is rendered to God in so far as it is possible for the laity to offer such worship. Such was the Christian home from the earliest times, and such it still is in more regions than some are inclined to admit. Even in our own land, especially in Catholic rural districts, the *ecclesia domestica* [1] has not yet disappeared, although some signs of weakening have begun to manifest themselves.

In order to demonstrate fully what a tragedy its disappearance

---
[1] Church of the home.

THE DOMESTIC LITURGY 263

would be, it may be useful to enumerate the features found in family worship that are based on, or an extension of, the Liturgy. The following short list of practices and devotions may be especially interesting to those who have had but little intimate contact with the Catholics of other lands, or whose acquaintance does not extend beyond the limits of the larger cities. There seems to be no suitable book in English dealing with these religious customs that could be recommended for more detailed information and explanation.

In most of the older Catholic countries there are, in addition to the Bible with family register, the Official Diocesan Prayerbook containing all prayers and hymns used in public, domestic, and private worship. At least one copy, printed in large or medium type, is available in every household. Another indispensable aid is the Church Almanac, with wall calendar noting the saints particularly honored as patrons and protectors of the region.

Furnishings of the Ecclesia Domestica

The furnishings of the *ecclesia domestica* include crucifixes, statues, sacred pictures, holy water fonts, books, especially the Family Bible (with its Family Register), Lives of the Saints, etc. Some of these articles are heirlooms or mementos of important events in the family life. As memorials of the death of progenitors, of the entrance into the priesthood or religion by sons or daughters, of jubilees, of sudden healings, or of accidents, they keep up the family traditions in a most edifying manner.

At present, statues, pictures, and framed memorials are no longer fashionable and, with their disappearance, their original purpose of keeping important religious events constantly before the mind of the family is no longer served. Would it be possible to introduce an efficient substitute? It seems so. In fact, in older Christian countries where illiteracy is fast disappearing, a beginning has already been made. The erstwhile diplomas, on which also the rules and regulations for the Third Order, Sodality, Christian Mothers and Holy Family Societies, etc. appeared, have been replaced by concise and very practical handbooks in which the records are written or inserted. These books treat of the Societies in their effects on the family.

Something similar could be done (and is being done elsewhere) in regard to the greatest religious events taking place in the Christian family. Memorial booklets might be issued (not necessarily expensive but strongly bound) for the following occasions: Baptism, with Penance as a restorer of baptismal grace; Confirmation, with Extreme Unction as a preparation for the final battle; First Communion, setting forth the Holy Eucharist in its three phases (Sacrifice, Holy Communion, and the Real Presence) and as Viaticum; finally Matrimony, with its effects and obligations. These booklets would cover the sacramental life of the family. Valuable, extremely practical, and for the majority of adults entirely unknown material should be assembled in these memorial booklets.[1]

Two objections to the foregoing suggestions might be raised. Firstly, will the people buy the booklets? Will they buy a catechism, veil, wreath, prayer book, rosary, flowers, and new clothing? Yes, if they can, and if the booklet is made a part of the requisites. The value as a permanent record to facilitate the acquisition of copies later on, must be stressed. It must be made a matter of routine. Secondly, will these booklets be read? Probably not by little children; they may, however, read them later. But the adults in the family, being psychologically prepared by the event, will read them at that time or never! The booklets must be written with this end in view. Even at the present time there are parents who want their children to grow up to be good Catholic men and women. For this purpose good reading in the home is necessary.

Daily Religious Practices and Sunday Observances

Family prayers, the evening blessing of children by a parent, the family recitation of the Rosary, religious reading, rehearsing

---

[1] The Liturgical Press, Collegeville, Minn., issued a series of booklets that could be used for this purpose.

the Catechism, etc. constitute regular elements of the daily domestic ritual.

The family Rosary should be zealously promoted. This is the express desire of the Blessed Virgin herself in her apparitions at Fatima. It is remarkable that Our Lady did not ask for pilgrimages or other public manifestations, but for the daily recitation of the Rosary by members of the family *gathered together at home*. This reveals the special purpose, not only that the prayer is enhanced by the number of the participants, but also that the family should be sanctified and should become a religious unit even as it is a physical unit. It is comparatively easy to start such a good practice, but it must be kept up for a long time before an expected reform will be brought about.

These exercises are not interrupted or dispensed with even if visitors happen to call. Visitors are invited to take part in them, or wait in another room, as the writer has experienced on several occasions.

When sufficient space is available in church, all the members of the family who can do so on Sunday attend the parochial High Mass, during which pastoral letters are read, important announcements made, and after which special blessings are imparted. At least one adult member of every family tries to attend as representative for the whole family. The longer sermon preached and the important announcements made are regularly discussed at dinner and so brought to the attention of all the members. Likewise, the family is represented at the devotions with Benediction.

Should any member be confined to the house, he always tries to make some compensation for the loss of Sunday Mass by following the signals given by the church bells, and by reciting prayers or reading the passages assigned for the particular day in his Goffine (a book translated into many languages and widely distributed).

During the week the children attending school represent the family at Mass, since school opens with Mass as an obligatory part of the curriculum. This beautiful custom holds for the schools of all grades.

It is regrettable that the church bells are practically out of service, except on Sunday mornings; and some churches have no bells at all. A church without bells would be unthinkable in most other civilized countries. There are of course reasons why church bells could not be rung too frequently in cities, but such reasons hardly exist in smaller communities and in the country. With the silencing of the bells there has also disappeared the salutary admonition of the bells when rung for the Angelus, for storms and sick calls, for events of public interest, and for rejoicing on feast days and their inauguration on the vigils. For such occasions the bells are rung in the old Catholic countries.

Seasonal Practices and Occasional Devotions

Very common in many regions are the following practices in the course of the Ecclesiastical Year. During Advent a circle or wreath with four candles is hung from the ceiling, and during the special Advent devotions one or more candles are lit according to the number of Sundays passed. The crib for Christmas, which is meanwhile being prepared, will be unveiled on the Vigil of the feast or after the Midnight Mass. Then, on the Feast of St. John the Evangelist a little blessed wine is presented to the members of the family at dinner with the words: "Bibite amorem sancti Joannis." On the Feast of the Epiphany the doors are signed with blessed chalk.

During Lent special prayers for the conversion of sinners are added. It is considered a disgrace for the whole parish if on the Second Sunday after Pentecost it is found that many have missed their Easter duty. On Easter and some other high feasts eggs, meats, or other foods are blessed for consumption at the family table. During the Octave of Easter prayer is added for the first communicants who are to receive their Lord on Low Sunday. The same practice is followed during the novena before Pentecost for the next candidates to be confirmed. On Sexagesima Sunday grains of wheat are blessed by the pastor, and are then planted, cared for, and watched by the children (cf. the Gospel).

Carefully observed, of course, are the monthly devotions: during March, to St. Joseph for a happy death; during May and

THE DOMESTIC LITURGY 267

October, to the Blessed Virgin for purity and protection (also to the Angels Guardian); and during June, to the Sacred Heart.

When storms are impending, the respective blessing is recited as soon as the church bell gives the signal. During pestilence, famine, and war the Litany of All Saints is recited repeatedly in common, or the prayers said regularly after Low Mass are substituted. These prayers give a most beautiful and full expression of our urgent needs to our powerful Mother and Advocate.

Reasons for the Ecclesia Domestica

In considering this long but still incomplete list of the elements of family worship, it must not be overlooked that the different activities are explained to the children, who naturally ask questions and whose minds as well as their hearts are in this manner satisfied. The influence which such a liturgical life exercises upon the family, and especially on the plastic character of the young, is easily understood. But the writer had two other important objectives in composing the list: first, to show how full the Christian life can be, and, second, to explain what a strong *ecclesia domestica* means in the life of the Church.

Some critic who has not given much consideration to the subject may, of course, say: "Why all these things? They are not necessary for salvation." This argument is more theoretical than practical. Those who have probed deeper into contemporary family conditions realize that the disappearance of these religious practices has left a complete spiritual vacuum in the members of a family that is very difficult to fill. Many pastors sense this, and strive to remedy the void by frequent Communions and attendance at parish devotions. These devotions, which are truly admirable in character, may alleviate individual longings, while the condition of the home and the family as a whole remains unrelieved. However, a single hour spent with God may not suffice to offset the worldly forces surrounding the faithful during the rest of the day, unless people are trained to turn their minds repeatedly to God. The less spiritual-minded, especially (but not exclusively) the young, may direct their pursuit of happiness into other directions that lead to neither temporal nor everlasting bliss.

Instead of retarding this progress of secularization and materialization, the churches are unconsciously promoting it by drawing the family more and more away from the home—by transferring domestic worship to the church. To attract greater numbers, the real liturgical functions like Vespers, rogation processions, etc., are curtailed, although these exercises are not domestic worship. But someone may object: "Is it not better for the faithful to have their religious exercises in church than not at all?" This question cannot be answered by a flat negation or a flat affirmative, as we shall see.

Already some purely domestic functions are being associated with purely religious affairs. For example, we have the Communion breakfasts; and as time progresses, we may have a dinner arranged to follow the Sunday High Mass, and some other function to follow the week-day Masses at noon. Now, it is not right to cite the example of the early Christians in this connection, since they had no churches of their own and the sacred mysteries were celebrated in *homes*. Nor can such functions be excused as affording the pastor an opportunity of addressing his people; if more favorable opportunities are not otherwise provided, something is obviously wrong, for talks given in purely secular surroundings can scarcely be classified as grace-giving sacramentals.

Add to these periodical gatherings all the social and recreational affairs fostered by many parishes, and we must concede that the home is being emptied of all that should be found therein. Many frankly recognize this condition, but say: "Well, the truly Christian home is gone, and something else must take its place." But nothing else can ever take its place. In regions where the domestic sanctuary is gone, the Church will disappear.

How was the belief in the one true God and in the promise of a Redeemer kept alive? How did Judaism survive despite shocks and trials, with its people expelled from their native land and scattered among strangers? How was every religion, true or false, maintained and propagated without the aid of priests and churches for centuries? How was the Catholic's faith preserved during the persecutions by the Romans in the early centuries, and the later persecutions by the Mohammedans, Japanese, and Turks? There is but one answer. In all these cases it was the sanctuary of the home, the domestic church with its worship, that *alone* prevented the destruction of the Church in certain areas where no priests or churches survived. Cut off entirely from the ministrations of the clergy, but remaining united with the universal and indestructible Church, the family could supply all that was absolutely necessary for salvation, and the participation in the Mystical Body of Christ furnished the graces needed for the maintenance and propagation of the Faith.

This is an important truth for us to realize at the present time. It supplies an answer to those who are anxiously pondering about the future of the Church in the countries overrun by aggressors. Fortunately, in nearly all these countries the sanctuary of the home is well cultivated. In some places where it was declining, it will again grow strong under duress; but where it has vanished entirely or is no longer known, the results will be truly deplorable. This is a truth which has been demonstrated again and again by history. As soon as the Church rose to importance and spiritual power in any land, the civil government despoiled her, but she could never be completely destroyed so long as truly Christian families remained.

Now, it is easy to say that no such things can happen among us. Serious thinkers and students of history can find no solid reasons why they should not come to pass even here, and the rejoinders of those who argue otherwise are unconvincing. However, a fuller discussion of this question is not opportune just now, and must be left to private consideration. Nations and governments may perish, but families, like the Church, will remain.

Conclusion

This chapter brings to a close our analysis of the program of Pope Pius XII for the spiritualization of mankind. The two parts of this book were devoted to this topic. The first dealt with the spiritualization of the individual in preparation for conjugal life, and the second described the spiritualization of the members of the family through the Liturgy, thereby placing society on a truly Christian basis.

Pope Pius XII adds a third postulate: "In every human society authority, discipline, respect for the social order, mutual rights, and the realization of moral obligations must be restored." This is a stupendous task, and it would require volumes to elaborate a detailed program and discuss practical means for carrying it out. Before this part of the papal instruction can become a reality, the individuals and families constituting society must first be reformed. When the whole of mankind is spiritualized, its groups and relationships will reflect the attitude of the whole. But so long as the public, in general, are not actual members of the Mystical Body of Christ, a perfect human society remains a thing to be hoped and worked for. At least, we must labor earnestly to create a better Christian mentality among our own people.

Preachers and teachers are confronted with no easy undertaking. They will have to overcome a strong secular mentality and the liberal principle of expediency first. People guided by such a mentality and acting according to such a principle will pay little attention to the preacher; and when his suggestions are inconvenient, they will utterly ignore him. However, hope and confidence in the power of the Holy Ghost will ever remain the heritage of the Church.

> "Holy Spirit, come, alight!
> From the clear celestial height
>   Thy pure beaming radiance give!
>
> "Come, Thou Father of the poor!
> Come, with treasures which endure!
>   Come, Thou Light of all that live!
>
> "Thou, of all consolers best,
> Thou, the soul's delightful Guest,
>   Dost refreshing peace bestow.
>
> "O Light of blessedness divine,
> Visit Thou these hearts of thine,
>   And our inmost being fill.
>
> "Thou on those who evermore
> Thee confess and Thee adore,
>   In Thy sevenfold gifts, descend!" [1]

---
[1] From the Sequence of Pentecost.

BIBLIOGRAPHY

Selected Annotated Bibliography

The Sacramentary, by ILDEFONSO SCHUSTER. 5 volumes. Benziger, New York. First printed in London, beginning 1924.

This is the most extensive work in English on the meaning, origin, and significance of the Liturgy, and of the greatest value to preachers and students. The first two volumes treat of the general concept and inauguration of liturgical forms. Thereafter the *proprium de tempore* is fully explained. The last two volumes consider the feast-days not treated before.

Christ in His Mysteries, by ABBOT MARMION, O.S.B. 441 pp. Herder, St. Louis; first printed in 1924.

In this work the author proves that the mysteries of Christ which we celebrate in the Liturgy are also our mysteries, and he shows our contact with them. The book is not only a source-work for preachers, retreat masters, and spiritual directors, but also an excellent means to form a deeply Christian mentality and a practical spirituality.

Christ the Life of the Soul, by ABBOT MARMION, O.S.B. 395 pp. Herder, St. Louis, 1922.

In this volume God's plans for us are explained and the foundation of the double aspect of Christian living—away from sin and closer to God—are laid. In this, the author makes good use of the rites of administering the Sacraments. Rather deep and learned, but interesting and consoling.

The Mystical Body of Christ, by DR. FRIEDRICH JUERGENSMEIER. Kenedy, New York, 1935.

The author presents an organic system of asceticism founded on the doctrine of the Mystical Body. Because faith and worship are its elements, the book is decidedly Christo-centric and rich in thought.

Christian Life and Worship, by GERALD ELLARD, S.J. Revised edition, 430 pp. Bruce, Milwaukee, 1942.

This excellent and popular book complements the present volume in several ways. This it does especially as far as living and thinking with the Church is concerned.

Liturgy and Personality, by DIETRICH VON HILDEBRAND. 218 pp. Longmans, New York, 1943.

The author discusses the influence of the Liturgy upon the human character in which a Christian mentality is required.

The Liturgy of the Mass, by PIUS PARSCH. 368 pp. Herder, St. Louis, 1942.

This complete and scientific work is very interesting and ought to be popular among all classes. It contains a wealth of practical material on its subject.

Catechetical Sermon-Aids, by BISHOP JOSEPH H. SCHLARMAN. 564 pp. Herder, St. Louis, 1941.

This rich volume contains much material selected from the Missal, Ritual, Pontifical, and Breviary. Its constant use would not only make sermons instructive and interesting, but also thought-provoking.

Catholic Morality, by JOSEPH I. SCHADE. 250 pp. St. Anthony Guild Press, Paterson, N. J., 1943.

Although this excellent volume does not directly pertain to the matter treated in this work, nevertheless indirectly it is of great help for pastoral application in the guidance of souls.

The Better Life, by KILIAN J. HENNRICH, O.F.M. Cap. 332 pp. Wagner, New York, 1942.

An international Franciscan, and a Cardinal Hayes Literature Committee, outstanding book selection. Although this work is a theology of Tertiarism, its contents can easily be applied to any mode of Christian life. The meaning and significance of the means of grace are explained from the Liturgy and this ought to make it a great contribution to the formation of the right mentality.

Werde Licht!, by BENEDICT BAUR, O.S.B. 3 vols. I: Advent and Christmas Cycle, 420 pp. II: Easter Cycle, 511 pp. III: Time after Pentecost, 687 pp. Herder, Freiburg (St. Louis), 1937-1938.

This invaluable, popular, and practical work is not yet available in English. It contains liturgical meditations for priests and religious for every day of the ecclesiastical year. Preachers, consulting the detailed topical indices, will find it an inexhaustible source of elevating and inspiring thoughts. It is strongly recommended for daily use and it will satisfactorily replace a shelf of other meditation books.

Christ, adapted by KILIAN J. HENNRICH, O F.M. Cap. 2 vols. I: Christ, Victim and Victor, 212 pp. II: Christ, Healer and Teacher, 206 pp. St. Anthony Guild Press, Paterson, N. J., 1940.

These two volumes, in a convenient size, contain meditations and readings on the Gospels intended for the laity. They cover the Liturgical Year except the Saturdays. The latter are covered in the volume, *Our Blessed Lady* (109 pp.), by the same author and publisher. A few good thoughts daily will improve the spiritual outlook.

The Psalms, with Introduction, Critical Notes and Spiritual Reflections, by Very Rev. Charles J. Callan, O.P. 695 pages, with Index. Wagner, New York, 1944.

The Reflections are an inexhaustible mine for Christianizing the mentality.

NOTE. In addition to the books enumerated, the author consulted the Missal, Pontifical, Breviary, and Rituals.

Supplementary Bibliography

A Short Breviary, St. John's Abbey Press, Collegeville, Minn., 1942.
ARENDZEN, J. P., *The Holy Trinity*, Sheed & Ward, New York, 1937.
CABROL, FERNAND, *The Year's Liturgy*, Benziger, New York, 1938.
CABROL FERNAND, *The Books of the Latin Liturgy*, Herder, St. Louis, 1932.
CARROLL, J. S., *God the Holy Ghost*, Kenedy, New York, 1940.
ELLARD, GERALD, *Men at Work at Worship*, Longmans, Green, New York, 1940.
FAHEY, DENIS, *The Social Rights of Our Divine Lord, Jesus Christ the King*, Browne & Nolan, London, 1932.
FILAS, F. I., S. J., *The Man Nearest to Christ*, Bruce, Milwaukee, 1944.
FORTESCUE, ADRIAN, *The Mass: A Study of the Roman Liturgy*, Longmans, Green, London, 1922.
Franciscan Supplement to the Daily Missal, St. Anthony Guild Press, Paterson, 1942.
HAFFERT, JOHN MATHIAS, *Mary in Her Scapular Promise*, Scapular Press, Sea Isle City, N. J., 1942.
HILDEBRAND, DIETRICH VON, *In Defense of Purity*, Sheed & Ward, London, 1936.
HILDEBRAND, DIETRICH VON, *Marriage*, Longmans, Green, London, 1942.
GILLET, M. S., *Innocence and Ignorance*, translated by J. Elliott Ross, Devin-Adair, New York, 1917.
GUARDINI, ROMANO, *The Church and the Catholic*, Sheed & Ward, New York, 1940.
GUARDINI, ROMANO, *The Spirit of the Liturgy*, Sheed & Ward, New York, 1940.

JAMES, FATHER, *Life and Religion*, Herder, St. Louis, 1932.
JARRETT, BEDE, *The Abiding Presence of the Holy Ghost in the Soul*, Newman Bookshop, Westminster, Md., 1943.
JUNGMANN, JOSEPH, *Liturgical Worship*, Pustet, New York, 1941.
KLEIN, FELIX, *The Doctrine of the Blessed Trinity*, Kenedy, New York, 1940.
KOCH, A., *Homiletisches Quellenwerk*. 4 vols. Herder, Freiburg im Breisgau, 1940.
LAURENTII A BRUNDUSIO, S., *Opera Omnia*, Ex Officina Typographica Seminarii, Patavii, IX vols., 1928-39. Vol. I: *Mariale*, 1928.
LEFEBVRE, GASPAR, *Catholic Liturgy*, Sands, London, 1937.
MCMAHON, JOHN T., *Building Character from Within*, Bruce, Milwaukee, 1939.
MERSCH, EMIL, *Morality and the Mystical Body*, Kenedy, New York, 1935.
NEUFELD, ANDREW, *Saint Brother Conrad of Parzham*, St Bonaventure's Monastery, Detroit, 1930.
O'MAHONY, D , *Panegyrics of the Saints*, Herder, St. Louis, 1924.
PARSCH, PIUS, *Das Jahr des Heiles*, Volksliturgisches Apostolat Klosterneuburg, Klosterneuburg (Austria), 1934.
POWER, ALBERT, *Our Lady's Titles*, Pustet, New York, 1932.
RUDLOFF, LEO VON, *Everyman's Theology*, translated from the Eighth German Edition by the Benedictines of St. John's Abbey, Collegeville, Minn., Bruce, Milwaukee, 1942.
STAPPER, RICHARD, *Catholic Liturgics*, translated and adapted from the German by David Baier, St. Anthony Guild Press, Paterson, N. J., 1935.
STURZO, LUIGI, *The True Life*, St. Anthony Guild Press, Paterson, N. J., 1943.
TANQUEREY, A., *Synopsis Theologiæ Dogmaticæ*, 3 vols., Desclée, Rome, 1922.
TERESA, ST., *An Autobiography*, Columbus Press, New York, 1911.
VILLIEN, A., *The History and Liturgy of the Sacraments*, Burns, Oates & Washbourne, London, 1932.
VIVES, FR. JOSEPH CALASANCTIUS CARD., *Summa Josephina*, Typographia Instituti Pii IX, Rome, 1907.
VONIER, ANSCAR, *The People of God*, Burns, Oates & Washbourne, London, 1937.
WALSH, WILLIAM THOMAS, *Saint Teresa of Avila*, Bruce, Milwaukee, 1943.
WEBB, BRUNO, *Why Does God Permit Evil?*, Kenedy, New York, 1941.

INDEX

Abbots, 243
Abel, 14
Abjuration, 8.
Abortion, 68
Abraham, 24, 120
Absolution, and birth-control, 92
Abstinence, 164, 170
"Acerbo nimis." See Encyclical on Christian Doctrine
Acolyte, quoted, 4-5
Adam, 19-22, 104
"Ad diem illum." See Encyclical on the Immaculate Conception
Adolescents, preparation for marriage, 61-74; spiritual guidance, 49-60
Adoration of the Cross, 183, 186
Adultery, 68
Advent, 108, 117-118, 258; home devotions, 266; Liturgy, 110-115
Advent, First Sunday of, 110-112
Advent, Second Sunday of, 112
Advent, Third Sunday of, 112, 114
Advent, Fourth Sunday of, 114
Agape, 179, 186
Agapitus, 166
Agar, 24
Agnosticism, 143
"Agnus Dei," 188-189, 197
Albert the Great, St., 231
Alleluia, 194
All Souls' Day, 231-232
Almanac, Church, 263
Aloysius Gonzaga, St., 250
Alphonsus Ligouri, St., devotion to Mary, 238; on prayer, 59
Altar privilege, 231
Altotting, shrine, 239
Amusement places, 96
Angels, 243-244
Angelus, 266

Anna, mother of Tobias, 81
Anna, prophetess, 134
Annunciation, 27. See Feast of the Annunciation
Anselm, St., 236, 238
Antichrist, 226-228, 231
Antonine, St., 238
Aperitio aurium, 170
Apostasy, 141
Apostles, 180, 234, 241-242; at Ascension, 206-207; coming of the Holy Ghost, 207-209; desertion of Christ, 155; foundation of the Church, 142; gift of tongues, 208; instruction by Christ, 199; liturgical Common, 243; miracles, 207; prophecies, 244
Apostles' Creed, 13
Archangels, 243
Ascension of Christ, 206-207
Ashes, blessing, 156-157; distribution, 156-157; imposition, 155
Ash Wednesday, 155-158
Assumption of the Blessed Virgin Mary, 225
Athanasian Creed, 13, 211
Atheistic Communism, 227
Atheistic totalitarianism, viii
Atheists, 146
Augustine, St., on bad Catholics, 36; on charity, 26; "De catechizandis rudibus," 167; on good works, 129; on Mystical Body, 176
Augustinians, devotion to Mary, 238
Avignon, 250

Balthasar, 122
Baptism, 138, 177; and Confirmation, 51-52, 207-208; days of administration, 207; effects, 28, 33-34; institution, 28; and Lenten Liturgy, 148,

275

INDEX

168, 189; and Mass, 56; and Matrimony, 65-66, 77-78; necessity, 33; obligations, 36, 195-196, rite, 31-33
Barnabas, St., 242
Beatification, 245
Beatitudes, 6, 230
Bells, church, 265-266; in Holy Week Liturgy, 179
Benedict XIII, Pope, 240
Benedict XIV, Pope, 239
Benedict XV, Pope, 236, 239
Benedictines, devotion to Mary, 238
Benediction of the Blessed Sacrament, 215, 265
Bernard, St., 216, 238, 239
Bernadette, St., 250
Bernardine of Siena, St., devotion to Mary, 238; on St. Joseph, 200, 239
Bernadone, family of St. Francis, 247
Bethlehem, 120, 133
Bible, The, vii, viii, 9-13; family, 45, 263; infallible truth, 12-13; and Liturgy, 14, 261; printing, 11; private interpretation, 11; reading, 10-11, 18-19; revisions, 10-11; study, 12, 18, 25; Bible and Tradition, 13, 15-16
Bible History, 40
Birth-control, 63, 92-93. See also Contraception
Bishops, on Christian mentality, viii; class of saints, 242; in Liturgy, 243; persecution, 227-228
Blessings, ashes, 156-157; baptismal water, 29-31, 189, 207; fire and light, 187-188; holy oils, 32, 52, 181; palms, 173-174; wedding ring, 80
Body and soul, a unit, 40-41
Bologna, 239
Bonaventure, St., devotion to Mary, 238; on Sacred Heart, 217; on stigmatization, 249
Bossuet, Jacques Benigne, on Liturgy, 107
Breviary, 14, 259
Bridal blessing, 83-86
Bridal examination, 64
Bridget of Sweden, St., 239
"Brotherhood of man," 211

Bull "Immensa," quoted, 107
Burial rite, 232
Byzantine Liturgy, 169, 243

Cain, 14, 22
Calendar, Church, 263
Cana. See Marriage Feast at Cana
Candace, Queen, 197
Candles, 134-135
Canonization, 245, 250, 251
Capital sins, 52
Capuchin-Franciscans, devotion to Mary, 199, 237-238; devotion to St. Joseph, 241
Care of the body, 5, 40-41
Carmelites, devotion to Mary, 238; devotion to St. Joseph, 239, 240, 241; devotion to Patriarchs, 244
Carmelites, Discalced, 240
Carnival, 158
Carrel, Dr. Alexis, on prayer, 59-60
Caspar, 122
"Casti connubii." See Encyclical on Chaste Wedlock
Catechetical instruction, viii
Catechism, vii, 39-40, 64, 106, 109, 204, 264-265
Catechumens, baptism, 29-31, 177, 187, 189; confirmation, 177, 189; in Easter week, 190; First Communion, 33, 189; instruction, 138, 165, 167-170, 176, 189, 204; probation, 151, 158
Catherine of Siena, St., 250
Catholic Action, and the family, 93-98; in Switzerland, 93; in the United States, 35-36, 50
Catholic Hour, 95-96
Catholics, bad, 36; errors endangering, viii, 6; social responsibility, 93-98
Celestine, Pope, 184
Celibates, 71, 84
Censorship, 96
Certitude in faith, 143-144
Chaldeans, 25
Cham, 120
Character, of marriage partner, 73-74

INDEX

Charity, 154, 177, 225
Charles Borromeo, St., 250
Chastisements of God, 159-160
Chastity, 71-73; preaching, 63
Childbirth, 188
Children, blessing of marraige, 79, 81-82, 92-93, 100; in Christian family, 99, 267; Jewish attitude, 23, 24; obedience, 89; rearing, 38-48
Chinese, 25
Chosen People, 14, 26, 243
Chrism, 181; in Baptism, 32; in Confirmation, 52
Christian living, 17, 43, 51, 53-54, 90-91, 109, 168, 252-255, 262-270
Christian Mothers Society, 263
Christian principles, 5
Christians, Early, 179, 268
Christian Science, 143
Christmas, 114-115; crib, 266; Liturgy, 108, 115-116
Church, The, 28; adversaries, 141; authority on Bible, 10, 11; custodian of faith, vii; divinity, 140; doctrinal basis, 144-145; and family, 100, 268-269; foundation, 15, 208; holiness of members, 91; and the Holy Spirit, 13, 208-209, 256; marks, 223; persecution, 223-224, 227-228, 268-269; preservation of customs, regulations and records, 14; protected by Christ, 140; replaces Synagogue, 117; soul-saving labors, 220; stability, 14, 141, 269; unchangeableness, 16; union with Christ, 77-78, 139, 142, 256
Church in the United States, spiritualizing activities, 35-36
Church Militant, 231
Church Suffering, 231
Church Triumphant, in the Liturgy, 234-251
Circumcision, 22; of Christ, 135
Civardi, Msgr. Luigi, on morality today, 253-254
Cologne, 122
Commandment, The Great, 20, 31, 37, 53; penalty of transgression, 21

Commandment of Christ, 177, 181-182
Commandments, 51, 54-55, 109
Communion breakfasts, 268
Concupiscence, 62
Confession, 54-55, 168
Confessors, 243, 244
Confirmation, 34, 51-52, 177, 207-209
Confraternity of Christian Doctrine, 35
Conrad of Parzham, St., 250-251; canonization, 245; devotion to Mary, 237, 238-239
Conscience, 3
Constance, Council of, 239
Constantinople, 150
Continence, 69
Contraception, 68; denounced by Pius XI, 67-68. See also Birth-Control
Converts, abjuration, 8; instruction for baptism, 32
Co-Redemptress, 236
Councils of the Church, 13
Counsel, Gift of, 52
Counsels, Divine, 6
Counter-Reformation, 250
Courtship, 71, 73
Creation of man, 19-20, 103-104
Creed, liturgical treatment, 109
Cross, and salvation, 171, 172, 179
Crucifix, 45, 263
Curé d'Ars, 107

D'Ailly, Peter, 240
Dances, 164
Death, 232; as punishment for sin, 20, 104
Decree "Sancta Mater Ecclesia," 243
Dedication of churches, 208
Descartes, 142
Devotions, family, 264-267; monthly, 266-267; public, 60, 259-260, 267-268
Diaconal Litany, 204, 260
Dispensation, Matrimonial, 64-66
Dissipations, 164
"Divini illius magistri." See Encycli-

cal on Christian Education of Youth

"Divino afflante Spiritu." See Encyclical on Bible Study

Divorce, 5, 63, 68, 160; words of Chirst, 77

Doctors of the Church, 14, 162; on Mary, 238; saints, 242, 245

Dogmatic definitions, 13

Dominic, St., 250

Dominicans, devotion to Mary, 238; devotion to St. Joseph, 239, 240

Don Bosco, St., 237, 238, 244, 251

Drink, 164

Duffy, Bishop John A., on youth, 49

Duke, Archbishop William, quoted, 4

Easter, home observance, 266; Liturgy, 108, 191-195, 258; Octave, 195, 198, 266

Easter, First Sunday after, 198-199

Easter, Second Sunday after, 199-200

Easter, Third Sunday after, 201-202

Easter, Fourth Sunday after, 202

Easter, Fifth Sunday after, 202-203

Easter cycle, 148-149

Easter duty, 168, 266

Easter Lamb, 177, 183, 184, 194

Easter Week, 195-198

Eastern Rites, 185

Ecclesia domestica, 262-269

Ecclesiastical Year. See Liturgical Year

Editors, and Catholic propaganda, 95; and religion, 35

Education, of adolescents, 49; of children, 40-42, 47; in Christian truths, 105-109; non-Catholic, 142-143; public, 49, 96-97

Egypt, flight of Holy Family, 121, 133

Egyptians, 25

Elements, controlled by Christ, 140; testimony to Christ, 125

Elias, St., 165, 244

Eliseus, St., 244

Ember Days, in Advent, 114; in Lent, 165-167; after Pentecost, 209-210; in September, 226

Emotion, and Liturgy, 258, 259-260

Encyclical on Bible Study, quoted, 12

Encyclical on Chaste Wedlock, 98; quoted, 63, 66, 67-68; vices condemned, 91

Encyclical on Christian Doctrine, quoted, 1

Encyclical on Christian Education of Youth, 98

Encyclical on Christ the King, 98; quoted, 101, 108, 229-230

Encyclical on Function of the State, 4

Encyclical on Reparation Due the Sacred Heart, 217

Encyclical on the Immaculate Conception, quoted, 113-114, 238

Encyclical on the Mystical Body, 98; praise of Mary, 114, 137, 173, 236; quoted, 88, 91, 114, 137, 142, 173, 228, 255-256

Encyclical on the Rosary, quoted, 238

Encyclical to the Church in the United States, 4, 6, 35, 253

End of the world, 227-228

Engagements to marry, 73, 74

Ephesus, Council of, 236

Ephrem, St., 238, 242

Epiphany, 119, 121-122; doctrines, 127; effects, 131-132; festal practice, 266; lessons, 128-131; Liturgy, 108, 122-127; manifestations, 119-121, 138, 139; Octave, 138

Epiphany, Second Sunday after, 134, 139

Epiphany, Third Sunday after, 139-140

Epiphany, Fourth Sunday after, 140

Epiphany, Fifth Sunday after, 140-141

Epiphany, Sixth Sunday after, 141

Error, 3; widespread today, viii

Espousals of Jesus and Mary, Office of the, 239

Eucharistia lucernaris, 188

Eucharistic Triduums, 158

Evangelists, 242, 243

Eve, 19-22

Evil, problem of, 158-161

Examination of conscience, 54-55, 231

INDEX

Expediency, 4, 229, 270
Exultet, 29, 104, 187

Faith, vii, viii, 9, 177, 202, 257; development, 14-15, fountains, 9-16, 261; and Holy Eucharist, 212-213, 214; necessity, 140; virtue, 143-144, 216
Fall of man, vii, 21-22, 26, 104
Family, 88, 99, 268-269; Christian, 48, 50-51, 90-100; first concern of Christ, 75; holiness and happiness, 86; the Holy, 89-90; memorial booklets, 264; natural factors, 99; sacramental life, 264; supernatural blessings, 100; Swiss program to uphold, 93; worship, 263, 264-267
Family prayers, 39, 46, 91, 164, 264-267
Family Weeks, 98
Famine, prayers during, 267
Fasting, 157, 164, 170, 209
Father, and children, 89; of Christian family, 99
"Fatherhood of God," 211
Fathers of the Church, 14, 162, 257
Fatima, 236, 237, 265
Fear of God, Gift of, 53
Feast of All Saints, 230-231
Feast of Christ the King, 228-230
Feast of Corpus Christi, 180, 212-216, 218-219
Feast of Mary, Mediatress of All Graces, 237
Feast of Mary's Divine Maternity, 236, 237
Feast of Our Lady of Lourdes, 237
Feast of Pentecost. See Pentecost
Feast of St. John the Evangelist, 266
Feast of St. Joseph, 239, 240
Feast of St. Mark, 203
Feast of St. Michael, 243
Feast of Sts. Peter and Paul, 222-223
Feast of the Annunciation, 237
Feast of the Ascension. See Ascension
Feast of the Assumption, 225-226, 237; Octave, 219
Feast of the Chair of St. Peter, 137-138

Feast of the Circumcision, 117
Feast of the Commemoration of St. Paul, 222-224
Feast of the Conversion of St. Paul, 137-138
Feast of the Epiphany. See Epiphany
Feast of the Espousals of Joseph and Mary, 240
Feast of the Holy Family, 89-90, 137, 237, 241
Feast of the Holy Guardian Angels, 243
Feast of the Immaculate Conception, 112-113
Feast of the Immaculate Heart of Mary, 219, 236
Feast of the Most Holy Trinity, 211-212
Feast of the Mother of the Good Shepherd, 237
Feast of the Nativity. See Christmas
Feast of the Nativity of Mary, 237
Feast of the Patronage of St. Joseph, 200, 239, 240, 241
Feast of the Purification, 134, 237
Feast of the Queen of the Apostles, 237
Feast of the Resurrection. See Easter
Feast of the Sacred Heart, 216-219
Feast of the Visitation, 237
Feasts, classification, 235; particular, 235
Federation of Churches of Christ, 224-225
Felicissimus, 166
Fichte, 142
Fidelis of Sigmaringen, St., 250
Fidelity, blessing of marriage, 79
Fire, 187-188
First Parents. See Adam; Eve
Fortitude, Gift of, 52-53
Francesca Cabrini, St., 237, 251
Frances of Rome, St., 244
Francis, Lon, quoted, 4-5
Franciscan Nuns of the Annunciation, 240
Franciscans, devotion to Mary, 237; devotion to St. Joseph, 239, 240,

241; foundation, 247; Liturgy, 249; Orders, 248; saints, 249
Francis of Assisi, St., 246-249; three Orders of, 248; Rule approved, 248; stigmatization, 249; Third Order, 36, 248
Francis Xavier, St., 250
Frankish ritual, 156, 204
Franks, 150
Frederick Barbarossa, Emperor, 122
Free will, vii, 21, 104, 159
Fruits of the Holy Ghost, 53
Fundamental truths, 105-106

Gabriel, Archangel, 27, 135, 243
Gabriel of the Sorrowful Mother, St., 237, 250
Gemma Galgani, St., 237, 244, 251
Gentiles, 112, 119, 121, 125, 128, 133
Germanus of Constantinople, St., 238
Gerson, John, 239, 240
Gertrude, St., 239
Gift of tongues, 208, 244
Gifts of the Holy Ghost, 52-53, 209
Gifts of the Magi, 120, 126
Gnostics, 198
Golden Rose, 169
Good and evil, causes of, 105
Good example, 45, 129-131
Good Friday, 183-187, 216
Good Shepherd, The, 200, 214
Good will, 178
Grace, actual, 127; in Christian family, 99, 100; and faith, 143-144; and the Holy Eucharist, 215; and the Holy Spirit, 256; liturgical treatment, 109; matrimonial, 65, 79; and merits of Christ, 155; necessity, 203; neglect, 62; and penance, 148; rejection, 153; restored to mankind, 104; sanctifying, 154
Greeks, 25
Gregorian Sacramentary, 31
Gregory I, Pope St., 150; changes in Liturgy, 138-139, 150; Homily, 125
Gregory XV, Pope, 240
Grignion de Montfort, St., 238
Guardian Angels, 243-244, 266-267
Guidance of youth, 50

Heart, vii; and Liturgy, 258-259
Heaven, 230
Hebdomeda paschalis, 175
Hegel, 142
Helena, St., 122
Henoch, 131
Herod, 120-121, 131, 133
Hierarchy, 222, 224
High school students, 49
Holy City, 111
Holy Communion, 56, 122-123, 180, 267
Holy Cross in Jerusalem, Church of the, in Rome, 112, 169, 183
Holy Eucharist, 34, 56, 177; feasts commemorating, 212; foreshadowed at Cana, 76, 139; institution, 180-181, 212; mystery of faith, 212-215; reception, 215-216
Holy Family, 89-90, 241, 260
Holy Family Society, 263
Holy Innocents, 230
Holy Orders, 77-78, 166, 207-208, 210
Holy Saturday, 29-33, 187-190
Holy Spirit, 208-209, 211; and Baptism, 28, 34; in the Church, 13, 15, 208, 256; Comforter, 210; and Confirmation, 52-53; Descent, 208; effects of coming, 202, 208; in the Liturgy, 255; needed today, 54; Pius XII on, 255-256; power, 270; and prayer, 60
Holy Thursday. See Maundy Thursday
Holy water fonts, 263
Home, 262; American and European, 46; Catholic countries, 263-264; cooperation with school, 42; influence on child, 39; protection essential, 43-44; religious environment, 45-46, 263-267; and virtues, 99
Home Weeks, 98
Hope, 178
Husbands, duties, 89

Ideologies, False, 5-6, 227
Idolaters, 211
Ignatius Loyola, St., 250
Images, 234

INDEX 281

Immaculate Conception, 113, 236, 237, 238
Immaculate Heart of Mary, 219, 236
Immaculate Mother of the Good Shepherd, 238
Immaculate Queen, 237
Incarnation, 27-28, 213
Incense, 188
Indefectibility, 16
Indians, Asiatic, 25
Indissolubility, of marriage, 79-80, 82
Indulgences, 231-232
Infallibility, 13-14
Innocence, in children, 38
Innocent III, Pope, 248
Innocent XI, Pope, 240
Intellect, vii, 3; and Liturgy, 259; sole objective of, vii

Jacob, 24
James, St., 196-197
Japanese, 269
Japhet, 120
Jerome, St., 11
Jerusalem, 111
Jesus Christ, 141; baptism, 121, 138; birth, 115-117, 121; at Cana, 75-76, 139; death, 183, 186; divinity, 121, 138, 211, 213; entry into Jerusalem, 173, 174; Eternal Sacrifice, 15, 193, 214; family life, 89; farewell address, 182-183; finding in the Temple, 136; forty days before Ascension, 199; founds His Church, 15; Giver of All gifts, 230; glorification, 206-219; Head of natural and supernatural order, 97-98, 127; hidden life, 134-137; High-Priest, 15, 171; Humanity, 213, 255; humiliation and glorification, 138; King, 127, 141, 228-230; knowledge, 135; miracles, 139, 140, 144, 166, mystical union with Church, 77-78, 139, 141-142, 256; name, 135, presentation in the Temple, 134-135; Prophet, 142, 144; public life, 137-141; Redeemer of mankind, 104, 112, 122, 127; revelations, 9, 13.
See also Ascension; Incarnation; Passion; Resurrection.
Jewish worship, 15, 187
Jews, 117, 119, 125, 165, 166-167; chosen by God, 14; marriage, 23-24, 26; perfidy, 213; veneration of holy men, 234
John, St., Apostle, 155, 236
John Chrysostom, St., on the Bible, 12; on training of children, 42
John Eudes, St., 238, 250
John of the Cross, St., 238, 251
John the Baptist, St , 112, 138, 244
Joseph, patriarch, 200
Joseph, St., 120-121, 133; model of fathers, 89; prayers to, 266; relation to Church, 136-137, 200; veneration, 234, 239-241
"Jucunda semper." See Encyclical on the Rosary
Judaism, 119, 268
Judas, 179, 180, 184, 241
Jude, St., 130-131
Judgment by God, 230-231, 232
June devotions, 267
Just, 160-161
Justin Martyr, St., 185
Juvenile delinquency, 4, 5

Kant, 142
Kings, Christians as, 53
Knowing God, vii, 25
Knowledge, Gift of, 52

Language of Liturgy, 57-58
Laborers, 90
Laetare Sunday, 169-170
Lamb of God, 138, 188
Lamp of the City of God, 188
Last Supper, 178, 180, 213
Lateran Basilica. See St. John Lateran
Latin, use in Liturgy, 57-58
Law, established by Christ, 15
Lawrence, St., 150-151, 196
Lawrence of Brindisi, St., 238, 250
Laws, concerning family, 97
Layman's Retreat Movement, 35
Legion of Decency, 50

INDEX

Lent, 162, 164; first day, 156; first week, 163-167; home devotions, 266; Liturgy, 148-149, 162-190
Lent, First Sunday of, 163-165
Lent, Third Sunday of, 168-169
Leo I, Pope St., Good Friday prayers, 185; liturgical prayer, 124
Leo X, Pope, 240
Leo XIII, Pope, on "Agnus Dei," 188-189; devotion to Mary, 236, 238; devotion to St. Joseph, 241; on family, 89-90, 262
Liberals, attitude toward family, 98
Light, 187-188
Light of the World, 134-135
Litanies, 185
Litany of All Saints, 60, 159, 187, 189, 203-204, 267
Litany of Good Friday, 185-186
Litany of St. Joseph, 241
Litany of the Holy Name, 219
Litany of the Sacred Heart, 219
Literary critics, and religious books, 35, 253
Literature Committees, 50
Liturgical books, 14
Liturgical Movement, 57
Liturgical Year, 110, 191-192, 258; lessons, 108-109; practices, 266
Liturgy, vii, viii, 14, 16, 103, 254-255; aid to faith and morals, 118, 261; appeal to intellect and emotions, 259-261; central theme, 256; and Christian living, 15, 86, 190, 224, 254-257; development, 15, 222; domestic, 262-267; educational value, 14, 107-109, 176, 204-205, 224; language, 57-58, 205; neglect, 35, 224; objective, 126-127, 252; pattern, 258-259; progression, 258-259; and ranks of feasts, 234-235; symbolism, 258
Lives of the Saints, 45, 263
Lombardy, 150, 250
Lourdes, 237
Love, of children for God, 39-40; and Christian perfection, 25; in creation, 20; of our First Parents, before fall, 20; and Sacraments, 56; uniting Blessed Trinity, 20, 211; uniting soul with Christ, 194
Low Sunday, 198-199, 266
Lukewarm persons, 6, 55-56
Lumen Christi, 188

Magi, 119-122, 128-129
Man, ages, in Liturgy, 258; dignity, 256; duties, vii, 103, 256; place in universal economy of God, vii, 7
Mandatum. See Washing of feet
Manifestation of the Lord, 120
"Manual of Catholic Action," quoted, 253-254
March devotions, 266
Margaret Mary Alacoque, St., 216, 250
Margaret of Hungary, St., 251
Marian age, 237
Marmion, Abbot, on baptism of Christ, 138; on glorification of Christ, 138, 206
Marriage, 77; among ancient cultured peoples, 25; civic obligations, 80; in earliest times, 22; economic aspects, 71; in Jewish history, 23-24; legal requirements, 80; as natural union, 78-79; nullity, 68; preparation, 61-74; purpose, 23, 26; in Roman law, 66; unity, 22-24, 26; validity, 68-69. See also Matrimony, Sacrament of
Marriage Feast at Cana, 75-76, 139
Martyrdom, 46, 230, 245
Martyrology, record of Christ's birth, 115
Martyrs, 242-243, 245, 246; Christians as, 53; early veneration, 197, 242
Mary, The Blessed Virgin, 113-114, 134-137, 192, 225-226, 237; at Cana, 75-76, 139; devotion to, 45, 266-267; feasts, 236-239; Immaculate Heart, 219, 236; our model, 45, 89; Mother of our Redeemer, 27; Mother of the Church, 45, 142, 200; Mother of the Divine Shepherd, 199; and Rosary, 265; sinlessness, 104, 113, 134; Sorrowful Mother, 173; titles, 236-238; veneration, 234, 235-239

ized INDEX 283

Mary Magdalen, 197
Masonic Liberalism, 227
Mass, 56, aid to salvation, 129, 221; attendance at High, 265; and Christmas, 116; daily attendance, 56-57; language, 57-58; Nuptial, 80-86; of the Blessed Virgin, 111; of St. Joseph, 240; Proper, 108; Requiem, 232, Rogation, 204; study, 58
Mass of the Presanctified, 183
Materialism, 90, 255, 268
Materialistic liberalism, viii
Mathias, St., 241-242
Matins, 108
Matrimony, Sacrament of, 76-80; and Baptism, 65-66; blessings, 79-80; Bridal Blessing, 83-86; contract, 80; essential quality, 68; graces bestowed, 65, 78-79; impediments, 64-66; Mass for Bridegroom and Bride, 80-86; and Mystical Body of Christ, 65, 77-78, 88, 100; Pius XI on, 63-64, 66; Pius XII on, 88; rite, 80; St. Robert Ballarmine on, 99-100. See also Marriage
Maundy Thursday, 178-183
May devotions, 266-267
McNicholas, Archbishop, quoted, 39
Mediatress of All Graces, 236
Melchior, 122
Mentality, vii, 3; Christian, viii, 3-8, 16, 103, 254, 270; pagan, 3, 4, 5; secular, 270
Mercy, Divine, 196, 199, 225, 232
Messiah, 119
Methodism, 143
Michael, Archangel, 243
Milan, 122
Mind, vii; and Liturgy, 259, 260
Miracles, 144-147; Christ at Cana, 75-76, 121, 139; Christ calming the tempest, 140; Christ curing the sick, 140, 166; Christ giving sight to the blind, 155; gift of Apostles, 207; persons favored, 7
Miraculous Medal, 237
"Miserentissimus Redemptor." See Encyclical on Reparation Due the Sacred Heart
Missal, 14, 111-112, 259
Missionaries, 129-130
Missions, 97, 98, 163
Mixed marriages, 65-67, 80
Modesty, 47
Mohammedans, 269
Monogamy, 23-24
Moral autonomy, viii
Morality, 9, 50, and civilization, 23; lack, 160; Penance as aid, 54-55
Moral skepticism, viii
Moral theology, vii
Mosaic laws, 24
Moses, 165
Mother, of Christian family, 99; responsibility, 47
Mother of Divine Grace, 237
Mother of Good Counsel, 238
Mother of Perpetual Help, 238
Mother of Sorrows, 238
Mysterium fidei, 213
Mystical Body of Christ, 28, 141-142, 201, 256; and Matrimony, 65, 77-78, 88, 100; membership, ix, 91, 138, 176, 194, 270; and the Mother of Christ, 113-114; and veneration of saints, 234
"Mystici Corporis." See Encyclical on the Mystical Body
Mysticism, distorted, 143

Nazareth, 133, 136
Neophytes, 195-198, 204, 257
New Dispensation, 109, 121, 139, 172, 178, 184, 203, 211
New Testament, 9-10
Nicene Creed, 13, 211
Ninivites, 165
Non-Bishops, 242
Non-Martyrs, 242, 245
Non-Virgins, 243, 244
Novenas, 60
Novitiates, 254
Nuptial Mass, 80-86

Obedience, required of Adam and Eve, 20-21; of Child Jesus, 89

Occasions of sin, 44
Octaves of feasts, 235
October devotions, 266-267
Oils, Holy, 181
Old Testament, 9
Oleum catechumenorum, 181
Oleum infirmorum, 181
O'Mahoney, Rev. James, quoted, 107
Order of Penance, 248
Ordination, 78, 166, 210

Pagans, 257; conversion, 129; marriage, 25
Palms, 174
Palm Sunday, 173-176
Panis dulcedinis, 213
Pantheists, 146
Parables, leaven, 141, 190; in Liturgy, 190; mustard seed, 141; sower, 140
Paraclete. See Holy Spirit
Parents, advice on marriage, 62, 64, 70-71; of Christian family, 99-100; custody of children, 47-48; duties toward children, 41-48
"Parish Devotions," 60, 260
Parochial functions, 268
Parsch, Dr. Pius, on language of the Liturgy, 58
Pasch. See Easter
Paschal Candle, 30, 188
Paschal lamb, 184
Passionists, devotion to Mary, **238**
Passion of Christ, 155, 171-173, 175-176, 177, 180, 182, 184-185, 213, 218
Passion-Tide, 171-173
Patience, 164
Patriarchs, 244
Patron of Catholic Action, 249
Patron of the Universal Church, 241
Patrons of Italy, 250
Patrons of Rome, 150
Paul, St., 137, 150, 152, 222-224, 242; on charity, 84, 154; on Christian living, 38, 40, 128, 151, 168, 201, 255; on concupiscence, 62; on faith, 9; on fall of man, 104; on family, 89; on Head of the Church, 127; on Kingship of Christ, 127; on matrimony, 77, 81; on persecution, 132; on prayer, 90; on preaching, 7; on the Resurrection, 191; on salvation, 127; on Scripture, 11-12, 18
Paul III, Pope, 240
Peace, 219
Penance, 256-257; in Lent, 148, 164; necessity, 160; public, 155, 178; and purgatory, 230-231
Penance, Sacrament of, 34, 54-55, 168, 177, 198-199
Penitential season, 148, 160. See Lent
Pentecost, 208-210, 258, 266
Pentecost, Sundays after, 220-222, 225, 226-228
Pentecostal gifts, 244
"People's Catechism," 224
Persecutions of religion, 5, 131-132, 269
Persians, 25
Personality, vii
Pestilence, prayers during, 267
Peter, St., 137, 150, 153, 199, 222-225, 242
Peter Canisius, St., 250, 251
Philip, St., 196-197
Philosophies, false, 142-143
Pictures, Holy, 45, 263
Piety, in children, 38-39; pre-marital, 71
Piety, Gift of, 53
Pilate, 229
Pius V, Pope St., 250
Pius VII, Pope, 240
Pius IX, Pope, on Christian mentality, viii; devotion to Mary, 236; devotion to St. Joseph, 240-241
Pius X, Pope, devotion to Mary, 236, 237; devotion to St. Joseph, 241; on doctrine of Christ, 1; on Mystical Body of Christ, 113-114
Pius XI, Pope, on Christ the King, 229-230; on contraception, 67-68; devotion to Mary, 236; on Liturgy, 101, 108; on marriage, 63-64, 66, 92; on Sacred Heart, 217
Pius XII, Pope, Address to Italian Youth (1940), 17; Christmas broadcast (1942), 17; Common for

Sainted Popes, 243; devotion to Mary, 236; on our Blessed Mother, 114, 137, 173; on Christ and the Church, 142; on family, 88; on holiness in the Church, 91; on the Holy Spirit, 255-256; on Immaculate Heart of Mary, 219; on mentality and morality today, 4, 253; on persecution of Church, 228; on prayer, 90; on Scripture, 12; on human society, 270; three-point program, 17, 51, 103, 269

Polygamy, 24

Poor, 7, 71, 90, 92

Popes, on Christian mentality, viii-ix; class of saints, 242; devotion to Mary, 236-238; infallibility, 13-14; Lenten ceremonies, 149, 174, 181, 183; in Liturgy, 243; on Tertiarism, 37; title of Patriarch, 244

Poverty, Franciscan, 247

Pragmatism, 143

Prayer, 90; aid to salvation, 129; congregational, 260; importance, 58-60; in Lent, 164; in preparation for marriage, 70, 73

Preaching, viii, 164, 260, 270; dogmatic sermons, 86-87; more fruitful, 106-107; ineffectual, 160, 253

Pre-Lenten Season, 149-155

Press, and religious propaganda, 95

Priesthood, foreshadowed at Cana, 76

Priests, Christians as, 53, 255

Procreation, 21-26, 67, 83-84, 100

Propaganda, on sanctity of marriage, 94-95

Prophecies, 9, 15; of Apostles, 244; of Christ, 144; Holy Saturday, 29

Prophets, 244; Christians as, 53; veneration, 244

Protection, of children, 43-44

Protector of the Church, 243

Protestantism, 202

Public opinion, Catholic influence, 94-98; destructive, 105

Public penitents, 155, 178, 179

Publishers, and religious books, 35, 95

Purgatory, 230-231

Purification of the Blessed Virgin Mary, 134-136

Quadragesima, 168

Quadragesima Sunday, 150

Quakerism, 143

Quasimodo geniti, 198

"Quas primas." See Encyclical on Christ the King

Queen of Heaven and Earth, 236

Queen of Mt. Carmel, 237

Queen of Peace, 236

Quinquagesima Sunday, 153-155

Rachel, 84

Radio, as means to uphold family, 95-96

Raguel, 81

Raphael, Archangel, 243

Rationalism, viii

Reading, indiscriminate, 62; in the home, 264; propaganda value, 95; spiritual, 35

Real Presence, 180, 212-213, 214

Rebecca, 84

Redeemer, Promise of a, 14, 27, 104

Redemption, 213; act of love, 28; effects, 28-29; in the Liturgy, 104, 110-112, 115-117; and Mary, 238

Redemptorists, devotion to Mary, 238

Reformers, 247-248; and Bible, 10; and saints, 234

Regeneration of mankind, 22, 27-29, 34

Relics, 234

Religion, 203; aid to parents, 99; endurance, 268-269; lack, 160; modern views, 143, 229; necessity of education in, 17-18, 47; and science, 145; in secular schools, 4

Religious vocations, 41, 46, 100

Religious writers, 10

Repository, 181

Reproaches, 186

Requiem Mass, 232

Respiritualization, 18, 254

Responsibility, of individual, 94, 97, 129-131

Resurrection of Christ, 177, 187, 189, 191, 192, 193, 256

Retreats, 35, 97, 98; annual Lenten, 162

Revelation, vii, viii, 9; in Bible, 10; and miracles, 147

Robert Bellarmine, St., 250, 251; devotion to Mary, 238; on Matrimony, 99-100

Rogation Days, 203-204

Rogation processions, 150, 203, 268

Roman Calendar, 235

Roman Catechism, on marriage, 78-79

Roman Emperor, 185

Roman Pontifical, 52, 181, 210, 259

Roman Ritual, 14, 108, 259

Romans, 25, 269

Rome, 111-112; cathedral, 163; patrons, 150; pestilence, 150

Rosary, 236, 237, 238; family, 46, 264-265

Rulers, 90

Sabbath, 15, 187

Sacrament of regeneration. See Baptism

Sacraments, viii, 209; aid to salvation, 129; dependence on Baptism, 33; fruitful reception, 43

Sacred Heart of Jesus, 216-219, 267

Sacrifice, 214-215

St. Anastasia, Church of, 116, 156

Sainted Popes, Common for, 243

St. John Lateran, Basilica of, 150, 163, 174, 178, 197, 207

St. Lawrence, Basilica of, 150, 168, 196

St. Mary *ad Martyres*, Church of, 197

St. Mary Major, Basilica of, 111, 116, 192

St. Pancras, Church of, 198

St. Paul, Basilica of, 152, 170, 196, 222

St. Peter, Basilica of, 116, 153, 171, 195, 206, 222

Saints, classes, 242-246; feasts, 235; hidden, 251; intercession, 234; some significant, 250; veneration, 234, 251; youthful, 254

St. Sabina, Church of, 157

St. Sylvester, Church of, 174

Salt, in baptism, 32

Salvation, vii, 7, 127, 194, 226

Sanctification of mankind, 34-37

Sara, wife of Abraham, 24

Sara, wife of Tobias, 81, 84

Saviour, Basilica of the. See St. John Lateran

Scapular of Our Lady of Mt. Carmel, 237, 238, 239

Scapular of St. Joseph, 241

Schlarman, Bishop Joseph, "Catechetical Aids," 261

School and Society, quoted, 54

Schopenhauer, 142

Schuster, Cardinal Ildefonso, on profitless sowing, 153; on true piety, 168; on worldliness, 172

Science, and religion, 145

Scriptural reading, viii

Scripture. See Bible

Seasons, in Liturgy, 258

Secret discipline, 170

Secularism, viii, 268

Self-denial, 37, 41, 47, 161, 164

Self-reform, 247

Sem, 120

Seminaries, 254

Septuagesima Sunday, 108, 150-152, 258

Sequence of Pentecost, 209, 270

Seraphs, 249

Sergius I, Pope, 186

Sermons, 86-87, 105-107; Lenten, 177; liturgical thoughts, 261

"Sertum laetitiae." See Encyclical to the Church in the United States

Serving God, vii

Sex, 23, 26; crimes among Jews, 24; disorders among ancient peoples, 25; safeguarded in earliest times, 22; spiritual meaning, 100

Sexagesima Sunday, 152-153, 266

Sex instruction, of children, 45; of youth, 58

Shepherds, at Bethlehem, 119

Simeon, 134-135
Sin, 159; avoidance, 257; mortal, 55, 230; original, 104; punishment, 159-160; venial, 55
Sixtus IV, Pope, 240
Sixtus V, Pope, on Liturgy, 107
Sodalities, 35, 263
Sorrowful Mother, 173
Soul, created to love, 20; faculties, vii
Spain, devotion to St. Joseph, 240
Spiritual Book Associates, 35
Spiritual books, 35, 45, 253, 263
Spirituality, of family, 90, 93; and Liturgy, 254-257; and mentality, vii; need, 36-37, 46, 267-268; nourishment, 34; of youth, 50, 54
Spiritual-mindedness, 254
Spiritual reading, viii
Standards, divine and worldly, 72-73, 96
State, and family, 99; supremacy, 229
State Absolutism, 227
Station churches, 111-112, 149, 195
Statues, Holy, 45, 263
Storms, 266, 267
Stephen, St., 196
Stigmatization, 249
Stritch, Archbishop Samuel, on laity in U.S., 254
Study clubs, viii, 87, 230, 261
"Summa Josephina," 241
"Summi pontificatus." See Encyclical on Function of the State
Sunday, 15; observance, 160, 265
Switzerland, family program, 93
Symmachus, Pope, 171
Synagogue, 117, 119, 172, 182, 185
Synaxis, 183, 186
Synoptics, 185

Temple of Jerusalem, 15; presentation of Infant Jesus, 134-135; finding of Child Jesus, 134
Temptations, 44
Teresa of Avila, St., on St. Joseph, 240
Tertiarism, 36-37
Tertullian, 207

"The Better Life," viii, 37
Theophorical procession, 215
Theosophy, 143
Thérèse of Lisieux, St., 237, 245, 250-251
Thief, Repentant, 179, 184
Third Order of St. Francis, 36-37, 248
Thomas, St., Apostle, 199
Thomas Aquinas, St., 238, 239
Three Hours' Service, 185
Tobias, 81
Totalitarianism, viii, 227, 229
Tradition, vii, 13-16; growth, 15; and Liturgy, 107, 261; necessity, 13; rejection, 15-16; and Scripture, 15; validity, 16
Transfiguration, 167
Transubstantiation, 180, 213, 214
Trent, Council of, on Bible, 10; on fall of man, 104; on Matrimony, 79
Tribulations, 159-161, 164
Trinity, The Holy, 20, 210-211, 213; presence at Baptism, 138, 198
Trinity Sunday, 108
True Cross, Relic of, 169, 183, 186
Truth, inculcation in children, 6-7; object of intellect, vii, 3
Turks, 269
Twelve Holy Apostles, Church of the, 196

Understanding, Gift of, 52
Unitarians, 211
Universities, Secular, teaching, 4, 5, 229
Uriel, Archangel, 243

Vatican Council, and devotion to St. Joseph, 240-241; on miracles, 146-147
Veneration of the Cross. See Adoration of the Cross
Veni Creator, 208
Vespers, 268
Vexilla Regis, 187
Viaticum, 215
Vicar of Christ, 224, 248
Vices, and fasting, 157; threatening marriage, 91, 160

INDEX

Vigil of Christmas, 114-115
Vigil of Easter, 187-190, 207-208
Vigil of Pentecost, 217
Vincent Ferrer, St., 239
Virgins, 242, 243, 244, 245-246
Virtues, divine, 28; domestic, 89, 91, 262; moral, 99
Vives y Tuto, Cardinal Jose Calasanctius, 241
Vocation in life, 46-47
Vulgate, 11, 13

War, 159, 228; cause, 5; effects, 5-6; prayers during, 267; and salvation, 232
Washing of feet, 180, 181-182
"Watchful Elders," 45

Water, changed into wine, 76; in designs of God, 30
Wealthy, 7, 71, 90, 92
Widows, 242
Will, vii, 9, 259, 260
Wine, in Scripture, 76
Wipo, 193
Wisdom, Gift of, 53
Wise Men. See Magi
Wives, duties, 89
Worldliness, 36, 153, 202
Worship, vii, viii; development, 14-15; personal, 262

Young men of today, 61-62
Young women of today, 61-62
"Youth Guidance," ix
Youth organizations, 50